thirtysomething at thirty

thirtysomething at thirty:

an oral history

by Scott Ryan

BearManor Media

2017

thirtysomething at thirty: an oral history

For information, address:

BearManor Media
P. O. Box 71426
Albany, GA 31708

bearmanormedia.com

Typesetting and layout by John Teehan

Published in the USA by BearManor Media

ISBN—978-1-62933-102-7

This book is dedicated to my wife, Jennifer.
You are the Dot to my George.

Contents

Foreword
by Ann Lewis Hamilton

thirtysomething at thirty? Thirty years ago? How is that possible? I must have been a ten-year-old writing prodigy.

Except that while writing on *thirtysomething*, I had a miscarriage and got pregnant again and had a son and wrote about those experiences on the show – so the ten-year-old writing thing doesn't exactly fly.

But thirty years flies. Faster than anyone can imagine.

When *thirtysomething* ended, my husband was thrilled. He explained how for years, he would be greeted every Wednesday morning at work with, "Hey, John. Guess I know what you and Ann were fighting about the other day."

Oh, no. Had I treated my husband like a laboratory specimen? Did I carry a hidden notebook to record our dinner conversations? After an argument, would I dash into the bedroom and write down the nasty things we'd said to each other? Of course not.

Well… okay, sometimes.

But that's one of the things that made *thirtysomething* so good – the honesty about what we were writing. Yes, it made my husband crazy, but I was writing about a real marriage (unfortunately for him, our marriage) - the good, the bad, the specifics. For example, once when I was grumpy (once?), my husband washed my hair and it was such a luxury. Later I wrote an episode where Gary washes Susannah's hair, because Susannah deserved that luxury, too.

Writing for the show was like therapy, only instead of going to someone's office and paying them hundreds of dollars to talk about our lives, we went to an office, wrote about our lives, and people paid us. How cool is that?

I'm a firm believer there is drama in everything. It doesn't have to be Lannisters killing Starks killing Boltons (yep, I'm a big fan of *Game of Thrones*). Drama exists in small things, too. Elliot being a goofball with his kids. Michael and Hope balancing Christmas and Hanukkah. Gary riding his bike. And sometimes larger things.

After my miscarriage, Ed Zwick and Marshall Herskovitz gave me the opportunity to write about one of the worst experiences of my life. It wasn't easy to do, but cathartic. We received mail where people told us about the comfort they felt because of that episode – and that felt nice, the idea that our show could make a difference.

As writers, it helped that we had wonderful characters to work with. They felt like people you knew or wanted to know. Ed and Marshall created them on paper and the actors brought them to life. They grew and we grew.

Working on *thirtysomething* spoiled me. I remember talking to Brandon Stoddard, the head of ABC Entertainment and a huge champion of the show. I told him how much I loved working in television and couldn't wait to work on other shows because they would be just as incredible as *thirtysomething*. Brandon laughed. He said, "A show like *thirtysomething* and creators like Ed and Marshall – they don't come around very often."

Of course he was right. I've worked with many other great people and on great shows, but *thirtysomething* was unique – the combination of actors, writers, crew, and the way Ed and Marshall functioned as executive producers – it was like film school. They wanted everyone to learn about the process – writers should spend time on the set. Talk to actors, hear what they had to say about the scripts. Melanie Mayron pointed to a line once and told me, "You don't need to write that, I can play it." What a lesson – we learned to write subtext. We watched a DP (director of photography) line up a shot. Saw the art director and props people make Hope and Michael's house look lived in, not like a page in a magazine.

Have I left anybody out? The editors, the composers, the directors, hair and makeup, the costume designer (Melissa's numbers coat – I still covet that coat), the writer's assistants – it's hard to explain the magic of the *thirtysomething* collaboration. I look back thirty years (thirty years!) and think of the experience, the generosity of Ed and Marshall as teachers. Wow. How lucky was I to be part of something so special?

I miss Michael and Hope and Elliot and Nancy and Gary and Melissa and Ellyn. Who knows what they're doing now? I guess all of us, in a way, will always be thirtysomething.

Introduction
by Scott Ryan

I watched *thirtysomething* the summer of 1992 on Lifetime Television. I was a 22-year-old male college senior. Probably not the demographic Ed Zwick and Marshall Herskovitz were aiming for when they created the series. Once I finished all eighty-five episodes, I instantly started again. This time I taped them on VHS. Most likely if you are old enough to remember *thirtysomething* you are old enough to remember what a VHS was. I wore out those tapes and replaced them with the DVDs. I just realized with streaming maybe no one knows what DVDs are anymore. Technology changes faster than Hope folds laundry.

Every few years, I would view the series again. Every time it played differently. The first time I paid attention only to Michael and Elliot. The second time I understood Melissa's journey. After I had kids, Hope and Nancy made perfect sense. When I worked for unscrupulous bosses, Miles turned from a fun character to my deepest fear. When I started my own business, my opinion on Miles changed again. When I was a stay-at-home dad, Gary's struggle became mine. How could one show mean something different with each passing year? When I watched it last year, Ellyn was hands down my favorite character. I hardly even paid attention to her the first time. What was going on?

Amazingly, by the power of the internet, I was moments away from talking with one of the creators, Marshall Herskovitz. I would ask him how he plotted to take Nancy from a weak character to a strong sexual woman only to try to break her once more. I would ask him how he created marriages on television that actually balanced the doldrums of parenting with the passion of love. I would find out exactly how they kept secret one of the greatest plot twists in television history. I had to know. As the co-host of *The Red Room Podcast* I had been studying television for years. No matter which series I covered, none had the honesty of *thirtysomething*. I needed to know why it was different from everything else. I had Marshall just where I wanted him. He would explain everything to me and I could put this mystery to rest. I could go back to trying to solve that other great mystery of life: my children. His response, when I asked him? He laughed. He let out a laugh and then another one. He said, "Plan? It was pure chaos. I don't think we planned any of it." It was that laugh that inspired this book. You can head out to iTunes right now and hear him laugh. It is there for the world to experience on *The thirtysomething Podcast* where this all began . . . where it can begin again, today. (If you got that reference you are really going to love this book. If you didn't you will soon.)

As I interviewed the rest of the crew, Susan, Joe, Richard, Ann, Winnie, Liberty, Ed, Scott, Ken, and Brandy all did their versions of the laugh. The truth is . . . well, that's the question isn't it? What is the truth? Where is the truth? In the episode "Guns and Roses" Hope says to Nancy, "You should tell me if you are going to write one of those books where you say humiliating things about your best friends." You are safe, Hope. This book has no gossip, no commentary from the outside. An oral history is just the words of the creators, writers, directors, and actors of the show. You will learn early on that this book is not fact. It is memory. I like memory better than fact. It is much more interesting and there are way fewer lawsuits.

The actors gave me plenty of "ask the writers, they will know." The writing staff gave me plenty of "I don't knows." You will read one person say the answer is "this" and the next person say the answer is "that." I like to think this book is found somewhere between "this" and "that." Marshall claims the show is about ambivalence. Why should the oral history pick a side if the writers never did?

The actors were everything you would want them to be. Polly Draper was hilarious and giggled just like Ellyn Warren. Melanie Mayron was so helpful just like Melissa Steadman. She reached out to be sure everyone knew about the book. Peter Horton was thoughtful and charming just like Gary Shepherd. Mel Harris was as smart as Hope Steadman from Princeton would be. Tim Busfield told stories with the energy of Elliot Weston. I could just see him pacing around that glass office building. Hearing Ken Olin talk about how much he loved Mel Harris made me believe that Michael and Hope were still very much in love. Patty Wettig had the spirituality and warmth that carried the soul of Nancy Weston.

So, with all due respect to Marshall's claim that there was no plan, here lies the blueprint of how the series that was based on all of our lifetimes was created. I started this book after working on *The thirtysomething Podcast* with my co-host Carolyn Hendler. I realized there was more to learn than could be covered in a one hour talk. I began conducting interviews for this book that dug deeper. This led to multiple emails, calls and even Facebook messages. Once the gates of memory were opened it was amazing what poured out. Everyone was so willing to share and to try to remember as much as they could. My inbox began to look like a *TV Guide* from the eighties.

I have arranged the interviews in episodic order. This way a reader can either read the book from start to finish and hear the story of *thirtysomething* in the order it happened or read about their favorite episode after viewing it. I have mixed all the interviews together to give the feeling that everyone is just sitting around in one big living room telling their story. Most of the participants performed multiple functions as Writers, Producers and Directors. I tried to give them credit for the task they performed with that episode. Richard Kramer may be listed as Director on an episode he directed, Producer when he comments on someone else's episode and Writer when he wrote the script. Eventually most of the cast started directing episodes as well. Tim Busfield goes by Tim, is listed as Timothy in the credits and everyone calls him Timmy. I have provided a Key that will explain what jobs each person held and the different names by which they are known.

Somehow I convinced two of the writers from the show to write original essays for this book. Ann Lewis Hamilton wrote the Foreword to start us off and Joe Dougherty wrote the Afterword that plays like a perfect end credits song. Production Designer, Brandy Alexander, generously shared her original models and personal set photos throughout the book. Director of Photography, Ken Zunder, also donated some personal photos that are on the front cover and a big surprise at the end of the book, but no spoilers.

I have attempted to provide you with the "this" as well as the "that." After thirty years there may not be a definitive answer for how the participants in this book built a groundbreaking series; however, you are about to read the closest version there is. The story of *thirty-something* told by the ridiculously talented people who crafted it. Cue Marshall's laugh.

Here is the main cast of the show: Mel Harris (Hope), Polly Draper (Ellyn), Tim Busfield (Elliot), Ken Olin (Michael), Peter Horton (Gary), Patty Wettig (Nancy), and Melanie Mayron (Melissa). Courtesy ABC Photography Archives.

Oral History

Key

ACTORS:

Timothy Busfield - Elliot Weston; Director; Referred to as Tim or Timmy
David Clennon - Miles Drentell
Dana Delany - Guest Star - Gary's Girlfriend, Eve
Paul Dooley - Guest Star - Bob Spano
Polly Draper - Ellyn Warren
Michael Feinstein - Guest Star - Musician
David Marshall Grant - Russell Weller
Mel Harris - Hope Murdoch Steadman; Director
Peter Horton - Gary Shepherd; Director
Patricia Kalember - Susannah Hart
Melanie Mayron - Melissa Steadman; Director
Nick Meglin - Guest Star - "Nick"
Ken Olin - Michael Steadman; Director; Referred to as Ken or Kenny
Corey Parker - Lee Owens
Charlotte Stewart - Guest Star - Peggy York
Patricia Wettig - Nancy Weston; Referred to as Patty
Lenny Von Dohlen - Guest Star - Roy MacCaulay

PRODUCTION:

Brandy Alexander: Production Designer
Joseph Dougherty: Writer, Producer, Director; Referred to as "Joe"
Liberty Godshall: Writer; Actress played "Madison"
Jill Gordon: Writer
Paul Haggis: Writer

Ann Lewis Hamilton: Writer, Producer, Director
Marshall Herskovitz: Creator, Writer, Executive Producer, Director; Actor played "Therapist"
Winnie Holzman: Writer
Richard Kramer: Writer, Producer, Director
Ron Lagomarsino: Director
Ellen S. Pressman: Producer, Director
Susan Shilliday: Writer
Scott Winant: Producer, Director
Kenneth Zunder: Director of Photography (DP); Referred to as Ken
Edward Zwick: Creator, Writer, Executive Producer, Director; Referred to as Ed

What is an Oral History? An Oral History is the story of an event told by the people who took part in it. This book is told from the people who crafted *thirtysomething*. Each person told what they remembered from those four years in their own words. There is no fact checking, no challenging of their recollections, only questions and answers. Since the majority of these interviews were conducted conversationally, the author has had to shape some of the sentences. Memories come back in spurts, not complete sentences. Every attempt has been made to make as few changes as possible. The intention of every sentence has been maintained. Dates of all the interviews can be found in the back of this book.

All pictures are used for editorial use only. This book is not affiliated with ABC, MGM or Bedford Falls. All photos and/or copyrighted material appearing in this book remains the work of it's owners. Marshall Herskovitz gave permission to use all *thirtysomething* pictures and scripts. He also said he wouldn't sue me. That was very nice of him. Photos were donated by Dan Steadman, Lisa Mercado Fernandez, Carol Gepper, Joe Dougherty, Ann Lewis Hamilton, Corey Parker, Melanie Mayron, Becca Ryan, Brandy Alexander, Richard Kramer, Todd Huppert, Dana Delany, Ken Zunder and Scott Ryan. Two photos were purchased from Photofest.

Front cover pictures from Ken Zunder. Designed by Becca Ryan.

Back cover pictures from Ken Zunder, Brandy Alexander. Designed by Becca Ryan.

Season 1
(1987–88)

"Pilot"

Directed by Marshall Herskovitz

Written by Marshall Herskovitz and Edward Zwick

September 29, 1987

The Beginning

Marshall Herskovitz (*Co-Creator, Executive Producer, Writer, Director*): Ed Zwick and I went through an extraordinary year before *thirtysomething* was even a glimmer in our imagination. From 1982 to 1983, there were a number of life events that happened to both of us. He got married. I had my first child. His mother was killed in a car accident. My father died of cancer. We won our first Emmy. It was a year that was filled with traumas and huge events. It cemented our friendship but it also gave us this sense that with every good thing a horrible thing was gonna happen. It pushed us for fifteen years into a way of looking at drama that basically said you have to shake the audience to its core in order to be a real artist.

Ed Zwick (*Co-Creator, Executive Producer, Writer, Director*): It was a year of living emotionally. There was a worldview that was formed that we shared. That in fact, the best thing and the worst thing happens, and they often happen at the same time. How do you reconcile

thirtysomething was created by Marshall Herskovitz and Ed Zwick in 1987. Viewers might notice the little child in this picture is only in the Pilot. Ethan was recast with Luke Rossi when the show went to series. Courtesy ABC Photography Archives.

that? How do you manage to find joy and celebration in the midst of grief and sorrow? The answer is we just do.

Marshall Herskovitz: What we were trying to do was raise the emotional stakes of everyday life to where they actually are for people. Our working theory was that you had to slow down. You had to take out the real events of life in order to show the true emotional impact of the normal things in life.

Susan Shilliday (*Writer*): It always amused me when I would read something that said they went for the demographic. Marshall and Ed were just inventing it as they went along. It was a new style. They didn't have enough ideas to pitch when they had to go to a Metro-Goldwyn-Mayer (*MGM*) meeting, so they added, "People in their thirties trying to invent a life."

Marshall Herskovitz: We were sitting in our office at MGM and we were less than a week away from our ABC meeting, where we came up with six television series ideas that were all awful. I had this anxiety that we might sell one and then we would have to do it. They wanted us to sell a television series and we didn't want to because we wanted to make movies. I said, "What we need is something that will never sell, but if it did sell we wouldn't mind doing it." Ed said, "What would that look like?"

Liberty Godshall (*Writer*): The very beginning was spent lying on our living room floor, which was what we did a lot back then. People were always hanging out at our house. Marshall was over talking about the nature of television. I remember saying, "I have never seen us on television." At the time, it was very true.

Marshall Herskovitz: Liberty starts telling about all of our friends and restating the idea I pitched to Ed. I got mad because when I said it, he was dismissive but when Liberty started talking about it, he bought into it. We wrote out a manifesto about what the series would be.

Ed Zwick: It had to do with the dialectic of experience that we had never seen on television. The idea that ambivalence and the struggle of everyday life was a thing that people rarely examined dramatically in television. We believed by addressing that, with its own greater truthfulness, would shake people up.

Scott Winant (*Producer, Director*): Ed and Marshall did the show because they wanted to see themselves on television. That is how they sold it. They didn't see people like themselves on television.

Marshall Herskovitz: There was the experience of *thirtysomething* from outside, which was to watch the show, and then there was the experience of *thirtysomething* from inside, which was the maelstrom of people, passions and pressures that we experienced in the making of the show. Being inside it was so different from watching the show. My wife Susan, at the time, and Ed's wife, Liberty, were writers on the show.

Susan Shilliday (*Writer*): A very important part of the show was having the characters in isolation. Not living in the cities where they grew up, so they didn't have a network of family but had friends. Where friends were their family. That was the basic idea.

Marshall Herskovitz: A lot of people criticized the show because they felt it was divorced from real life. That was our intention. We had to take these things out in order to talk about the stuff of everyday life. It's very important to talk about how people communicate with each other. How people resolve conflicts with the people they love. How they deal with their own ambivalence.

Scott Winant: A friend of mine told me about this project called *thirtysomething*. I called up Ed Zwick and said, "I want to talk to you about your show." I just talked my way in. I actually think they hired me just because they liked me. It clearly couldn't come from any other reason because I certainly hadn't produced a series before. We were all faking it. They were both writing and Marshall was directing. I knew Ed was going to take the producing credit. I convinced Ed to hire me as a producer. If you watch the pilot, you will see that Ed takes the credit in the front and I take the same credit but in the back. I did that because I didn't want to step on Ed. Then when we went to series I came on as producer.

The Writing Staff

Richard Kramer (*Writer, Producer, Director*): It may have been one of the last series that didn't have a writer's room, because Ed and Marshall were bored by a writer's room. We would work with them individually. No one other than them ever weighed in on a script of mine. They just felt why have writers around if you are gonna tell them what to do.

Ann Lewis Hamilton (*Writer, Producer, Director*): Ed and Marshall are really smart guys. They assembled a bunch of writers willing to sell out their husbands and families. "Yeah sure, we will write about that." Then later you go, "Really, I did that?" I think some writers are afraid to do it, but *thirtysomething* was such an environment that made you want to explore real marriage.

Ed Zwick: Marshall and I wrote the outline beat by beat with the writer and then they wrote draft after draft. Because we had a meeting of the minds in that outline, we knew that it wasn't going to stray too far from

The writers wrote each script from an outline by Ed and Marshall, who took no story credit. The individual writers did their own rewrites. There was no writer's room. Courtesy of Carol Gepper's TV Guide Collection.

what our intentions were. The execution of it was entirely the writers with notes on what that should sound like. We exercised a very firm control over the storytelling but the writing itself was individuated.

Richard Kramer: One of the reasons the show was good was that we were allowed to work out our own stuff. No one ever told me what to write. How the story was told was pretty much left to us with strong support and supervision from Ed and Marshall. They'd take what we wrote and make it as good as it could be. They were interested in our version.

Joe Dougherty (*Writer, Producer, Director*): We took the show very seriously. I always said there should have been two signs on the door at the office. One when you walked in that said, "It's not TV; it's *thirtysomething.*" and the sign on the other side that said, "It's just a television show." I think we did some stuff that no one else did.

Paul Haggis: (*Writer*) I had recently been fired as head writer/executive producer of *The Facts of Life* (1979) with good reason and had become disenchanted with the world of network situation comedies. My agent at the time, Mark Harris, submitted my work to several new tv series, among them *thirtysomething*. Marshall and Ed shot a terrific pilot and it had been picked up for a six episode order. They read my work and decided that I would be a good fit as their right hand. When we met, I told them that they were likely just mistaken but I loved what they were doing and if they were dumb enough to hire me, I would be thrilled to join them.

Scott Winant (*Producer*): Basically writers would pitch and meet with Ed and Marshall. The writer would deliver a script. They would give notes. The writer would go back and do the rewrite. Everyone was allowed to bring a voice.

Jill Gordon (*Writer*): Ed and Marshall stand out as truly extraordinary show runners. It's a common practice for a writer to write several drafts, only to be automatically rewritten by a higher level producer, who is simply prepping their drafts for the show runner to ultimately rewrite the final script. That was never the case with Ed and Marshall. They never touched a single word of any of my drafts, or anyone else's that I know of. They would give thoughtful, respectful and incredibly insightful notes that always pushed me to dig deeper and find a stronger way to approach a scene. I am so deeply grateful to them for what they taught me as a writer and as a showrunner.

Ed Zwick: I can see the value of a writer's room in comedy but I question its value in drama. We believed that one writer's unique sensibility is impossible to replicate with a group enterprise. Marshall and I sat down and wrote every story with the writer. There has been a tradition since then that the executive producer takes a story credit and then takes money for it. We took no credit and that was deliberate because we wanted the writer to have ownership.

Ann Lewis Hamilton: *thirtysomething* was my first big job. I thought every show was run by two people who were really super smart. This was the way television must be. It was a pretty unique experience.

The seven main characters would be crafted by a different writer each episode who would bring a separate voice filtered through Ed and Marshall. Each actor also added personal events that informed their characters. Courtesy ABC Photography Archives.

Liberty Godshall: Marshall and Ed were so unusual in the way they constructed the infrastructure of the show. I think it is why they have such devotion from all the writers. They worked as story editors with each writer but never took a story credit. It was huge in terms of respect for the writer and economically because the writers got all the money.

Ken Olin (*Played Michael Steadman*): A few years ago, I went to visit Ed and Marshall. This was after I had worked on *Alias* (2001) and *Brothers and Sisters* (2006) and they said, "What is a writer's room? What is it like? We've never been in a writer's room." The scripts weren't coming out of any sort of collective. They didn't gang bang an episode at the end of a season. Joe and Richard didn't sit in a room with Susan and Ann.

Scott Winant: I grew into the business believing that was how it was done. It was kind of shocking to work on shows where writers pitch and write scripts as a collective. That was not the case on *thirtysomething.*

Ann Lewis Hamilton: I have always said it was sort of run like a film school. I certainly never worked on another show where the executive producers said, "Go to the set. We want you to talk to the actors. We want you to sit with editors." They wanted to teach us how to make television.

Susan Shilliday: There were moments after the fact when I would realize that 40 million people just heard what I wrote. The one time it really landed on me was when I used something that I said about my daughter. I used the line, "Do all kids radiate light or is it just her?" I then saw it quoted in an article about what was so wonderful and what was so horrible about the show.

The Title

Marshall Herskovitz: I said to Ed, as we were writing the pilot, "What should we call this?" He said, "*thirtysomething*." I said, "Okay." That was the whole conversation. There were lots of conversations afterwards because the studio and network hated the name. They said, "We will pick up the show if you change the title to *Grown-Ups*." We said, "That is a terrible title. We are not going to change it."

Ed Zwick: They said, "We are the network. We decide the name." We said, "Fine. Then maybe you should get someone else to do the show

The show with the lowercase "t" was a name that confused the Network and fans. Now it is part of the lexicon. Courtesy of Carol Gepper's TV Guide Collection.

because that is what the show is called." We were willing to throw our body across this show and our intentions from the beginning in order to succeed.

Marshall Herskovitz: They couldn't get the rights to *Grown-Ups* so they said, "Okay, we will pick it up."

Brandy Alexander (*Production Designer*): I was renting some hardware for the show and I told the person it was for a show called *thirtysomething*. They said, "thirty what?" I said, "*thirtysomething*." They said, "You forgot what it is called?" They just couldn't understand that it wasn't thirty and then another word. It was *thirtysomething*.

The Casting

Marshall Herskovitz: Ed's wife is named Liberty. So, the female lead character could have been called Faith or Hope; we wanted a play on words like that.

Liberty Godshall: I have a concept name as well. The picking of Hope's name was not willy nilly. It says something about the show.

Marshall Herskovitz: We had no discussion about Hope's name. Ed said, "What should we call her?" I said, "Hope." He said, "Okay."

Liberty Godshall: I did not feel that Hope was me. During casting Marshall said, "I want you to play the character of Hope." I was an actress for about six years and had just segued to writing. My son was about nine months at the time. I wanted to see him take his first step. I just couldn't miss raising him because it was compelling stuff. Marshall said, "All the stuff you are saying is how we envision the character, so you would be perfect for it."

Richard Kramer (*Producer*): Hope represented Ed and Marshall's feelings about their wives. Both wives were involved on the show and hugely important. Hope was deeply supportive, sometimes judgmental, sometimes impossible to read, utterly reliable and indispensable. Michael wouldn't have any idea of what to do in life without her. The show was really ruled by women. The women were much more together than the men.

Mel Harris: (*Played Hope Murdoch Steadman*): My son was a year and a half at the time. One of the things I said to Ed and Marshall was, "How long have you been living in my house?" It was so representative of being a new mom. They are such wonderfully talented writers, and the pilot nailed that in a big way.

Mel Harris played Hope Murdoch Steadman. While Hope was created as a mixture of Ed's wife, Liberty and Marshall's then wife, Susan, Mel made the character her own. Courtesy of ABC Photography Archives. The Lisa Mercado Fernandez Collection.

Liberty Godshall: We were doing a pilot where the plot was trying to get a babysitter so they could go camping. It was unheard of to use that as a plot.

Tim Busfield (*Played Elliot Weston*): I was impressed with Ed and Marshall in that the biggest conflict in the pilot was a stroller that costs $270. They went on to win an Emmy for best series and used that episode.

Susan Shilliday: I was always asked if I was the basis of the Nancy character. We were all Nancy, Hope, Michael and Elliot just being that age at the time. It was based on our lives, but it was based on everyone's life. I am not any one character. Patty Wettig and I used to say Nancy existed somewhere in between us.

Patty Wettig (*Played Nancy Weston*): Now I see that Liberty and Susan were a great part of Nancy. I didn't think of it then. I was so involved in creating this character. I felt very possessive of Nancy. I felt so in the center. I see now it was such a combination of all their energies. I maybe was too egocentric. (*Laughs*)

Marshall Herskovitz: Susan and I had become friends with Ken Olin and Patty Wettig before we did the show because our kids went to nursery school together.

Patty Wettig (*Nancy*): Our son, Cliff, was very verbal. I knew he had to find some little kid to talk with. Suddenly, this chair fell over and a little blond girl jumped and said, "That startled me." That was Lizzie Herskovitz. They became best friends. A few weeks later, Ken and I had dinner with Susan and Marshall. They told us about this pilot called *thirtysomething*. We met because of Lizzie and Cliff.

Ken Olin (*Michael*): There was nothing like the pilot script out there at that time. I had done a movie of the week for ABC called *Tonight's the Night* (1987). I had also done a small part on *Hill Street Blues* (1981) but I wasn't known. I was on the radar in terms of young actors who were in a position to get pilots. It was a different time then. Movie stars weren't doing television. Television made stars; they didn't cast stars.

Ken Olin and Patty Wettig are married in real life but were cast in opposite couples as Michael (married to Hope) and Nancy (married to Elliot). Courtesy of the Dan Steadman Collection. TV Guide.

Marshall Herskovitz: There was a lot of discomfort as to how we were going to handle the casting because, all of a sudden, Ken and Patty were coming in to audition for the parts of Michael and Hope.

Patty Wettig: I read for the part of Hope because Nancy literally had one sentence in the the pilot. It wasn't that I preferred Hope as a character, but in the pilot it was all about Michael and Hope. I don't know that I totally liked the idea of Ken doing this intense part with someone other than me. Who were they gonna cast as Hope?

Mel Harris (*Hope*): In terms of playing Ken's wife in front of Ken's wife that is more of Ken's wife's problem than it is mine. I don't mean that in a bad way at all, we are all friends. Kenny and I got along from the get-go. The network didn't mix and match Hope and Michael. We were their only choices at that point.

Marshall Herskovitz: Deciding that Patty should not play Hope was very difficult because Ken and Patty wanted to play Michael and Hope. We felt Patty wasn't the right person for Hope. It was a difficult conversation to have with her. Nancy was really not established in the pilot.

Patty Wettig: After I had auditioned for Hope, I went in to talk with Marshall and Ed. They talked to me about Nancy and explained her journey.

Marshall Herskovitz: We said to her, "You'll be as important as anyone else on the show." She believed us but it was not easy because the pilot didn't reveal much about her.

Patty Wettig: They said, "We want to take Nancy's self-esteem all the way down until she finds the resources within herself to basically start her life again." That kind of journey interested me.

Tim Busfield (*Elliot*): Patty and I knew each other. We were both members of Circle Repertory Company in New York with Jeff Daniels and Judd Hirsh. Kenny took over for me at shortstop on the softball team on the Broadway show league because I was doing *Brighton Beach Memoirs* on Broadway. We'd always chat and hang out. I didn't read with Patty when we went in for the network. I read with Kenny, but we already had some history.

Richard Kramer: The only actor that was a little bit younger was Tim Busfield. He was thirty-one when he did the pilot. They loved him for good reason. Before the pilot was shot, they decided that he should have a beard. It became a great part of the character.

Polly Draper, Peter Horton, and Melanie Mayron were cast as the three single characters. Their characters would develop slowly through the first season while the show focused on Michael and Hope. Courtesy ABC Photography Archives.

Tim Busfield: My agent called me and said they want you, but they don't know if they want you for Gary or Elliot. I said, "I don't know anything about being single, unattached, and good-looking, but, boy I can screw up a marriage. Let me play Elliot."

Peter Horton (*Played Gary Shepherd*): I was friends with Ed and Marshall before *thirtysomething*. They had called me up and said, "Do you wanna do a pilot?" I said, "No, I am not acting anymore, just directing." They said, "It's really good; will you just read it?" I read it, called them back and I said, "That is the best pilot I have ever read, but I am not acting anymore." They said, "Come read with some of the actors." We read and had a really good time.

Polly Draper: (*Played Ellyn Warren*): I remember Marshall calling me and saying, "Please come in and read for the part of Melissa." I said, "I really like Ellyn. I don't want to read for the other part." Melissa only had one line in the pilot, so I wanted the bigger part. (*Laughs*) I said, "I think the perfect casting would be me as Ellyn and Melanie as Melissa." Melanie always credits me with giving her the part. I think Marshall finally just gave up and did it. I think he always wanted both of us.

Melanie Mayron (*Played Melissa Steadman*): When we did the pilot, Melissa was Gary's ex-girlfriend. When the show was picked up they didn't know how to bring Melissa into the group. They decided that she should be Michael's cousin.

Polly Draper: Melissa was written as a kind of wild party girl and then it evolved to be more like Melanie. She wasn't even supposed to be the cousin.

Richard Kramer: Melanie was basically the classic television character Rhoda in the pilot. Melanie came to me and said, "Please help me not be Rhoda."

Melanie Mayron: They didn't know what Melissa's career path was. I suggested she be a photographer. I had played one in a film called *Girlfriends* (1978). I was also doing photography as my fall-back money maker to take pictures for actors for their agents. I was very comfortable with the camera. This way they could hire her for the print ads for Michael and Elliot's commercial company.

Polly Draper: I liked Ellyn because she was complex. She was a person who was really ambitious, judgmental, and bright but she also wanted people to like her. The part of me that wasn't like the character was the part of me that they decided would enhance the character. Ellyn initially alienated everyone. One of those friends that we all have that is difficult but you still love her. I was Hope's friend and one of those people that the husband doesn't get why the wife still likes this person.

Mel Harris (*Hope*): It wasn't like Ellyn was jealous of Hope. Ellyn was on a very driven career path. That was the way Ed and Marshall set her up. It was reflective of what happens to two single women who are friends. One gets married and you add a child to that friendship. I think for her it became, "Why is your time going where it is going?"

Polly Draper: I am guessing the Ellyn laugh was added by me. When I say the line in the pilot, "I have twenty-seven people reporting to me." You can't be quite as self-important as the line sounds because she is basically apologizing for bragging. So, I guess I just put in the laugh (*Laughs*) like I am doing right now.

Liberty Godshall: I had a major affinity for Ellyn. She reminded me very much of my best friend in real life. I hadn't seen that character on television before. Someone who is tough and vulnerable at the same time.

Peter Horton: I remember we were doing an acting exercise on the pilot. We would lay down on the floor, relax, and stand up as our characters. Ed and Marshall would come around and ask questions. Ed asked me, "Gary, how many of your students have you slept with?" I said, "None." He got this look on his face that said, "Oh shit." They created Gary and he wasn't as nice as I made him. When I came on the scene to do Gary I had just gotten divorced and was longing for a family. I wish I had spent the first couple of seasons having him be a little less nice.

Winnie Holzman (*Writer, joined the staff in season 3*): I saw every episode before I worked on *thirtysomething*. I was overwhelmed by the show. Ken Olin was someone I had known personally. We had gone to acting school. We had done scenes together. I knew Patty, but not as well. I knew Polly Draper. We had a mutual friend. It was really intense because I was very taken with the show, but was also jeal-

Ken Olin remembers it being a struggle to create Michael in the shadow of Woody Allen. Ed and Marshall have a different view of the creation of Michael Steadman. Courtesy of ABC Photography Archives. The Lisa Mercado Fernandez Collection.

ous. I was seeing all these people who I knew in various amounts of intimacy. I had the feeling that everybody I knew was on a television show except me.

Richard Kramer: One secret of *thirtysomething* was Ken Olin. He was very polarizing for people because the initial criticisms of the show were centered around him. Ken was brilliant on the show. He was fearless. He was willing to be an asshole. He was willing to be Jewish. He was willing to do anything. He was a real bonus and I loved writing for him. If we didn't have Ken, the show wouldn't have worked.

Ken Olin (*Michael*): I think Ed was looking for more of a Rob Lowe and Demi Moore look. Marshall had wanted Michael to be quirkier and more Jewish than he thought I was. I remember I asked Marshall if we could take a day trip with the kids because I wanted him to see me as a father and less as an actor.

Dana Delany (*Guest Star, Episode 10*): Marshall and Ed had such a vision. Every generation has a show that defines them and I think that fit into that era. They just captured it. I remember people complaining that the characters talked so much. This was a generation that grew up watching Woody Allen movies. When I met Ed, he had been a production assistant on a Woody Allen movie and he was telling me about it. He was very much influenced by that.

Ed Zwick: Woody Allen's work definitely influenced us by his willingness to trade on his personal experience and how to turn that into comedy or drama. I happened to be given by him the first script to *Annie Hall* (1977). I couldn't believe what I was reading. I had come to know Diane Keaton and him a little bit. He basically turned their relationship into an artful, comic script. The idea that one could do that was so mind blowing. I know it had an effect on what we did.

Ken Olin: In the beginning, they had an idea of who Michael was and that was very different from who I was. It was difficult during the filming of the pilot. They had certain behaviors they wanted me to do. They were looking for more of a Woody Allen type. There were moments where I dropped my shoulders and head. They wanted those particular movements. It was odd for me. There was a struggle between my desire to make Michael more grown up and a little less neurotic in his behaviors. I am not talking about his insecurities but his body movements. I think they were frustrated with me.

Woody Allen was a major influence on Marshall and Ed. Ken says he was also an influence on Michael Steadman. Was he? That is the question. Courtesy MGM DVD.

Ed Zwick: I am not sure that the intent was to have the character have those more comic neurosis that describe a Woody Allen performance. I think that is probably Kenny's way of describing a struggle that I am sure we were having about an expression of his feelings. It just doesn't inform what our intentions would have been. I love the fact that he would have this specific memory of which I have none.

Marshall Herskovitz: Ken never disappointed. That is Kenny being dear and being an actor. We pictured Michael being Peter Riegert from *Animal House* (1978) very droll, funny, clever, and ironic. It wasn't Woody Allen, but it wasn't a guy as great looking as Ken Olin. We knew the kids in highschool who were that good looking and they didn't talk like this. They didn't have to. Kenny was the only person who auditioned that actually understood who Michael was.

Ed Zwick: We were writing in a voice that was starting to become a little bit more generationally acute. Not everyone that we met as an actor could do it. We had to find people who could pick up on the rhythms we were going for. I remember Kenny walked in and had a wry, dark humor. He was a very smart, great looking guy who had a certain amount of insecurities that made him endearing. He was not conventional in that television way.

Ken Olin: Stylistically, Woody Allen had the greatest influence on the way the show was filmed. I deeply understood Michael's emotional side, but not the mannerisms. I think Marshall really related with those. It was primarily his voice on the page in the pilot.

Marshall Herskovitz: Ken and I had a problem in the final scene of the pilot. There was a very intense speech that Michael gave. It really was the climax of the episode. It all fell on his shoulders. The first time we shot it, Kenny wasn't emotional enough and I didn't realize he wasn't emotional enough. This was essentially my first time directing and I made a mistake. We felt we had to reshoot it. That was painful for both of us. He felt he disappointed me. I remember we left the set and he said to me, "I feel so awful, I am not giving you what you want." I think there was a level of fear that held us both back, but he did get it. That scene stands out as an amazing scene for the pilot. It cemented the show when you saw this guy break down and talk about his life. You

The script called for actors that would bring a new brand of acting to television. Ed and Marshall were interested in making television more like film. Courtesy ABC Photography Archives.

saw his vulnerability. We both moved into uncharted territory. Kenny is remembering that part of the process and not remembering that he actually got it.

Ken Olin: I liked acting from a place of vulnerability and sensitivity. The neurotic mannerisms and behaviorisms were something they wanted. It was the struggle with the fact that I am not by nature that sort of Jewish self-image. In their minds, Michael was much more a Woody Allen guy who married a gorgeous shiksa. While I was actually a Jewish guy married to a gorgeous shiksa, my relationship with Patty was entirely different.

Mel Harris: In terms of playing Susan Shilliday or Liberty Godshall, I felt really lucky that they picked a brunette shiksa instead of a blond one like they were.

Ed Zwick: Mel looks one way, very beautiful, but she is really a Jersey girl who has real spunk. She has some darker hues to her. We were as interested in the inner lives of the people we were casting as were are in their abilities to say our words. I knew we had to plumb their natures and steal from their experience. The actors would define the characters as much as we would, if what we were going to to do was going to be as intimate as we wanted it to be. We needed actors who were substantial and not just one thing. The complexity and contradictions would be the most interesting things about them.

Richard Kramer: I adored Mel Harris. Her journey was wonderful to behold because as an actress she had never carried a series before. I think she is the secret sauce. Hope polarized people and she was meant to.

Polly Draper (*Ellyn*): That is why I love the show. It is so unforgiving, but so human. It gives the warts and all of everybody. As annoying, vulnerable, and shallow as people can be they have that certain thing about them that makes you fall in love with them. That was one of the first series that I had seen that showed flawed people.

The Reaction

Susan Shilliday: I remember them filming the pilot and all the chaos of it. I was deep in it. I don't even remember seeing it for the first time. It was just what was going on. When I look back on it, the pilot is not one of my favorite episodes. I think they were still inventing it. They hadn't landed on the voice yet, which makes sense.

Mel Harris: The reviews were 50% positive and 50% negative. Then we debuted and became this demographic hit. The people who gave us those negative reviews were forced to go back and review us again. It gave us another wave of publicity. Back then you couldn't fake publicity like you can now. Being reviewed negatively to begin with was probably the best thing that happened to our show.

Ed Zwick: There were as many people that were put off by the show as there were that admired it. I think it is because to talk about the examined life is something that is controversial. The way to do that is to try to get down to a granular level of experience, to really try to look at the dynamics and break it apart. That was the agenda.

Scott Winant (*Producer*): In those days, shows went to a preview house to test a pilot. They sat down a full audience of people. They gave everybody a device with a knob on it. When the audience was happy they turned it to the right. When they were not happy they turned it to the left. They watched a Mr. Magoo cartoon to modulate the audience to see if they were a receptive audience. Then they showed the pilot. I think we might have been the worst tested show ever. People at the preview house said, "It is hard for me to remember a show that tested worse than this."

Ed Zwick: I think they showed a Daffy Duck cartoon to use as a median score and we tested less than Daffy Duck. We went into this room behind a mirror and watched a focus group talk about the pilot. They were saying, "Who is that guy? Why was that person upset?" It was terrible. I had just bought a brand new car after driving a beat up

Reactions were split when the show premiered, but it went on to win the Emmy and People's Choice the first year. Courtesy of Carol Gepper's TV Guide Collection.

one for years. I was so shaken by the experience that when I pulled out of the parking lot, I backed into a post.

Scott Winant: We had to watch a test group where they said, "I don't want to see my life on television. What is this show?" I remember how deflated Ed and Marshall were. It was a bad evening. We slumped our way into the elevator and Brandon Stoddard, the head of ABC Entertainment, stepped in with us. Brandon turned to Ed and Marshall and said, "You know, I don't care. I like the show. I am gonna put it on." I don't know if that could happen anymore. Where a network executive, simply because he understands and likes a show, could go against electronic testing. If Brandon Stoddard had not decided to go against convention and put it on, it never would have made it to air. We won the People's Choice Award a few months later.

Liberty Godshall: We were so criticized for focusing on ourselves. Which was what we did. We thought we were the first people who ever had children, for God's sake. (*Laughs*) At least we knew it. In writing it we said we know it is ridiculous. Now, this is what millennials do all the time.

Ed Zwick: When the show was about to premiere, they played us a bunch of promos for the series. They were loud, brassy, and in your face. They were really quite horrible. We went to them and said, "Guys, these suck. Let us make our own trailers." We did a set of monologues of characters talking. The camera was outside of a room and would slowly reveal the characters. The intention was to go from a loud commercial to something still and quiet. When the viewer's television was suddenly quiet for a moment, they didn't know how to react. They actually listened for a bit.

Richard Kramer: We explored using the Stephen Sondheim song "Our Time" from *Merrily We Roll Along* as the theme song. It was expensive and we couldn't afford it. I remember I sat at the piano and played "Our Time" for Ed and Marshall. Instead, we got Snuffy Walden and that wonderful theme music, which I love.

Scott Winant: The only reason I brought Snuffy in was because an agent called me and said she had a client named Snuffy Walden. I literally wanted to meet a guy named Snuffy. When I found out Snuffy had no experience doing scores, we arranged for him to meet with Stewart Levin, who was an established composer and understood composition and arrangements. Snuffy had the identifying sound because of his slide guitar that was almost unique to his playing style.

Marshall Herskovitz: So much of the show was about the importance of telling the truth to yourself and someone else. The only reason to do that is to resolve something. I feel that was a theme of the show that was very important to us. It had to do with the idea of the power of love. The necessity of solving your problems with other people as opposed to against other people.

Ed Zwick: There is a certain temerity and presumptiveness that you have when you are young. I think it came out of a spirit of our generation to try to be a little bit radical in the approach. There were several moments in the process in which we encountered these rubicons. It was charmed in the beginning, in that we went in to pitch the show to a group of people who were our age. They understood what our intentions were but that was only the first step.

Ken Zunder (*Director Of Photography. Joined series in Season 2*): Most of the people working on the show were actually in their thirties. The cast and the crew had little kids. Normal television shows started at 8:00 a.m. We started at 6:30 a.m. This meant we would be home earlier to spend time with our kids. Every day at 5:12 p.m. Lindsley Parsons, the Production Manager, would come down to the set and call last shot. It meant we could get out of there by 5:30 and get to see our kids at night.

Ed Zwick: Then we had to actually write it and tell the studio we were gonna cast unknowns. We were going to have someone shoot it who had never shot before and Marshall was going to direct it and he had never directed a pilot before. Each step we had to take the moral high ground. "This is how we are going to do it and if you don't like it, then let's not do it." There were many different skirmishes and then a couple of real battles along the way.

"The Parents Are Coming, The Parents Are Coming"

Directed by Edward Zwick

Written by Marshall Herskovitz and Edward Zwick

October 6, 1987

Ed Zwick: We turned in "The Parents are Coming" and went into Brandon Stoddard's office who was a wonderful guy. He said, "I read the first couple scripts. They are great but don't you think they are a bit dark? Don't you think we could lighten them up." We said, "We think they are funny." He said, "Don't you think you are going a little bit deep as far as the angst of the characters?" We said, "No." It wasn't exactly a rope-a-dope, but to a certain degree it was saying this is what we intended. I think they were unaccustomed to someone saying "No" to them. Somehow that willingness to hold to our convictions gave them the courage to hold to their convictions because they actually did like the show. They were just trying to do things the way they had always done them. They looked at us with our hubris and just somehow buckled.

Mel Harris (*Hope*): Shirley Knight played my mother. She was one of the most wonderful actresses. George Coe played my dad. I was so lucky to have them. The dynamic that we saw with Hope and her mom was a real examination of a young woman who was now a mother trying to make her way and not be criticized. Being a mom empowered her to speak back to her own mother. Maybe her mom was a meddling pain in the ass who she loved anyway. I don't think that Hope wished for a different mother. I think as she became a mother herself, she was looking for a different kind of support and communication.

Richard Kramer (*Producer*): Shirley Knight told us, "Do you know who your genius is? Mel Harris."

Susan Shilliday (*Writer*): When the show was picked up, Ed and Marshall didn't know how to explain to others what they were trying to

The first regular episode focused on Hope and her mother's relationship. This relationship is continued in Season 3. Courtesy of Carol Gepper's TV Guide Collection.

do. Liberty and I knew what they were trying to do. They just looked at us and said, "Go, start writing." Richard, Liberty and I came in early. Ed and Marshall were working on the first episodes. There was a vague idea of what the season was going to look like.

Patty Wettig (*Nancy*): After we did the pilot, they decided to recast the kids. I said to Marshall and Ed, "If I don't ask you for anything else," which of course I did ask them for other things but I said, "Please let me help cast the kids. Bring in some boys and audition them with me. The chemistry between me and my son, Ethan, is going to be as important as my chemistry with Elliot." They decided to let me. The moment Luke Rossi (*Ethan*) walked in, my heart exploded. I can still feel it. That was my son, I knew it. When we read, he was great. I am sure some aspect of him reminded me of my own son. I thought he was fantastic.

Episode 3

"Housewarming"

Directed by John Pasquin

Written by Edward Zwick and Marshall Herskovitz

October 13, 1987

Marshall Herskovitz: After the third episode, my brother called me and said, "Do your friends just drop in like that all the time?" I said, "Hell no." He said, "Thank God. I was so jealous." That was just a convenience of writing, you have to get people in the same room. Every show has some kind of wish fulfillment behind it. I think it was a big wish fulfillment in *thirtysomething* that these friends had become a family in this way. They were so involved in each others lives that they dropped over.

Ed Zwick: We wanted these kind, smart, thoughtful people who were nonetheless beset by all the things that we had now discovered life was defined by. They seem enviable by first blush, but in fact they, like everyone else, had to deal with the things that challenge you everyday. There was a sense that these people were committed to communication and a willingness to get below the surface of "Hi, honey, I'm home."

Marshall Herskovitz: We had people before every shot who would just go through the set and throw old clothes, toys, and mess things up all over the floor. You had to do twice as much stuff before anyone would notice it at all. It was important to us to see if you could do that on television.

"Couples"

Directed by Marshall Herskovitz

Written by Edward Zwick and Marshall Herskovitz

October 27, 1987

Patty Wettig: One of the first episodes we filmed was the episode where I twirl the baton. That was a baby step to learning who Nancy was.

Susan Shilliday: I wouldn't say that anyone figured out in great detail how Nancy was going to develop. It was clear that we would explore her finding herself. We didn't know how. As opposed to Hope, who starts out a little more strong and has to figure out how that works in a marriage, Nancy was someone who had much less a feeling of self worth. She had children earlier and made that a large part of her identity.

Marshall Herskovitz: There wasn't one source behind Nancy. Patty Wettig was a very passionate woman, incredibly smart, and had a lot to say about her character. We had other writers working with us as well. One of the things that defined the experience of *thirtysomething* was the passion about it. I think every single person was passionate about it and that was exhausting. It was a crucible for all of us. It was four years of this incredibly intense commitment to one thing. Believe me, everyone had their own opinions.

Mel Harris: The wonderful thing was that Ed and Marshall's door was always open. You could compliment or complain. We read through every script before shooting them. There were scripts where I would say,

"Couples" focused on the two married couples as we see the same date night viewed from each of the four characters. The final shot of the episode contradicts all versions by showing a far away view of the four of them laughing and having a great time at a restaraunt. Courtesy of the Dan Steadman Collection.

"I just don't think Hope would do this." I am very good at picking my battles.

Patty Wettig: I felt very possessive of Nancy. If I read a scene that didn't go the right way, I would go to the office and talk to the writers. It felt like she was mine.

Marshall Herskovitz: I can't even begin to tell you how Nancy went from one thing to another. It was helped along by the very strong creative contributions of these various people whether it was Susan, Liberty or Patty.

Susan Shilliday: When Ed and Marshall wrote "Couples" they would have already read "Separation" (*Episode 13*) because it was one of the first episodes that was written. So, the people inside the show knew what was coming.

Marshall Herskovitz (*Director*): When we first cut "Couples" together according to the script, the show didn't work. I did a huge restructuring in the editing room to make it more comprehensible. We did a lot more inner cutting in the original script between everyone's point of view. It was just a big mess. I decided to follow one character's point of view and then another character's point of view.

Patty Wettig: The network mandated that the first episodes had to be centered around Michael and Hope. They didn't want any other character other than Hope or Michael to lead an episode. They felt the audience had to attach to them before you can go to the other characters. We filmed "Couples" early, but didn't play it till later because they felt that one had a little too much Nancy and Elliot. Well, I have heard it was because the network didn't want anyone but Michael and Hope in the first ten episodes, but it might have been Ed and Marshall's way of saying, "Patty, you are not getting an episode for awhile so be quiet." (*Laughs*)

Marshall Herskovitz: We spent an hour going deeply into each person's point of view and how widely varying those perceptions were. Just remember when you're at a restaurant and you see four people laughing, there is a world inside those people that can be very dark. From the outside it looks like everybody's fine. We remember the dangers, but we don't remember when things are fine. Maybe the evening wasn't as bad as each character thought it was. For all I know, we may have disagreed among ourselves what that last shot meant.

"But Not for Me"

Directed by Tom Moore

Written by Richard Kramer

November 3, 1987

Scott Winant (*Producer*): I had Michael Feinstein commissioned to do incidental music and play the entire score for this episode. It was about Michael and Hope going out on a date.

Michael Feinstein (*Musician*): Richard Kramer, friend of a mutual friend, wrote the episode with me in mind. When I went to meet the producers they actually said something to the effect that they weren't sure if I was the right one for the part, which made me laugh. When we filmed, it was done before the series had premiered, so I had no idea that it was going to be such a big deal. There was one lyric I sang in "I Could Write A Book" that they changed because of the plot, something I wouldn't have done otherwise.

Scott Winant: I said this was a unique episode. It was about this space out of time where Michael and Hope actually tried to pretend they could have a normal life. We did two things that were unusual. Everybody they encountered was played by the same two actors (*Lucy Webb, Timothy Stack*). Also, I had Michael Feinstein playing the piano and doing cabaret songs between the scenes. That had nothing to do with the show or how we did it. I collaborated with Richard on that.

Richard Kramer (*Writer*): Scott was the producer. He made those things happen. Ed and Marshall didn't get on the phone and find

Episode five was the first script not written by Marshall and Ed. Richard Kramer wrote the backstory of Gary and Melissa with the B story of Michael and Hope's night out. Courtesy of ABC Photography Archives. The Lisa Mercado Fernandez Collection.

Michael Feinstein. I don't remember if I wrote Michael's name into the script. I just know we had a friend in common that allowed me to reach out to him to see if he would do it. He liked the script and was interested in doing it. I recently saw Tom Moore, the director of that episode. He said, "You changed the voice of the show with that episode." At first, Ed and Marshall were not delighted with that fact. It brought in a different note. They were hard to please. It was the first episode not written by them. They had standards in their mind that we were trying to meet. I didn't always succeed.

Scott Winant: We would never be discouraged for being inventive. Ed and Marshall loved that. We had to earn it. We had to prove our point. They were bold and anxious to experiment. The collaborations we had were very strong and stimulating.

Richard Kramer: I got great pleasure out of writing for Peter Horton and Melanie Mayron. I was given carte blanche to make up their backstory.

Peter Horton (*Gary*): The relationship between Gary and Melissa was so much about longing. They were really good for each other and it should have worked. For Gary, that is why he would run from it. That would make him happy and there was a part in him that wasn't able to accept that. I don't want to speak for Melanie because she will get mad at me. (*Laughs*)

Melanie Mayron (*Melissa*): Melissa wanted Gary in a way she couldn't have him anymore. When people break up, they don't see each other for a long time because they have to not have that person in their sight. I think that was the dynamic with the Melissa/Gary story at that point.

Peter Horton: When you get in those deeper places things get irrational. You could see them working, but Gary wouldn't let her in. He kept sabotaging it.

Richard Kramer: I was told to write a scene that was fifteen pages long to mess with the pacing of a normal television script. So, I wrote a one act play that contained the Melissa and Gary story. We were trying to grab television by our mouths like a dog and shake it back and forth.

"We Gather Together"

Directed by Mark Cullingham

Written by Susan Miller and Richard Kramer and Edward Zwick

November 17, 1987

Polly Draper (*Ellyn*): Gary and Ellyn started out as pure hatred. Gary was so annoying to Ellyn. We just could not have gotten along worse. I loved it.

Episode 7

"Nice Work If You Can Get It"

Directed by Claudia Weill

Written by Paul Haggis, Story by Jean Vallely

December 1, 1987

Paul Haggis (*Writer*): When pitching ideas there always comes a moment of desperation, a moment where your mind just stops functioning and your mouth spits out whatever lame thought shoots through your brain. So, I could absolutely identify with Elliot and Michael as they ground away in search of anything that passes for original thought. It is in these desperate moments where we convince ourselves that the worst idea imaginable could indeed be that groundbreaking expression. And in that moment, "Yo, it's your Art Center" was born.

The show started off as a fan favorite, despite the Network being unsure and test audiences giving it a bad score. thirtysomething*'s first TV Guide Cover debuted at the end of Season 1. Courtesy of Carol Gepper's TV Guide Collection.*

Joe Dougherty (*Producer*): Paul Haggis wrote a scene that explains everything you need to know about life. Michael is talking to Hope about watching the home shopping network. Michael says he is in advertising and he knows that if he calls in he can buy the duck but they won't let him. I think it was a porcelain duck. What he learned about life is that if you keep trying to get the ducks you'll miss out on the kitchen knives. I might have the items wrong.

Writer Paul Haggis came up with Michael and Elliot's slogan for the Art Center. Ellyn was not pleased and didn't hire them for the job. It may not have been what Ellyn wanted but you try to stop thinking about it when you visit a museum. Artwork by Becca Ryan.

Paul Haggis: One of my great pleasures is finding truth in absurdity and absurdity in truth. I pictured Michael at this point in his life where he is questioning every decision he made, everything that brought him to this moment. Like many people, when I am troubled I have difficulty sleeping. In the eighties, when you turned on the television late at night, the programming you found on your local stations was mostly infomercials. One could hear "Wait, there's more!' so many times without realizing that there truly was no more. So, flipping through the channels quickly brought you to the Home Shopping Network. It was here that I thought Michael might discover the meaning of life, that nothing is permanent, that if you wait too long, life and the item you weren't even sure that you wanted, truly does pass you by.

Joe Dougherty: Ken intensely played this like it's was an epiphany and Mel looked at him like he was out of his mind. You could actually live your life by that philosophy.

"Weaning"

Directed by John Pasquin

Written by Liberty Godshall

December 8, 1987

Liberty Godshall (*Writer*): This was the first thing I ever wrote for television. I had written a screenplay and had the good fortune of selling it. I was actually weaning as I wrote it. I was on rocky ground and I think that episode is on rocky ground. It is all over the place, which is how a mother feels at that moment.

Mel Harris (*Hope*): I was playing a non-working mother while I was a mother with a young child. I am a better person and mother when I work. It challenges me and challenges my mind. My son grew up on the set. My daughter was born at the end of the third season.

Liberty Godshall: The episode was politicized at that moment and taken out of context into women working outside of the home instead of inside of the home. It got so ridiculous because there was nothing stated in that episode one way or the other. I was working when I wrote it with my child at home. It was about so many different issues. It is amazing how much ground we have lost just in the various aspects of motherhood. I am more proud of the episode now because weaning would never be picked for a topic of a television show today.

Mel Harris: I remember my last breastfeeding with my daughter to this day. Sitting there, knowing it was gonna be the last time and crying. It was so powerful. She is now twenty-five. We became a breastfeeding nation in the eighties. My mother threw a bottle at me and

"Weaning" is an episode about a new mother deciding when to go back to work at the same time her child is weaning herself. Writer Liberty Godshall wanted to focus on female topics that are rarely discussed on television. Courtesy of ABC Photography Archives.

I was supposed to catch it. That is what you did. You pumped. You froze it. That episode was at the forefront of an activity that people engaged in raising their children. I didn't receive any how dare you stop breastfeeding your child hate mail.

Liberty Godshall: There was a book released that mentioned "Weaning." The author got very riled up at this episode. She felt that Marshall and Ed were saying that women should be stay-at-home mothers. She was very angry about it. She missed about a thousand beats in that script.

Mel Harris: You don't want to lose the women who have to work or chose to work; they were an important part of who our audience was. But you want to honor those who stay home which we all know is an incredibly hard job. There was a balance of being true to who Hope was. She gave up a career to raise the kids. Michael certainly had great success at times during the series. For Hope it was about when the children got older. She looked to fulfill the things that were filled by the children. The early nest syndrome instead of empty nest.

Liberty Godshall: What happens to women who have been out there in the workforce and are warrior women in that arena is the physicality of having a child puts you in a slightly different world from your mate. As a person who was raised in the sixties, I didn't think there were any differences between men and women. It is an awakening. You are in this alone. Your mate isn't gonna understand what you are feeling and there is some sadness because you have not had this type of isolation. That is what happens in the scene in the kitchen when Hope starts crying out of nowhere. Poor Michael, he was trying to understand and was very loving.

Ken Olin (*Michael*): I think they started to accept the way I played Michael. The fact that the show was popular right out of the gate didn't hurt. The public certainly accepted me as Michael.

Mel Harris: The feedback overall in general was amazing at how people felt about the show but "Weaning" in particular certainly garnered a lot from women specifically.

Liberty Godshall: It is so much easier to go back to work. The stress is lower. Luckily going into it, I wasn't aware of how dicey it was going to be to talk about all these things. There is no judgement and Hope basically ends up saying I don't know.

Scott Winant (*Producer*): I got a call at 5:30 in the morning. An actor couldn't make it because his wife went into labor. It was a scene where Elliot and Michael were doing a commercial. They needed an actor for the director in the scene. John Pasquin insisted that I play it. That was my first acting gig. I got dressed and came in. They put me in make up and I played the director. That was when I realized I was going bald. I could see it so clearly.

"I'll Be Home for Christmas"

Directed by Robert Lieberman

Written by Richard Kramer, Story by Susan Monsky

December 15, 1987

Richard Kramer (*Writer*): Ed and Marshall, who were never anything but supportive, were troubled by the big blow out scene between Melissa and Michael. That episode was shot before we went on the air. The scene was at a level of intensity that the show had not explored before. The brief of Ed and Marshall was that they wanted it to be about little moments and things that were not ordinarily seen as drama on television. Marshall said, "I don't know if this is the show."

Marshall Herskovitz: Richard remembers that incorrectly. I looked at that scene and said, "Oh my fucking God, this is so brilliant." I was knocked out by how brilliant they were. I was over the moon about it.

Melanie Mayron (*Melissa*): We had a wonderful Director, Rob Lieberman. He wanted us to really go for it. I remember there was a beat where I smacked the door. He just wanted us to not hold back at all.

Ken Olin (*Michael*): Everything shifted in that episode. Rob Lieberman came from a very different film background. They wanted the director to bring their own sensibility to the episodes. He was a hip, contemporary commercial director. He brought this vibe to the episode. It was really liberating for me. The struggle for me was how do I bring this character to life when I am not in synch with what Ed and Marshall wanted? They wanted a quirky type of performance. Rob really helped, we had a great relationship.

Michael and Melissa fight over work and their relationship in a visceral scene that changed the trajectory of the series in the fan favorite, "I'll Be Home For Christmas." Courtesy of ABC Photography Archives. The Lisa Mercado Fernandez Collection.

Richard Kramer: We really blew the lights out with that. When I was writing the fight scene for Melissa and Michael Ed said, "Take it as far as you can." I remember Ken and Melanie shaking on the set after doing it because they were so overwhelmed by finding this in their characters.

Melanie Mayron: Rob had two cameras and they had the longest lens he could find which meant the cameras were really far away. It felt like it was just Ken and I on the set. The crew was back where the cameras were. When he said action we just went for it. It was like being on stage. We could play it as big as we wanted to the balcony because the people were sitting far away on the other side of the orchestra pit. It was the only time we shot the show that way.

Richard Kramer: Ken and Melanie had the most wonderful chemistry. It was as strong as the chemistry between Mel Harris and Ken. They were familiarly convincing. That was just a gift that we got. It was also part of the genius of the casting that Ed and Marshall did. It was intuitive because you never know when you are casting a pilot.

Ken Olin: That was the best scene. I think that episode allowed me to bring something fully of myself to it. Maybe from there I could understand the other parts of Michael. Whatever limitations I had as an actor were gone. That scene with Melanie was everything that made doing the series incredible. Melanie was wonderful in it. People were not writing full on fights like that.

Melanie Mayron: Ken is a terrific actor who is bright, giving and so present. He also has the most wicked sense of humor. He is just wonderful and really keeps you on your toes.

Richard Kramer: That was a story about the need for acknowledgment. There was a very key scene in the alley where Melissa was wearing her numbers coat. That alley was on the lot in Studio City, California. Gary tells her it was Michael that sent her art to the gallery. That moment was then paid off in the final moment when she came to Michael's house. Melissa came out of the shadows. She was letting him know that she knew that he stood up for her.

Before Carrie Bradshaw made shoes the most coveted fashion accessory, Melissa Steadman wore a numbers coat and one earring. Artwork by Becca Ryan.

Melanie Mayron: I didn't keep the numbers coat when the show ended. Patrick Norris was our custom designer. A few years ago we were both directing *Pretty Little Liars* (2010). He said, "I've got something for you." He handed me the numbers coat. Patrick had saved it and gave it back to me.

Winnie Holzman (*Writer*): I really lost my heart to the show with that first Christmas episode. That was a turning point. At first, I admired it and was a little bit almost weary. I just slipped into a much much deeper level of admiration. I was overwhelmed by what they were accomplishing on television.

Richard Kramer: Mel Harris was so beautiful in that velvet dress. The menorah scene was gorgeously lit. My favorite moments were where the moment was so loaded and so understood that it could be conveyed wordlessly. That is the thing that has changed in television. Now they have what is called a Tone Meeting. You get on the phone with the studio or network and they tell you what they want the tone to be. It is very awful.

Melanie Mayron: I think Melissa was the one that was following her dream. Michael wasn't at that point. He had a wife, a baby and had responsibilities. He had the fear of not ever being able to break out and do what he wanted.

Ken Olin: Ed and Marshall wanted to defy certain conventions as writers. In that episode, we realized what kind of requirements we needed to hit. We weren't going to be able to change storytelling. We had to accept the terms of the medium we were working in as well. A lot of credit goes to Rob and Richard for hitting it. Ed and Marshall deserve credit for containing that and moving forward with it. Ed and Marshall never made arguments for their limitations. They wanted to learn and they wanted to teach. That episode is an example of them changing their focus. From then on, that season really took off.

Marshall Herskovitz: I was learning something from Rob. I had never seen someone shoot with 400 millimeter lenses. Shooting with that kind of lens made it so intense. Ed and I said, "Holy shit, look at that. What lens is that?" The longest lens you shot with in those days was 75.

Mel Harris (*Hope*): The first Christmas show was incredibly powerful. It became this period of mostly fabulous moments.

Richard Kramer: I think what really lands that episode is Gary walking off alone. It was a nod that I did to the end of the play *Bus Stop* (1955) by William Inge.

Scott Winant (*Producer*): The network would say, "We want to come down to the set and take a picture of Michael bringing the Christmas tree home." I told them, "We don't want you to show that. That is relevant to being a surprise within the context of the episode." We started to lie so that they wouldn't give away our stuff.

Episode 10

"South by Southeast"

Directed by Dan Lerner

Written by Paul Haggis

January 5, 1988

Dana Delany (*Played Gary's love interest Eve*): I had done a sitcom called *Sweet Surrender* (1987). It was my first and last foray into sitcoms. Paul Haggis was a writer on it. Paul and I connected because we weren't really comfortable in that world. He wrote the part of "Eve" for me in "South by Southwest." They came to me and just offered me the part. I used to joke that the only person that worked at ABC longer than me was Bob Iger. He was head of the network when I did *Moonlighting (1985), thirtysomething*, and *China Beach (1988).*

Paul Haggis (*Writer*): I had the great pleasure of working with Dana on her first situation comedy. Dana is smart, funny, terrifically talented and beautiful. I thought that if Gary were ever to fall deeply in love, she would be the worst possible candidate because there was simply no easy way to dismiss her, no box to put her in that would rule her out. Gary would have no option finally but to look inward for the cause of his problems with relationships.

Dana Delany: I already knew Ed Zwick because when I was working in an antique store in 1980, he came into the store and we met there. He was a writer on *Family* (1979) and we became acquaintances. It all came full circle when I worked for him on *thirtysomething*.

Ann Lewis Hamilton (*Producer*): Some of the episodes in the first season were so funny. Paul Haggis wrote "South by Southwest." It was

Dana Delany played Gary's girlfriend one year before she starred on China Beach. *This episode ends with a fantasy of the cast playing parts in a multitude of Alfred Hitchcock films. Courtesy of Dana Delany.*

just hilarious. He was sort of put on the show. I think he helped in the beginning. When I was there, Paul was very kind and wrote good scripts.

Paul Haggis: I asked myself what was the worst thing that could happen to a man like Gary, who bedded multiple beautiful women a week and never found one who was "right for him." The answer was quite obvious - falling in love with the perfect woman. There are many things that bring fear into the hearts of men, but the idea of finally getting exactly what you've always said that you wanted has to be at the top of that list.

Dana Delany: It was not a typical episode. It was a nod to Alfred Hitchcock. It was Dan Lerner's directorial debut. He has gone on to be a big television director. We rehearsed the episode at Peter's house on a weekend with Dan. I remembered thinking, "Wow, they really take this seriously." Dan shot for seven days and then Marshall came in and directed extra scenes for the episode. I think Marshall directed a scene with Peter and I that they wanted in a very specific way. I think it was more of an intimate scene.

Peter Horton (*Gary*): I loved Dana Delany. I think I had a crush on her in that episode. She was so sexy and grounded in such a unique way. I was just in love with her. It made it so easy to play.

Dana Delany: Peter was sort of every girl's dream. The freewheeling bachelor that all the girls had a crush on. He was sort of the original boy-man. I am still friends with all those people. I see Marshall, Ed, Tim, Ken, and Patty. We travel in the same circles. Peter really was that free spirit. One weekend, we went to see Tim Busfield's children's theater group do a performance. Peter didn't have the address or a map. He said, "We will just sort of figure it out." He really was like his character. Peter is also a killer hugger. He will hug and crush you. You better be sure you are not wearing glasses. They will be destroyed. (*Laughs*)

Ken Olin (*Michael*): From the Pilot to a Rashomon ("Couples") episode to a Hitchcock episode, we were doing wildly different things. The challenge of acting to a script was like being in an acting class working on different plays. You had to change towards the material and try to realize the demands of that script. Most of us had trained in the theater. We would change our approach to fit the material.

Paul Haggis: I had long admired Hitchcock and his ability to manipulate our fears. The thought struck me that, being unable to face his fear of being loved, Gary could easily find himself in one Hitchcock film after another. From that point on, it just became pure fun. Marshall and Ed were always great with the writers, giving us all the rope we needed to hang ourselves, and I took the end of that rope and ran right over a cliff. Again, with my love of finding truth in absurdity and vice versa, I thought this might be a way for Gary to finally dig into his subconscious and find out more about himself than he could if he threw himself into years of therapy. And, boys being boys, I thought Michael and Elliot would leap at the chance to momentarily escape lives that they feared were becoming ordinary.

Peter Horton: The Hitchcock stuff was all from Dan, the Director of the episode. He was our Director of Photography on the pilot so he came out of a real visual discipline. It was the first time I saw people pull out low angle prisms and dolly shots. Where they pull out and zoom in at the same time, all of the Hitchcock tricks. It was a fun thing to do. I remember distinctly the scene we shot in Westwood where I knew I had blown it with Dana Delany and I get on my bike and ride.

Dana Delany: I don't even remember that I played the *Psycho* (1960) mom in the Hitchcock fantasy sequence. I am so happy to hear that I did. No wonder I have such affection for it. The *Psycho* house is on the Universal lot so when I was shooting *Desperate Housewives* (2004) I would go sneak off and sit at the *Psycho* house. I must have felt a deep connection.

"Therapy"

Directed by Marshall Herskovitz

Written by Susan Shilliday

January 12, 1988

Susan Shilliday: I started writing "Separation" first. Then we realized we needed an episode before that. By the time I wrote those two episodes, I was pretty deep into the Nancy and Elliot characters. I probably wrote all of "Separation" and then we realized we needed "Therapy." Nancy was the person I gravitated to. It wasn't a decision. It just kind of happened.

Patty Wettig: Susan really wrote a great episode. I didn't feel like Nancy until we filmed "Therapy." Tim, Marshall and I were gonna do all the therapy sessions in one day. It was my birthday the day we filmed them. I remember driving to the set that day thinking, "Don't think about your husband today. Don't think about your kids today. You just need to focus with all your force on your work." Which I don't think I had done in a few years.

Tim Busfield (*Elliot*): Patty knew my ex-wife. She loved playing her in scenes when she knew it would get a reaction. In the "Therapy" episode, there were many times when I called her by my ex's name. Patty would beam ear to ear because she knew that she was getting to me.

Patty Wettig: That used to crack me up. I love Tim. We did have really good chemistry together. You either do or you don't. As much as I would remind him of his first wife, who I knew because I had done a play with, for me, his arms reminded me of my father. My father had died about six years before *thirtysomething*. I would look down at his arms and there was something so familiar to me. It was an odd thing. It just always vibrated in me. It was very particular. We just trusted each other.

Tim Busfield: We have been great life long friends. My wife (*Melissa Gilbert*) has fallen in love with Kenny and Patty. Any time you have that kind of chemistry, and you can maintain it, there's a lot of love there.

Patty Wettig: When you are acting and you are going to be raw and vulnerable you have to not protect yourself. You know that the person

Patty Wettig went from two lines in the pilot to a tour de force performance that won her an Emmy for Best Supporting Actress in "Therapy." Courtesy of ABC Photography Archives. The Lisa Mercado Fernandez Collection.

you are working with is equally invested and no one is trying to win. They aren't going to try to get more attention. Actors have their issues. I never had issues with Tim. I think that he is phenomenal.

Tim Busfield: Every actor loves to play conflict because that's when we feel like we're actors the most. Acting that kind of stuff is easier than acting the more subtle stuff. When you're doing some of the more subtle stuff you may not know what you did. If you're doing it right, you don't really know what you did. When you're yelling at each other, it's a little easier. We just took off and Marshall didn't need to guide us so much.

Marshall Herskovitz (*Director*): There was a take in this episode where Timmy really got upset and started to cry. He said, "Do I mean anything, am I anything?" and tears were coming to his face. It is one of those moments that is just gold, when somebody's soul is just revealing itself right there on camera. Sitting in the room when he did that, I thought it was over the top. I said, "Timmy, you have to pull it back from that." He said, "Really?" I said, "Yeah, I think so." So, he pulls it back. When we got to dailies I said, "Oh my God, I am an idiot." I don't know if it was because I was sitting there or I was doing too many things. What he had done was utterly brilliant and I thought it was too much. The blessing of film is that you do multiple takes so he had already done it and we had it. As soon as I saw dailies, I thought I can't believe I thought this was over the top.

Patty Wettig: It just was happening. It was like one of those feelings of flight. There was no work involved, it was all muscle. There was no thinking involved. It was just spontaneous.

Marshall Herskovitz: That was just Tim and Patty being great actors, responding to the material and just being present.

Richard Kramer: I will never forget them shooting that sequence with Marshall playing the therapist on this little tiny set. It had gone late and we were all gathered around silent and knowing this was something else. The extent to which Tim and Patty went for it was fearless.

"Therapy" has a B Story of Ellyn trying to keep a secret about having a tattoo. The way this story collides with Nancy and Elliot's therapy perfectly displays how the writers crafted their scripts. "Therapy" won a Writers Guild Award for drama. Courtesy of Carol Gepper's TV Guide Collection.

Marshall Herskovitz: I made the bizarre decision to act in that episode. So, there I was playing the therapist, trying to direct them when in fact this was the first time I had ever acted on camera. I had acted a lot in college but I had never been on camera. I was having my own reaction. Acting on camera is really difficult. The first time the camera was on me it was a piece of coverage and I was looking at Timmy who was talking. All I could think of was, "There is a camera behind him. Oh my God, I'm looking in the camera. Don't look into the camera."

Tim Busfield: He would apologize to us for his acting.

Marshall Herskovitz: I was so completely distracted by the ridiculous nonsense of real life at that moment. It gave me incredible respect for what these people do. That they can actually stay in character when there is so much distracting stuff going around. There I was dealing with that while at the same time trying to deal with directing the show.

Tim Busfield: A few weeks ago, my wife told me how despicable I was as Elliot. He was such a great opportunity to play a character that evoked that response. There were things that they wrote into Elliot which elicited severe frustration from women. I was in the supermarket reaching for cream cheese, I turned around and a woman gave me a big slap on the side of my face. She was upset at Elliot for saying to Nancy "Don't you ever shave your legs anymore?" It was brutal but I didn't write it. Susan Shilliday wrote it. I laughed at the read through when I saw it and everybody groaned. So, you knew it was gonna have some impact.

Patty Wettig: Timmy and I could work incredibly well without offending each other. I remember afterwards on the drive home feeling satisfied as an actor for the first time in five years.

Tim Busfield: The B storyline in "Therapy" is brilliant. They tied the scenes together. The secret of the tattoo and what happens when you break those secrets is what it was about. Going in there and digging up the marital problems.

Susan Shilliday: I have no idea how I came up with the B story of Ellyn's tattoo. I know I wanted the fact that nobody could keep a secret to be in there. It was important that one character would look at it as totally trivial and not something that you would worry about keeping a secret, but the other character would think of it as highly personal. It was revealing of Nancy because someone else would just brush it off but she feels horrible about it.

Patty Wettig: I was nominated for an Emmy for "Therapy." Ken and I got out of the car at the Emmy awards and nobody knew me. They knew Ken. All the reporters screamed, "Ken, who's your date?" Then I won the Emmy and I felt perfectly fine about it. (*Laughs*)

Episode 12

"Competition"

Directed by Rob Cohen

Written by Joseph Dougherty

January 19, 1988

Joe Dougherty (*Writer*): I was a playwright in New York and my representation sent a copy of my play to Ed and Marshall. They were putting together the writing staff of the show. They wanted a staff that wasn't polished at television. They said, "There had been some kind of clerical error at ABC and the show was going to get on the air and would probably disappear immediately. If I wanted one, I had better move pretty quickly." I read the first four scripts that night. I said, "Yeah, cut me off a slice of this."

Ken Olin (*Michael*): How do you have Joe, Richard, Susan, Liberty and Ann writing on the same show? Paul Haggis was there for a while as well. They were all very different writers.

Ann Lewis Hamilton (*Producer*): I have this presumption that people thought the show was whiney yuppies. I certainly never saw it like that. Michael was so hyper sensitive. I thought he was awesome. All my female friends wanted to be married to Michael. The characters were introspective. Gary, Elliot, and Michael seemed like real guys to me.

Ken Olin: I thought they had Michael softer than he had to be. His behavior was a little cuter than it had to be. There was a tendency to be a little more adolescent, a little mushier.

Elliot gets to outshine Michael in Joe Dougherty's first script, "Competition." Does this episode mirror the relationship between Ed and Marshall? Courtesy of ABC Photography Archives. The Lisa Mercado Fernandez Collection.

Joe Dougherty: "Competition" came out of Ed and Marshall's personal competition. What it was like for them to be partners.

Tim Busfield: That was them dealing with their successes as well. You can flip back and forth on who does what. Ed was a feature director and was directing *Glory* (1989) and Marshall wasn't. So, they naturally had to deal with the male ego and competition. They had to deal with it in their friendship and partnership in owning Bedford Falls, their production company.

Liberty Godshall: I see starting points of both of Ed and Marshall in each character. It is a jumble and a lot of it is creatively drawn and idealized. The process of writing is such an alchemy. What I see now is what the actors brought to the characters. I don't see Ed in Michael. It really is just a note in a very big song.

Brandy Alexander (*Production Designer*): Marshall and Ed are very similar to Michael and Elliot and not just in first initials of their names. They may not even own up to how similar. Ed would lay on the floor and bounce a basketball in the air. Marshall would sit at his desk like he was ready to play chess. I loved the differences between them. You would ask Ed a question and he would answer, "Sure, let's do that." Marshall would answer, "What is the last possible day that you need the answer by."

Scott Winant (*Producer*): Face it, Michael and Elliot were Marshall and Ed. They wanted to talk about the things that scared them. Petty jealousy and triteness are part of us. I honestly believe that they picked advertising because it was so similar to making film. When you create television it is there to mount a platform to play commercials. You are, at the end of the day, selling toilet paper. What Ed and Marshall did was cut out the middle man and actually have them sell toilet paper. Let's have them care deeply about how they sell the toilet paper.

Marshall Herskovitz: I think both Ed and I identified with Michael. People would ask us which one is Michael and which one is Elliot and we would say we are both Michael and Elliot is the id. Michael was a composite of the two of us. We would address Michael with our particular emotional issues, but we related to all of them in a very intense and personal way and over time even more so.

Joe Dougherty: I think Michael was human in the episode. He was fine with competition as long as he won. Werner Breslow (*Richard Masur*) was kind of like an early draft of Miles Drentell in terms of how he used people. He played people against each other.

Liberty Godshall: Joe's writing is so important because the seeds he planted in "Competition" are the intonations of Michael's ambition. That script brought out something important in Michael.

Ken Olin: Having a different voice for Michael wasn't a new experience on that show. As an actor, you had to adjust to the stylistic demands on all their scripts. There wasn't the same thing of "I have to protect my character or my character wouldn't do that." It didn't have the same kind of consistency where there was a model that we had to

This episode starts the fan argument of whether Hope supports Michael enough or if Michael supports Hope enough. An argument that still wages thirty years later. Courtesy of ABC Photography Archives.

adhere to. The constant would be Michael's emotional point of view of things which probably remained the same. In this episode he gets a little small minded.

Joe Dougherty: I think Michael discovered part of himself that he would have preferred wasn't there. One of my favorite lines is when Elliot said, "You're not gonna write a letter to *The Times*, are you?" I was kind of ready to play these two guys against each other just to see what rotten things I could do to them. I doubt sincerely that I have done anything nastier to a character than letting that microphone stay open at that recording session. That may be the worst thing I have ever done to anybody. It is arguably the most aggressively male episode of the first season.

Ken Olin: I never felt that Michael couldn't behave badly out of a sense of protecting him. I don't think they thought of Michael as perfect.

Mel Harris: People often say Michael was right or Hope was right. There was no middle ground. I would have people come up to me and say, "How can you treat him like that?"

Joe Dougherty: The main reason that I wanted to do the show was the relationship between Hope and Michael. At the time, there was no depiction on television of the fact that you could be angry at someone that you loved. People have a hard time accepting their own reality unless they see a version of it on television. We would look at the mail that came to the office and it was, "I wish my friends would talk like this. I never knew people would be like this." It was the idea that Michael and Hope could be angry at each other but still be in love and they would work it out. That was the kind of marriage we hadn't been privy to on American television at that point.

Episode 13

"Separation"

Directed by Peter Horton

Written by Susan Shilliday

January 26, 1988

Tim Busfield: The guys called me to their office to talk about "Separation" before the script came out. They told me what the character arc would be and that Nancy and Elliot were going to split up. Peter Horton directed that episode.

Peter Horton *(Director)*: The very first scene I shot in "Separation" was the scene where Elliot is sitting in the car with Nancy and he wants to get out of the car. It was very much trial by fire.

Patty Wettig: I loved working with Peter. Beauty is the word that comes to mind. He had a kindness and a way of appreciating Nancy. The way he directed was in tune with Nancy's spirit in some lyrical way.

Peter Horton: I have this vivid memory of Ed taking me down to the set so I could go over the shots and what I was thinking. I got the infamous Ed Zwick sigh. Finally, he walked away and passed somebody and he told them, "He is just not getting it. He is just not getting it." (*Laughs*) The good thing about him was that he wouldn't leave it there. I went to him later, he explained it and he was right. Once I had directed "Separation" and they gained confidence, the next episodes were easier.

Susan Shilliday (*Writer*): Elliot feels he doesn't love Nancy anymore and can't forgive her for that. Nancy feels so wounded by him and betrayed. She feels there is nothing else to do. She is trying to take a strong position but feels wounded. It is what the show is about: how does any marriage survive? It is always on a knife edge. I was just talking last night to my daughter who was born when I was writing this stuff. I was nursing with one arm and writing with another. You never know what goes on in anyone's marriage and I have always been interested in that.

Peter Horton: You can have a great movie as long as you have a good cast and good script. You can have a shitty director and still be okay. Tim was so good. You really couldn't go wrong with him. He was bringing so much to that part, especially at that time. All you would do as director with him is turn the knob; he already had beautiful music playing. Directing Tim was easy. Ken Olin was a different story. (*Laughs*)

Tim Busfield: The scene where Elliot tries to explain to Hope why he left Nancy was great. I loved playing that stuff, a husband explaining to his best friend's wife why they separated.

Hope becomes the confidant of Nancy and Elliot as the Westin's marriage crumbles in "Separation." Peter Horton becomes the first of the cast to direct an episode. Courtesy of ABC Photography Archives. The Lisa Mercado Fernandez Collection.

Susan Shilliday: That is one of the things in writing that I am fiercest about. I do a lot of writing workshops with people at Sundance. I am always trying to tell writers that people do not talk to each other. Conversations are often really monologues and people rarely actually listen to each other. To find that moment in a scene where they do communicate is very important, but they don't have to answer each other all the time. The moment when they do hear each other becomes incredibly weighted. It is something I do consciously.

Tim Busfield: Peter shot my talk with Hope as one long shot with a super long lens that just keeps creeping in. It was very emotional and moving.

Susan Shilliday: It comes back to the idea that they don't talk to their family, they talk to their friends. I didn't want Elliot to go to Michael. I wanted him to go to Hope and to have her be put on the spot with her getting confidences from both Nancy and Elliot, which happens to friendships during divorces.

Tim Busfield: The episode also was mixed with the fun of me living at Michael and Hope's house. I take a bite of an English muffin that hasn't been toasted. You read that and think that is great. It is not me jumping out of a moving car onto a moving truck to save the day. I am playing an idiot that tries to eat an English muffin without toasting it. Mel Harris was so good in those scenes with me. Hope's reaction to Elliot was so great. She gave me so much room to play. She was a tough New Jersey girl and when she glared at you, you felt it.

Mel Harris: My husband's children call it the look of death. In the pilot it wouldn't have worked as well as it does in a later episode.

Patty Wettig: My mom called and was mad at me. She said, "What are you doing? You can't look that bad and have such low self-esteem on television. That isn't how other people on television are behaving." She was embarrassed by revealing those female aspects. I said, "Well, I am sorry but I know too many women who behave like this." If we had just exploited Nancy then I wouldn't have played it. I wanted to play it with that full expression until she figured out how to get her life back. It made people nervous to watch Nancy.

Susan Shilliday: I think young women today don't realize how much at that time people were trying to invent second wave feminism and be strong and have children. It wasn't clear. We were trying to figure it out as we did it. Most of us grew up watching very conventional marriages. We wanted to explore the different variations of women.

Tim Busfield: My favorite comment on the show was when people would say I feel like you were looking in my window. I feel like you were watching my life. That's the ultimate when you have movement in other people's hearts.

"I'm in Love, I'm in Love, I'm in Love with a Wonderful Gynecologist"

Directed by Scott Winant

Written by Ann Lewis Hamilton and Richard Kramer, Story by Ann Lewis Hamilton

February 2, 1988

Ann Lewis Hamilton (*Writer*): They were looking for another writer and I was recommended. My agent said, "Do you wanna go meet on *thirtysomething* to write a script?" I said, "Let me think about it." My agent said, "Don't be stupid. Go take the meeting. It's a really hot show." I said, "I really like it and if I don't get the job I am gonna be bummed out." I met and they assigned me an episode. Melissa and Ellyn fall in love with the same guy. He is a gynecologist. The scene that I really remember is a cut fantasy in the gynecologist office. It had a giant cold speculum that the doctor takes out of a refrigerator. When I went in the office to meet everyone, Susan and Liberty were telling me, "We love this. We love the giant ice cold speculum." Ed said, "You certainly fell in love with our fantasies." The first draft was filled with wildly over the top fantasies, but they hired me. That was a fun episode to start with.

Scott Winant (*Director, his directorial debut*): Ed and Marshall knew what my ambitions were. I wasn't assigned that episode. A director fell out. It was a script that was not finished. It was troubled. It would be filmed on one side of Christmas and finished on the other side. Nobody wanted to do the episode. All of a sudden they said, "Hey Scott, you've got an opportunity. We are gonna give you this one." I felt a lot of pressure jumping into that.

Polly Draper and Melanie Mayron share the spotlight as Ellyn and Melissa try to date the same guy, a gynecologist, in Ann Lewis Hamilton's first script and Scott Winant's directorial debut. Courtesy of Carol Gepper's TV Guide Collection.

Marshall Herskovitz: When Scott started directing he brought a style that was very lyrical to the show. We didn't even know how he did it. I would only learn afterwards the train wreck Scott Winant saved me from. He was what he turned out to be; a creative Director and Producer functioning as a Line Producer on *thirtysomething*. He was bringing his creativity to solving problems. He was solving problems that we didn't even know were problems.

Polly Draper: Initially when Ed and Marshall were writing for me, they wanted Ellyn to be that person that everyone groans when she entered the room. Once Melanie Mayron and I got to be such good friends off the set, they realized that we were funny and started writing comedy for us. I became a character that had a lot of comic quirks instead a very serious one which is what they intended.

Polly Draper was hired to play the serious best friend to Hope. Her natural comedic sensibilities seeped into Ellyn Warren. She became an avenue for the writers and directors to add a small amount of physical comedy to the series. Courtesy of ABC Photography Archives. The Lisa Mercado Fernandez Collection.

Scott Winant: Just have Polly Draper sit on a gynecologist's table in a paper dress, you really don't have to do much. She is just so funny.

Melanie Mayron (*Melissa*): There was tremendous humor in the show. I think it surprises people when they watch it again. The ensemble was good at drama and comedy. You could turn it on a dime and get a lot of comedic stuff from everyone.

Polly Draper: I know they were getting complaints that the show was too serious, so Melanie and I were the perfect people to strut out there to make fools of ourselves. Ellyn was the type of person that wanted to be serious. She wanted to have things be just right and she would mess them up.

Richard Kramer: Polly Draper is a great comic actor in the tradition of Maggie Smith

Episode 15 "Business as Usual"

Directed by Claudia Weill

Written by Paul Haggis and Marshall Herskovitz

February 9, 1988

Episode 16 "Accounts Receivable"

Directed by Edward Zwick

Written by Richard Kramer

March 1, 1988

Ken Olin: Stephen Schiff (*Played Leo Steadman, Michael's father dying of cancer*) for me was out of that legendary New York period of great actors that came out of Stella Adler and Strasburg. He was amazing. Casting him was like, "Oh shit, this is real." The show was really taking off at this point. That episode was a very personal, autobiographical script for Marshall. He never said, "This is my story." I think whatever pressure I felt was put on myself. I don't think that Patty felt pressure during "Therapy" when that was very personal for Marshall and Susan. By this episode, I was inspired and working hard. It felt very much like my story at that point.

Paul Haggis (*Writer*): I frankly struggled with "Business As Usual." My parents were both alive, but since I was a boy I had been trying to come to grips with the death of my grandfather. I took the first pass at the script, but I cannot say that I did it justice. I came from the tradition where men did not talk to men about their feelings, and that may have informed the script but it also hurt in its telling. We then met on the draft, and Ed and Marshall shared their own very personal experiences with death, and dealing with the dying. Marshall took the next pass at the script, and really elevated it to the point where, in his hands, it became one of our best episodes.

Richard Kramer: I was stuck while writing "Accounts Receivable." Ed came into my office and said, "Just don't think. Write the script as if you are writing a letter to the three people in the world who know you and love you the best." What I took from that was never explain yourself, never worry about how you are coming across, never try to manipulate anybody else's responses. The people who are gonna get it are gonna get it.

Episode 15 and 16 almost play as a two part episode, although they each have a completely different feel. Ken Olin takes center stage as he deals with the illness of his father. Courtesy of Carol Gepper's TV Guide Collection.

Ken Olin: "Accounts Receivable" is so different than "Business As Usual." It was a great run of episodes. Claudia, who directed part one, is completely different than Ed, who directed part two. I loved being directed by Ed. Richard's writing always had this muscular lyricism to it. To me it was all sort of personal. My friend Danny Stone (*Brad*) played my brother.

Tim Busfield: What I loved about *thirtysomething* was that they were small problems. They were the kind of stuff that you don't want anybody to know about. You don't want other people knowing that you have marital problems. You don't want other people to know that you're not handling being a mother very well. You don't want other people to know that you're struggling with your brother over your dad's death. They can be festering splinters in our soul, but they aren't high stakes.

Richard Kramer: This is another episode about acknowledgement. That was a very personal episode because it was sort of about my own brother. I was trying to acknowledge my brother and his efforts in life. His efforts had nothing to do with Brad Steadman's efforts. You try to do things in your work that you haven't been able to do in your life. Ed and I never mentioned that this was about my brother, James, until ten years later.

Joe Dougherty: Michael always seemed to be the doctor who understood every symptom he had but couldn't seem to do anything about it. His brother and father relationships are pretty central and key, as I think they were to Ed and Marshall.

Richard Kramer: Barbara Barrie, who played Ken's mother, was just wonderful. I would see them huddled in the corner of the set just talking like they were mother and son. Her brother had been an architect in real life. In the scene she has with Ken and the model of the house, she starts to lose control and then pulls it back. She knew when she read the script that she would have a hard time doing it and was gonna save it for the day to see what happened. I remember the way she said, "Look at this, look at the detail." Barbara was such a fine actress.

Ken Olin: Richard and I were really close and would talk all the time. We did not hold ourselves out as a representation of our generation but it was a representation of who we were as people.

Ken Olin was willing to share stories from his childhood to inform the character of Michael Steadman. He shared how he found out that his parents were getting divorced and it became how Michael found out as well. Courtesy of Carol Gepper's TV Guide Collection.

Richard Kramer: The story Michael tells about hearing that his parents were getting divorced was pure. That was how Ken found out that his parents were getting divorced. I may have added a detail or too, but not that many. We always did a read through of the next script while they were shooting the previous episode. You gathered around a table and all the production people are there. The actors have not seen the script before that. I remember Ken read the scene, just put the script down and looked at me and said, "Fuck you, Richard."

Ken Olin: He completely stole it. It was great. That story was the story of me being away at school in Vermont. My father came to school to tell me that my parents were separating and I had no idea. I don't even remember how much of the story Richard put in the script, but it is my real story. I was completely mercenary by that point. We were all in as a mode of self expression.

Richard Kramer: I said to him after, "I hope you are cool with that." He said, "I can't wait to do it." There are probably ten examples of that happening. I put that in Michael Steadman's history, which is not Ken's history but Ken and every other actor were very generous about lending themselves privately with their character. It was safe and no way was used to embarrass somebody. It was the deal that we were all making.

Episode 17

"Whose Forest is This?"

Directed by Peter Horton

Written by Richard Kramer, Story by Kathleen Tolan

March 15, 1988

Peter Horton (*Director*): Luke Rossi (*Ethan*) was the lead in that episode and was a little kid. We got to the scene where Nancy was on the bed with him and telling him the story. He had a few lines in the scene, but he was just burned out.

Richard Kramer (*Writer*): One of my favorite moments was when Ethan gets Nancy to tell the story of his birth differently.

Patty Wettig (*Nancy*): Peter directed it and we had a long day. We were doing Luke's coverage first. I had told him the story of the baby in my belly many times. They turned the camera around to get my close up. I started to tell him the story again. Luke says, "I can't stand hearing that story one more time."

Peter Horton: Patty basically acted that entire scene by herself and improvised it because he was just too worn out to speak. We asked him to just lay on the bed. She was so sensitive about it and handled it so graciously.

Patty Wettig: I said, "Luke, if you can hear it just one more time. We will get it." I told Peter, "Do whatever you have to do to get this in one take," and we did.

Tim Busfield (*Elliot*): The stuff with the kids was always easily emotionalized for me because I had a son who had been through a divorce and was the same age as Luke. It really crushed me not being in the same house with him. Once Nancy and Elliot split up, that stuff had a lot more meaning for me.

Peter Horton directed Patty Wettig multiple times as he became the go-to person for the continuing story of Nancy and Elliot's marriage. Courtesy of Carol Gepper's TV Guide Collection.

Richard Kramer: Timmy gave me one of the nicest compliments. He said that he wouldn't have to look at one of my scripts twice because he would memorize it because it made such sense. I cherish that.

Patty Wettig: There were so many episodes that had stories from our lives that it is almost embarrassing. The story I tell Ethan is the story I told Richard Kramer about me having a baby with Ken. So, it is me telling the story to Richard. Richard writing it as if Elliot says it and then me playing Nancy telling it differently to Ethan. That is a perfect example of loopings in the show that made it so personal.

Richard Kramer: That was a thing that Ken had said to Patty when she was pregnant. I don't know why but when I was sitting down to write the episode I remembered what Patty told me.

Patty Wettig: Is the story about Marshall and Susan or Nancy and Elliot or Ken and I or Richard and someone? It was such a melting pot. Even within the story it is hard to know. That is what gave the series the reality. I would go to the grocery store and the butcher would say, "That is exactly what happened to me."

Patty Wettig shared a personal story with Richard Kramer that Ken used to tell to their child in utero. Richard put the story in the script for Nancy to tell Ethan about Elliot. And you think your life is confusing? Courtesy ABC Photography Archives.

Tim Busfield: I love that episode. It is a really strong episode. Richard would write some great stuff.

Episode 18

"Nancy's First Date"

Directed by Ron Lagomarsino

Written by Susan Shilliday

March 22, 1988

Ron Lagomarsino (*Director*): I was living in New York and had just directed the world premiere of *Driving Miss Daisy* on Broadway. Richard Kramer was recruiting theater talent to work on the show because it was such a character driven piece. It was a dream to get to direct a show that I would actually watch if I wasn't working on the show. This was my first experience with the world of television. It started when we were casting the smaller roles. I was amazed at how in and out the casting part was. These actors, who had been driving an hour from Santa Monica to Studio City, would read three lines and then hit the door. I felt so bad.

Susan Shilliday (*Writer*): As usual, I did research after the fact and found that many couples who are separated do have sexual encounters. I have since talked to couple's counselors who said it is a common occurrence. Not a lot of thought went into the decision to have Nancy and Elliot have sex when I wrote it. It just seemed like Nancy would suddenly seem a lot more attractive when she was no longer available to Elliot. Nancy would be finding her own life and he would want to make a claim. Nancy would be feeling better about herself and she would respond to that.

Tim Busfield: The book Nancy is writing is actually Elliot's story. It isn't Nancy's story. He knew that she needed that so he didn't press the subject. Elliot never said, "This is my fucking story." I love that

After weeks of being separated, Nancy and Elliot have a sexual encounter moments before Nancy's first date with a new man. Courtesy ABC Photography Archives.

he was proud that she had something. He didn't want the pressure of a wife at home without having a life. For Elliot to see that she found something was really fun and great to play.

Episode 19

"Undone"

Directed by Dan Lerner

Written by Joseph Dougherty

April 12, 1988

Mel Harris: There is an episode where somehow Michael kisses Emily Birch (*Chelsea Field, Played Michael's College Girlfriend*). I told Ed and Marshall, "That wasn't right." I thought Michael should tell Hope. They said, "No way. That is not gonna happen. He didn't do anything wrong." I thought that was interesting.

Ed Zwick: Michael is tempted in Emily's hotel room. There was an extraordinary fight about whether they should kiss among the men and the women. Whether you could have adultery in your heart. Whether it was a crime or misdemeanor.

Joe Dougherty: "Cheats" is a loaded and subjective word. That said, he shouldn't have kissed her. Not that I was wrong to write it, but that the character made a mistake when he did it. Did he? I kind of forget.

Marshall Herskovitz: I think it was part of our willingness to say that people are very ambivalent. It's about the fact that people have differing and conflicting feelings in their lives. They love their wife. They hate their wife. They love their job. They hate their job. We wrote a manifesto when we first pitched the show that talked about being torn. You want to be a kid but you want to make a living. You want to sleep with other people but you love your wife. Life is full of these conflicting desires and feelings. You have to figure out how to negotiate that path. That is really what the show is about.

When Michael shared a kiss with his college sweetheart in the episode "Undone," there were fights behind the scenes as to whether this was the right plot point to explore. Courtesy ABC Photography Archives.

Joe Dougherty: When Michael read the poem that Emily wrote in the notebook, Richard Kramer said, "Why don't you write the poem so he says it out loud?" I said, "I can't do that." If I would have done that it would just be a poem, but if I just showed his face while he read it then it became the best poem ever.

Episode 20

"Tenure"

Directed by Ken Gilbert

Written by Ann Lewis Hamilton, Story by John Olive

May 3, 1988

Peter Horton: Gary had shame as all of us do. His drive to succeed and get tenure was based on that shame. We all have to dethrone our fathers. Gary was not talking tenure because he didn't want to play the game. He wanted to pretend he didn't care and to admit that he did care would violate Gary paradigms of caring about money, power or prestige. He came out of the seventies. He had long hair. His fingernails were clawing back in the seventies.

Ann Lewis Hamilton: I don't think that script is my shining success. I couldn't wrap my head around tenure. I was much more comfortable writing about giant speculums than tenure. I didn't quite succeed. I think Susan Shilliday did a rewrite of "Tenure" and made it better. I think my draft was probably not astounding. Susan can do anything. I'll give her many props for helping that episode. It just wasn't the best thing that I did.

Susan Shilliday: We actually wrote our own episodes unless people ran out of time or were ill. We knew the voices of the characters and you jumped in and did it. To me, re-writing is like putting all the puzzle pieces together in the right way. I don't understand people complaining about re-writing. It's easy. You have all the stuff there. It's writing for the first time that is hard.

Trying to get the academic stuff to be believable was hard to do on a television show. To do anything that is remotely authentic about

Gary runs out of time to get tenure at his university in an episode that Ann Hamilton and Susan Shilliday worked on. Courtesy ABC Photography Archives.

higher education is not done. I wanted to try to make it feel authentic in terms of the highly political situation that goes on.

Peter Horton: Riding the horse in "Tenure" was the most fun.

Ann Lewis Hamilton: It was sort of always a mystery as to why I got hired because I had done mostly action and low budget cop scripts before I got hired on *thirtysomething*. At the end of the first season when I sat down with Ed and Marshall, I wondered if I was gonna be asked back. They were really very kind and said, "Let's try another year." I then had the good/bad misfortune to have a personal crisis that led me to really dig into my life. I finally learned how to access emotions and that was the tipping point for me.

Episode 21

"Born to Be Mild"

Directed by Ron Lagomarsino

Written by Jerry Stahl

May 10, 1988

End of Season 1

Brandy Alexander (*Production Designer*): When I walked onto the bed and breakfast set Mel Harris said, "Brandy, I don't have to act. I feel like I am in a bed and breakfast." That was a nice complement to get in front of the crew. That was the kind of family atmosphere it was.

Season 1 wraps up with a light hearted episode of Michael and Hope going to a cottage for a weekend away while Ellyn and Woodman watch Janey. Courtesy of Carol Gepper's TV Guide Collection.

Scott Winant: Most people think *thirtysomething* was a very realistic, grounded show. You get that impression, but we did a lot of weird shit. I was constantly fighting with the studio for money for all those weird things. I had the editors cut together all the fantasy sequences that we did from season one. I used "The End" by The Beatles. I had horses coming into sets, reproduced anxiety by making little creatures, Nancy's first date fantasies and guys with guns storming Michael. We went into the subconscious quite a bit, but people didn't realize it was happening because it was so tied to the characters.

Patty Wettig: I believe Nancy was a bit of an outsider. In the first year I did feel like I was a little bit on the outside. When the seven of us gathered, I wasn't quite sure where I fit into the group. I am not sure why that was. Maybe originally it came from Susan. I never thought of it before. Susan isn't someone who needs to belong to the group. I wouldn't say she was an outsider. She just isn't going to be the soccer mom. She carries her own universe with her. That may be part of Nancy.

Mel Harris: We were on a television panel and Ed and Marshall were telling about how green they all were. I said, "Hell, if I knew you were all so green I wouldn't have been so scared myself." It was this lovely laboratory of creative artists and the right show at the right time. Not always easy, but it was great.

Melanie Mayron (*Melissa*): We won the People's Choice and the Emmy award for best show the first season. We all got to go up on stage. None of us could believe it. We were going to Studio City where we go to one or two sound stages. The world of where we were working was very small, then we go outside that space and people recognize you. It gets translated on television, but it is not part of your reality.

Marshall Herskovitz: I think the first season we were trying everything we knew. We tried every kind of format. We quickly discovered that there were certain limits with which the show functioned with best. We could still do a lot of of interesting things but there were some things that were not worth doing. Doing a Hitchcock takeoff wasn't going to work for our show. We had to do one to learn that. There was a lot of experimentation. Mid-way through the first season we hit our stride.

Joe Dougherty: I think they were surprised that our ratings were okay. We were the first demographic hit on television where people started to look at who was watching. We had a valuable audience. Hence the large number of diapers and Saabs we sold for the network as a 10 o'clock show.

The first season turned Ken Olin and Mel Harris into stars as well as the poster faces for the yuppie movement of the 1980s. Despite the fact that they were not rich, the media kept saying the characters had everything. Season 2 would prove that not to be true. Courtesy of ABC Photography Archives. The Lisa Mercado Fernandez Collection.

Season 2
(1988–89)

"We'll Meet Again"

Directed by Scott Winant

Written by Richard Kramer

December 6, 1988

Scott Winant (*Director*): Marshall gave me the second season premiere. Richard Kramer wrote the script and we collaborated on it over the summer. I just kept making it bigger and bigger. I built an indoor garden. I changed the wallpaper on the main set for a flashback. I made visual transitions going from one time period to another. I got in trouble for doing that episode because I couldn't get it done in the allotted time. I went over.

Richard Kramer (*Writer*): Scott was famous for going over schedule. The kind of detail in which he worked made it impossible for him to do it in eight days. Everyone else managed to do it for the most part. It became a joke between us that he always took nine days where everyone else took eight. I believe this episode went nine or ten days.

Scott Winant: I used to do that all the time, but Ed really got on me. He said, "You are the producer of the show. How can you tell the other directors to stay on schedule when you couldn't?" It got to a point where he was leaning on me so much I had to go into his office and confront him. It was literally at a point where I was having a break down and

The second season premiered with an episode focused on the Steadman house back in the 1940s. The theme is about Michael and Hope deciding if it is time to have a second child. Courtesy of Carol Gepper's TV Guide Collection.

wanted to quit. Ed totally fooled me as he always did. He acknowledged it, apologized and that was it. It was over.

Richard Kramer: I doubt if Scott would have flowered had he been on another show. He was the perfect person to have as the producer on that show. His relationship was very important to me.

Scott Winant: However, it was the first episode to get an Emmy nomination for directing. I was vindicated, but it took eight months. (*Laughs*)

Richard Kramer: I had to rewrite it many times. Much more so than anything else I worked on. We couldn't quite figure it out. Years later someone told me that it was taught in a television writing class as a perfect episodic script. That is ridiculous because it was pure chaos.

Lenny Von Dohlen (*Played Roy MacCaulay*): As a New York actor visiting Los Angeles, I was tickled to be cast on what was then such a popular and important show. The vibe was welcoming and fraternal. On the very focused set the bar was high for truth and character integrity, with a smoothly functioning crew working at the top of their game. With our episode having all those 1940s flashbacks, it seemed to stoke everyone's fires. I loved working with Jo Anderson (*Played Sally Spangler*) who, like myself, slides smoothly and comfortably into period stories. The most memorable scene was having a romantic dance in the back garden of Hope and Michael's future home. I had this idea of using the standard "Stardust." It was my grandparent's favorite song from their early courtship. I asked Scott or Richard if we could please use it. They did. So my ninety year old grandparents in Kenedy, Texas, were able to watch on the night it first aired.

Scott Winant: "Stardust" was my favorite song. I actually ended up naming my production company after the song.

Richard Kramer: I remember that Ellen Pressman took all the photos from the past of Sally and Roy.

Ellen S. Pressman (*Producer*): Did I get credited for the photos? I might have done that. I don't remember. I wasn't supposed to do things like that, but I probably did. I am sure I didn't get paid as a photographer. (*Laughs*)

Lenny Von Dohlen: All the period still photos of Jo and I that are in Hope's scrapbook were shot on the Santa Monica pier and at a nearby English pub.

Mel Harris (*Hope*): We couldn't show Hope's diaphragm when she went to get her birth control. She was a married woman with a child in the late eighties and we couldn't show her diaphragm on television. Mind boggling.

Richard Kramer: That episode was about fruitfulness. It was about getting past the first step of ambivalence where you can make a decision. It was metaphorically an attack on Hope's ambivalence about having another kid.

Mel Harris: I think for me Hope's issues weren't black and white. They were a rainbow of colors. It all goes in there and you got what came out. I tried to be very moment to moment. I will go back to the fact that we had wonderful writers, producers and actors to work together with.

Richard Kramer: I remember writing the words for Michael, "Okay, I'll pull out." He was fundamentally raping her. It was supposed to be iffy.

Scott Winant: This was an important scene. This became a bone of contention between Ed and myself. Ed wanted it to be a little more violent. He wanted Michael to push himself onto Hope to be more physically

There was much debate about the scene where Michael wants to have sex without using contraception. How much force was appropriate to get the point of the story across? The answer changes depending on who was asked and what they remembered. Courtesy of ABC Photography Archives. The Lisa Mercado Fernandez Collection.

adamant about this moment. I knew that. He told me that. We discussed it in our meetings, but on the day when I was directing the scene with Ken and Mel, I went another way. We always strived for real honesty at the moment. I had to concede to the moment and how it felt for the actors.

Ken Olin (*Michael*): I don't remember anything about that. The idea of me forcing myself on Mel is ridiculous. I wonder how much of that was shared with me.

Richard Kramer: Scott interpreted that scene in his way, in what he felt was best for Michael and Hope. That came out of the fertile field that these shows came out of and whether Ed got mad or not doesn't matter. Ed completely respected Scott.

Scott Winant: We'd been living with these characters and the scene that I directed was what I believed to be believable. I know we did make the point that Michael was trying to force her to conceive. I remember how disappointed Ed was when he saw the dailies. How he felt that I chickened out and that I didn't push the actors stronger. It's funny that I still feel guilty about that because of how important it was to Ed.

Ed Zwick: If what Scott feels he failed to do was to have pushed to the more controversial part of that scene, that is what a lot of us faced in how revealing we could be. Scott's work was uniformly wonderful. He kept raising the bar for each of us. We often approached the third rail of things that were very uncomfortable and confronted us all with our own inhibitions.

Scott Winant: It is rare that show runners are that invested in the nuance of performance the way those guys were. It was a daily lesson and we were always challenging ourselves. That moment was not just my moment but it was Ken's and Mel's.

Mel Harris: You play it in a way that you feel is true to the character you constructed.

Ken Olin: I would doubt that Ed wanted Michael raping Hope. You are making me become Michael again, which is so weird. I think Ed would want the intellectual exploration of what happens when a person's libido supersedes their rationality. A moment from Michael that would have surprised him would be something to explore.

Scott Winant: Michael was a real living breathing person to me, not just a character. I had a huge investment in all the characters. I took every moment as precious. I wouldn't do a scene because we wanted to be outrageous or to be gratuitous. It had to be truthful to that moment. I know that is what the boys always insisted on and what I always encouraged other directors to do.

Joe Dougherty (*Producer*): I had an argument with Richard Kramer on "We'll Meet Again." Hope found the diary and you saw the former inhabitants of the house. At the end of the episode, she came down the stairs and talked to the woman who was leaving. I read the scene and went to Richard. I said, "It seems to me like the woman in the past knows that she is talking to the woman in the future." And he said, "Yes, that is what is going on." I said, "Would you have more resident subtext if the woman in the past thought she was just talking to the next woman who was moving into the house? They could just have this wonderful conversation about pipes." He said, "No." It was one of the places where we were all very different writers. You could tell the difference between my scripts and Richard's scripts and Ann's scripts. Sometimes those different approaches meshed and sometimes they were in direct conflict. To Richard that wasn't the way to do it. If I had written it, it would just be about pipes and let you take the subtext.

Episode 23

"In Re: The Marriage of Weston"

Directed by Peter Horton

Written by Susan Shilliday

December 13, 1988

Peter Horton (*Director*): That episode was daunting for me because I was still a young filmmaker. The challenge of that one was the contrast of now versus what is breaking up. What were Nancy and Elliot losing? The typewriter was key because of the cold mechanistic sound of it almost being like a clock ticking, going forward, unable to go back, typing out their future and their irreparable circumstance. The blueish cold light of that, contrasted with the warmer yellows of the past.

Susan Shilliday (*Writer*): The typewriter was in the script from the beginning. I remember the words were very important. It had to be written as though there was no possibility for Nancy and Elliot to get back together, otherwise the episode was not going to work. If I am talking to writers who are starting out, I say don't use flashbacks and don't lean on them, but we wanted to tell more stories of what happened before the opening of the series.

Patty Wettig (*Nancy*): Even though there was the low self esteem, Nancy was always connected with her heart to her children. I think that made her a better mom. When she became stronger as a human she had even more to give them.

Peter Horton: Patty and I ended up working a lot together which I loved. The Nancy and Elliot relationship was the richest on the show because it was the most tragic. Those episodes were the nuggets of the show where the gold was found. If Ed and Marshall weren't directing those, they wanted someone in house to do them. I lobbied for them because I loved

The current state of the Westin marriage is examined while we see flashbacks of how Nancy and Elliot fell in love in this hour meditation on the disintegration of a marriage. Courtesy of ABC Photography Archives.

them. I also was light in them as an actor. I didn't like acting and directing in the same episodes. Those are such different head spaces for me.

Patty Wettig: I loved it when Peter would ask me to transition something that made it better. When he was inside directing my character he came from a place that I fully trusted.

Susan Shilliday: It is funny that Rita Wilson (*Adrienne*) plays Elliot's lawyer in that episode. I don't think there was a personal connection. I think she just won the part through casting. Later, our kids went to school with her kids. I remember meeting Tom Hanks when we were doing that episode.

"The Mike Van Dyke Show"

Directed by Ron Lagomarsino

Written by Marshall Herskovitz and Edward Zwick

December 20, 1988

Ron Lagomarsino: I loved directing episodes written by Ed and Marshall because they were the heart and soul of the show. It must have been the luck of the draw because I was not the most seasoned of all the directors, but I ended up directing the most episodes. It was challenging but with such great material it made my work easier.

The thirtysomething *cast becomes the* Dick Van Dyke *cast during one of Michael's fantasies as the show does their second holiday episode. Courtesy of ABC Photography Archives.*

Marshall Herskovitz: When I look back on the show, what really amazes me is that we were allowed to talk about the small stuff. For some reason television doesn't see itself as playing that role. Every week was a meditation on some particular aspect of life. I am amazed that they let us do it and we got away with it. We wanted to talk about the fear of losing a spouse in the Christmas episode where Hope was in a car accident and Michael was worried about her. To just be able to talk about fear was a great gift.

Liberty Godshall: That car accident happened to me. It was a big deal at the time. I was in a horrific pile up on the 405 when I was seven months pregnant and went into labor. It was bad. When I got to the hospital all I could think of was how can I call my husband, who I was standing next to when he got the phone call that his mother had died in a car accident? How quickly can I say I am okay? Ed picked up the phone and I said, "I am okay." He said, "Okay." I said, "I am totally okay." I did that for twenty minutes. Then I said, "I was in a car accident, but I am okay."

Ed Zwick: It had to become axiomatic that we were pilfering from each other's lives. It was such a searing moment that I am not sure I even asked Liberty if she minded if I wrote about her accident. I just assumed that she would understand. We were working so hard there were times that my writing was a way of talking to her and her writing was a way of answering me. That was true with Marshall and Susan as well.

Ken Olin: The episode's theme was life viewed from the fifties where everything was supposed to be perfect, but it actually wasn't. That is a pretty high concept. They were never forced to think in terms of we better dumb this down. I am sure we were insufferable for some people. The intellectual rigor that was being applied to the work.

Ed Zwick: You think it is about Christmas and Hanukkah, then you think it is about mixed marriage, then you think it is about television, but ultimately it turns out to be belief in God. I am sure it was something that I was reckoning with when I got that phone call from Liberty. I couldn't help but write the thing that was so much on my mind. It was profoundly important to me.

An episode that appears to just be a lark of a fantasy turns quite serious when it talks about the loss of a loved one and the belief in God. Courtesy of Carol Gepper's TV Guide Collection.

Ron Lagomarsino: I am pretty sure we filmed the Dick Van Dyke section of the episode in one day. We wanted it to feel like a sitcom. We shot it with a second camera getting a side angle and one dead on. We had a lot of discussions about how we were going to make it feel like a sitcom while making sure the scenes worked. I think there were varying degrees of success of finding the acting style of the sitcom. Some of the actors were more comfortable than others in playing that heightened style.

Ken Olin: I wasn't comfortable in that episode. I wondered if I would be able to do it well. Tim, Melanie and Patty were very funny in it. They were comfortable doing comedy. It just wasn't something I had done. I was anxious about the episode.

Ed Zwick: The actors are so good in doing those imitations. They are wonderful. We had done a Christmas episode the year before and we wondered how to top it.

Ken Olin: I don't think Marshall and Ed were afraid of examining their own shortcomings through Michael. I don't know how much of this was Richard's influence. Michael would start off at one point and then he would learn to be a better person. Maybe he was idealized.

Richard Kramer: Ken was owned by all the writers. Michael was the idealization of equal parts me, Marshall and Ed. He was a perfect vessel for us to pour feelings about ourselves into.

Ken Olin: Episodes like "Mike Van Dyke" showed how you can use this medium. Television has a cinematic freedom that doesn't exist anywhere

The crew worked to be sure the set matched the Dick Van Dyke set as well as reminded us of the Steadman house. The episode ended in a camera trick where Michael walks from being black and white into color; a trick that is easily achieved now but was groundbreaking in 1988. Courtesy of ABC Photography Archives. The Lisa Mercado Fernandez Collection.

else. You are using an ensemble and can do different genres with them. The show wasn't just emotionally ambitious, it was cinematically and intellectually ambitious as well.

Brandy Alexander (*Production Designer*): I asked the Director of Photography for a lens that I could look through and it takes out all the color, so I just see black and white. I was able to match the shades of black and white from our set to the *Dick Van Dyke Show* (1961). I wanted it to be as close as possible. We even made the little step so Ken could trip over it just like Dick Van Dyke did.

Ron Lagomarsino: The scene where Michael walks from black and white to color was done in post production. I don't remember what the requirement was on the set. By today's standards, it was quite rudimentary. I recall we had to shoot it in a certain way. I loved having the wonderful Jack Guilford play Santa Claus and the Rabbi. That was a thrill for me.

Ed Zwick: We had initially asked Carl Reiner to be the Rabbi. He said yes, but then he was unavailable. That would have been the final metta of the entire enterprise.

Ken Olin: I think some of the episodes that aren't talked about as much are the genius of what Ed and Marshall were doing. Those episodes had real impact on younger writers. When I got hired as a director on *Felicity* (1998), JJ Abrams was a huge fan of *thirtysomething*. He was a young writer when we were on and our show was significant because it offered a scope for television writing that wasn't there. You could write a sitcom into an episode. That is an ambitious idea. Many writers who were about ten years younger were influenced by the possibilities the show opened up.

Ron Lagomarsino: You just cross your fingers when you are directing kids. When I directed *Once and Again* (1999) I worked with Evan Rachel Wood when she was ten. She was amazing. You knew she was going to be somebody. Working with Claire Danes at thirteen on *My So-Called Life* (1994) was staggering at what she was able to bring to Angela. It was a tandem of working with Luke (*Ethan*) directly, but also having Patty and Tim. They had a better rapport with him because they knew him better.

Tim Busfield: I would end up directing the kids most of the times in the scenes because they knew me and not the director.

Ron Lagomarsino: If you can find the way to make the scene organic it is better for a child actor. It is like finding the trigger that would unlock something for them in the scene. Instead of giving them ten notes, I try to give them one.

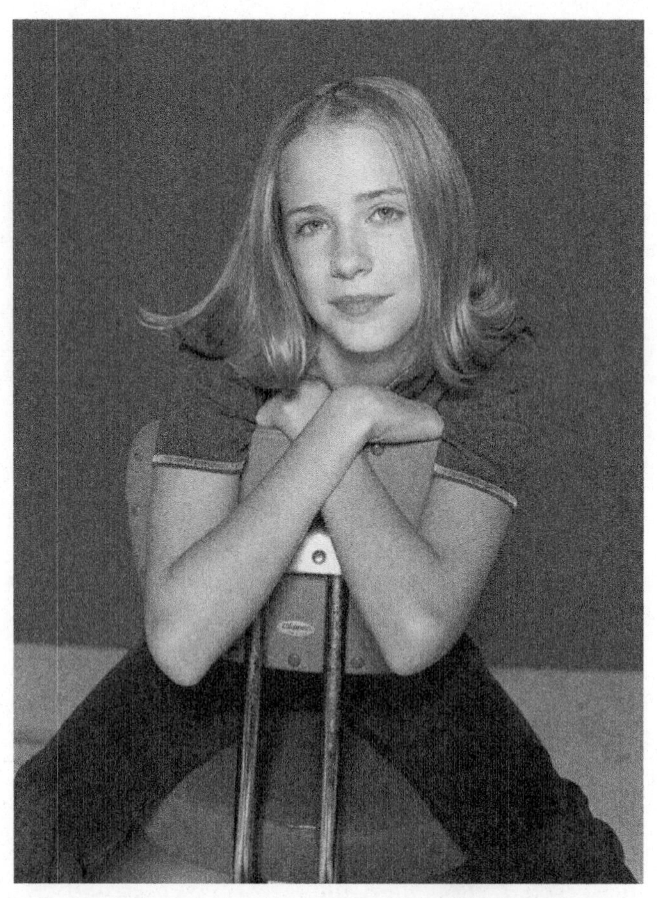

A young Evan Rachel Wood (Westworld) was directed by Ron Lagomarsino on Once and Again, another show from Marshall and Ed. Courtesy of ABC Photography Archives.

"Trust Me"

Directed by Steven Robman

Written by Richard Kramer

January 3, 1989

Richard Kramer: I had to introduce Russell and Susannah and do the Gary and Melissa story, but I never worried that it was a lot of plot to cover. I just did it. I also wrote a scene where Shakespeare gave Gary advice and the entire thing was in iambic pentameter. It was very funny, but it got cut.

David Marshall Grant (*Played Russell Weller*): I was a fan of *thirtysomething* as a viewer. I knew Richard Kramer because I had acted in a television movie called *Kent State* (1981) that he wrote. Richard and I went to the same gym at the time he wrote "Trust Me." He told me he was going to write a gay character who would be Melissa's friend and would I be interested. I said no.

Richard Kramer: He didn't want to be perceived as a gay actor who could only play gay parts. He was gunning for a big movie career. His representation was sending him down a road to be a young leading man. To play a gay character was something that was not part of the plan. People just weren't doing it. After he said no, we talked to Peter Gallagher about playing the part. I went back to David and showed him the scene that I had written. He agreed to do the part.

David Marshall Grant: You have to put this in context. The AIDS epidemic had ravished the gay artistic community. I don't think the virus had even been discovered at that point. It was a tough time being gay and to be a successful gay actor was a nonstarter. Openly gay back then meant if anyone knew you were gay in the entertainment industry. It was a career risk.

Richard Kramer: I wanted to create a gay character that wasn't in distress. He wasn't beaten, diseased or an outcast. He was just someone that the characters would take in stride.

David Marshall Grant: I feel like this seeded *Will & Grace* (1998), if you wanted to diagram the arc of the stereotypical gay best friend. In the beginning, it was the bachelor in old movies. He was the gay best friend until finally we had to name it. He wasn't a bachelor. He was gay. Then the gay best friend disappeared. Next there were effeminate gay characters. When Russell came along he was just a guy who was gay. He had no qualities that would single him out. That was a novel approach. Now sexuality and masculinity are more fluid. Gay men can appear straight and straight men can appear gay.

Richard Kramer: I am not sure if he was the first gay best friend. Where I was coming from in creating Russell was I said to Ed and Marshall, "They don't have a single gay friend? They would." They said, "Go make one up." I didn't go to David because he was gay. I went to him because he was a great actor. I had worked with him before.

David Marshall Grant: My agent, Ed Limato, didn't know I was gay. So, he wasn't really against me taking the part of Russell. It was one of those moments that I look back on as a choice that I made that finally just came from my heart instead of my head. There was a part of me that couldn't take it anymore. I didn't want to be afraid. It was a great part, a great writer and a great show. It was a turning point in my life.

Richard Kramer: When you are writing, you don't think about television history. You just think about what would be honest. You can't be important. You just want what is real.

David Marshall Grant: Russell seemed like me. He seemed like a guy who was gay who had hang ups about it, had fears and was much more invested in his humanity than he was with the identity of being gay. He was an important person to put out there in that tragic time for gay men. No reporter ever called me up and asked, "You are playing Russell on *thirtysomething*,

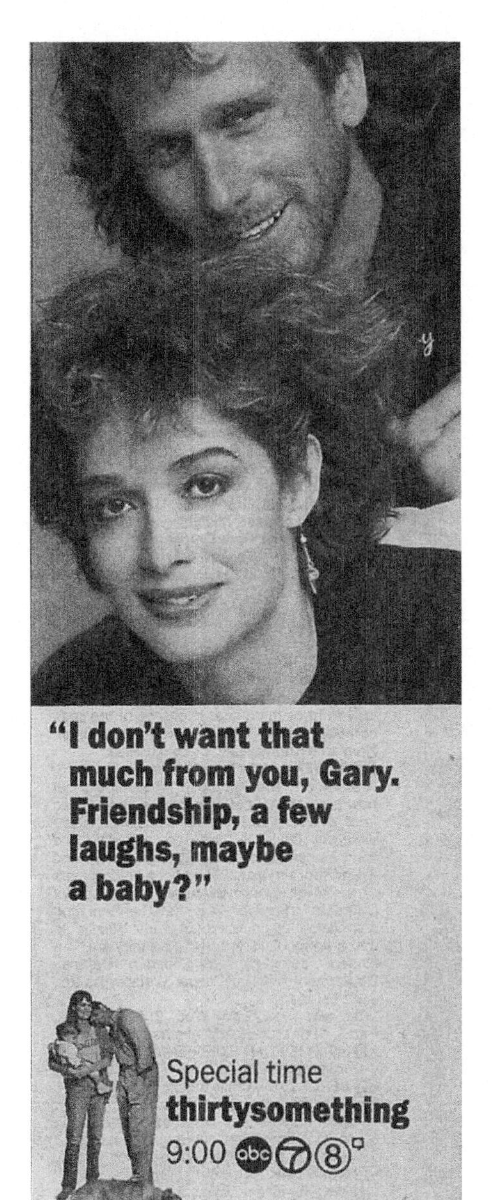

In "Trust Me," Melissa and Gary think about having a baby together. This episode also introduces Susannah and Russell. All three plot points influence the trajectory of the series. Courtesy of Carol Gepper's TV Guide Collection.

are you gay?" God knows what I would have said, but it was never asked of me. I wasn't famous, so no one really cared. (*Laughs*)

Richard Kramer: David is very elegant in life. I was honored to be able to contribute to the conversation at the level that I did. There was no controversy bringing him on the show. There was none of the noise of today at all.

David Marshall Grant: It was a different time. There wasn't any internet. Fan mail was the only access to the reaction. Once a few episodes aired, I started to get mail addressed to me at the studio. Almost all of it was very moving to me. To this day I talk to people who were affected by Russell.

Richard Kramer: I took David and Melanie out to dinner to see if they had chemistry together. Of course they hit it off immediately. They had a great connection as people and actors.

Melanie Mayron: David was Melissa's best friend out in the world. He was so sweet and we had a great working relationship. Having a gay man as a best friend just wasn't done. We got to do stuff that actors didn't usually get to do and we knew it.

David Marshall Grant: The joy of working on that show was that I was embraced by this family. When I watched the show as a fan, I wanted to be their friends and live in that world. Then I got to walk into their houses. It was like a fantasy to be able to enter a world you wanted to live in.

Richard Kramer: I remember the challenge of creating Susannah. I really wanted to make her someone who didn't fit in with the rest of the group, to make her the odd woman out. The actress had to fit into the group. You look at the person and think how do they make sense in the ensemble. There had to be a level of visible intelligence. She had to be somewhat classy. That was Patricia Kalember.

Patricia Kalember (*Played Susannah Hart*): My take on Susannah from the beginning was that she was one of those profoundly shy people. Most arrogant people are incredibly shy and sometimes deeply insecure and that was my take on her. This was someone who had no social skills whatsoever and had a chip on her shoulder.

Peter Horton: When we were casting Susannah we had a choice of going one of two ways. We had Patricia Kalember and an African-American actress. Either way it was going to be a girlfriend that my friends didn't like.

Richard Kramer: Lonette McKee (*Malcolm X, 1992*) was the other actress. She was beautiful. I went to New York and saw maybe twenty actresses. It came down to Lonette or Patricia. In the end, they weren't ready to take on a biracial couple. I don't know if it was the network or what, but they weren't going to do that yet.

Patricia Kalember: I was trying to wrap my mind around who this person was. I saw her like somebody with Aspergers. They just say what they think. They just don't have that ability to see the affect they might have on people because they are working so hard on their own stuff. Richard thought that sounded great.

Peter Horton: Patricia had this spirit to her. This solid center to her. She is a whole person underneath which was perfect for Gary because she was a grown up and he was not.

Patricia Kalember joined the show as Gary's love interest, Susannah Hart. They had immediate chemistry despite that her character was not the easiest person to warm up to. Courtesy ABC Photography Archives.

Patricia Kalember: I am nothing like the character. The first time I went in and talked with Marshall I was being Susannah for the first couple of read throughs just in case they would find out and fire me. When I got in his office he said, "You are nothing like this character are you?" I said, "No, I am not." It is the little things we do when we get something on a piece paper. It is the actor's job to decide who the person is and what they want to do with it.

Richard Kramer: I remember researching the character that Courtney B. Vance plays, Curtis. I felt that he was a bit too old to play the part. He is very good in the episode, but a bit too old.

Patricia Kalember: Courtney was up and coming. He had just come off a Broadway show. He was so lovely and a wonderful character. They had such a great collection of writers on that show with Winnie, Joe, and Richard; the list goes on and on.

Richard Kramer: The soul of that script is what Susannah says to Gary. When he is going to show up with Curtis, she says, "That is good. He needs a good man in his life." She is really talking about herself. That is serving the needs of Gary who was doubting whether he was a good man or not.

Peter Horton: Patricia and I just hit it off as people. I think if we met each other in different circumstances we might have dated. We were a good match for each other. She had a tough, strong, take no prisoners personality.

Patricia Kalember: Peter is a mensch. He is a sweetheart and a nice guy.

Episode 26

"No Promises"

Directed by Ken Olin

Written by Liberty Godshall

January 10, 1989

Liberty Godshall: I looked at Ellyn as this brave warrior and such a babe, so sexy with a gravelly voice. So many of my friends were going through that exact storyline. I saw in various friends a combination of drive and self judgement that was very poignant to me. When I started to find out these women's relationships with their fathers, I had to write about it.

Ken Olin (*Director*): That was my directorial debut. I was so unprepared. It wasn't from lack of trying. I just didn't know how different it was to initiate something as opposed to modify it. They had to schedule an episode where I wouldn't be heavy in the episode that preceded it so I could do prep work and I couldn't be heavy in the actual episode I was directing. That was how I got "No Promises."

Richard Kramer: We were privately convinced that Polly Draper was the most talented person in the cast. This episode is pure proof of that. They were all great, but there was something about her. She was an acting genius. She is a very intense and trained actor. I was challenged by working with Polly because there was nothing she couldn't do. Ken Olin's directing is extraordinary in it.

Ken Olin: I loved directing Polly. I am sure it was much harder on her than me. She had to deal with a director who had never directed before. I didn't know what I was doing. Scott Winant was really helpful to me. Today, I pride myself at never asking actors to do something that is unnatural, but in that episode I would have these cool ideas for shots that

Ken Olin had his directorial debut in this episode and became the second cast member to direct. He would go on to direct for Alias, Brothers and Sisters and This Is Us. Courtesy ABC Photography Archives.

would force actors to do weird stuff. I was so nervous. If you listen to the dailies before every single take you hear me yell, "Alright, settle down!" No one was making any noise. It was perfectly quiet. At one point, the Director of Photography walked outside and kicked a dumpster he was so sick of hearing me say it.

Brandy Alexander (*Production Designer*): I remember getting out of a van on a scouting location with Ken on his directorial debut. He turned to me and say, "Oy, what am I going to do? I am not directorial material." It was so funny. I said, "Calm down, we are going to look at the location and see if it works for the script." He became an excellent director and producer.

Polly Draper (*Ellyn*): Ken was really supportive and adorable. Right from the get go he was a great director. He is good with camera movement and great with actors. He is incredibly supportive, sweet and wise. We knew each other so well. He understood the show better than a lot of the new directors that came into the show.

Ken Olin: On the first day, I had done the first two scenes and was ahead of schedule. I had watched Ed and he never had shot lists. So, I didn't make one. I got to the scene with Polly and her mom making the bed. I froze. I had no idea how to shoot it. This was just two people making a bed. It wasn't a hard scene. The word went up to whoever and Scott came down to help me. At the end of the day, Scott and I sat down to make a shot list for the next day. I should have been doing this in the days of prep before. Scott saved my life that night.

Scott Winant: Although Ken may have had a rough start that day, he was a natural and a born director. I knew it from directing him as an actor. He was always curious and his mind required a tremendous amount of creative stimulation, so I knew directing was in his future.

Polly Draper: Ellyn grew to have a really deep friendship with Michael aside from the one she had with Hope. They grew to have a mutual respect that they didn't initially have. She started out jealous of Michael and his relationship with Hope. Then, she realized what a good guy he was. He was the first person Ellyn told about her parents getting divorced and he was really kind to her.

Liberty Godshall: Ellyn and Michael's friendship was a silent river running through the series. The way he would ease her fears as a big brother.

Richard Kramer: Betsy Blair (*Played Ellyn's Mom, Marjorie Warren*) was married to Gene Kelly for a very long time. That was just Liberty's brilliant intuitive move to give her a speech about being married to a dancer.

Liberty Godshall: I did not know that Gene Kelly's ex-wife would be cast for the part. That is one of those things that happens when you tap into your subconscious. I had no idea when I wrote it.

Richard Kramer: I think Betsy Blair's performance was extraordinary. There was something that was terrifying about her. You so understand what that mother/daughter relationship was. I had written a film for her director husband at the time. She wasn't working then. She had been nominated for Oscars and led this interesting life with Gene Kelly. I asked her if she wanted to work. She came in and read and that led to Liberty being able to write about being married to a dancer.

Liberty Godshall: I just tried to get back to the forties which is always perceived as very romantic. I talked to people about their parent's romances. I know that my husband's father talked about having a convertible and how he kept these scarves in the glove box and would give them

Polly Draper is wonderful in this hour that focuses on Ellyn's reaction to her parents getting divorced. With time and multiple viewings this episode resonates with fans and the writers. Courtesy of ABC Photography Archives. The Lisa Mercado Fernandez Collection.

to women. What we think of as romantic was actually pretty superficial but the dancing part of it never was to me. Big bands were such a huge part of my parent's life. It just came to me that it would be as good a way as any to pick someone to marry. In Ellyn's mind, she is hearing this speech too late. So, she breaks down.

Richard Kramer: I watched it the other day. Ellyn was in every single scene. I don't think we ever did that. Usually, there was some second story or interweaving plot and there wasn't in this. This was like Bergman.

Liberty Godshall: That was the type of story that was easy for me to do. I dont think it is natural to think of four different stories that are concurrent. I think we knew this was a story with emotional weight. I think it is easier for me as a writer to focus on one story.

Richard Kramer: I saw Ed and Liberty the day I watched it and I told them there was not one dated moment in it. It does not seem like an eighties artifact outside of the clothes. Moment to moment, it is happening right in front of you. Polly was brilliant at not playing a neurotic character but playing someone who was very complicated. Liberty's script was superb. Polly's performance was extraordinary. I turned it off and said, "This episode was a real accomplishment. God, this was fucking great!"

Liberty Godshall: I think Ellyn was heart breakingly lovable in this episode. Polly got into that part very deeply and revealed stuff that I was so moved by her.

Richard Kramer: It wasn't like watching Polly Draper it was like watching Ellyn Warren. I got lost in watching it. It's like a John Cheever story. It is so smart about how wasps live and torture each other. It was timeless. I am happy to say that about an episode I had nothing to do with.

Polly Draper: Don't forget Woodman the wonderful actor Terry Kinney who I loved so much, yet they kept writing for me to be such a bitch to him.

Episode 27 "Politics"

Directed by Claudia Weill

Written by Susan Shilliday, Story by Jerry Stahl

January 17, 1989

Susan Shilliday: That episode is a blur to me. Fortunately, we had Patricia Kalember who was terrific.

Patricia Kalember (*Susannah*): I read a quote that said you shouldn't engage in an argument unless you are prepared to change your mind. Sometimes we get so hardened in our political views it is hard to talk about it. The idea of going into a discussion and to be willing to give up your position is kind of missing these days. Susannah was not an empathetic person and such an ideologue. It was probably hard for her to see the other side.

Polly Draper: That was initially the way they had seen Ellyn going, a little more hard edged. In a television series, you evolve with the people and they wanted to make the most out of other qualities that I had. Susannah was a recurring character so they could get away with her being more cold.

Gary brings Susannah to meet the gang. It doesn't go well. The episode is memorable to the producers because of ABC's reaction to a line Susannah says to Gary. ABC cut the scene without telling the producers. Courtesy ABC Photography Archives.

Susan Shilliday: I remember the line where Gary realizes Susannah was from Pittsburgh because she said, "She needs walked home." I am from Pittsburgh. Everyone says, "The floor needs vacuumed and my hair needs brushed." I thought that was perfectly normal. It was only later that I learned that other people don't say that. It comes directly from Scottish dialect that came with the coal workers to Pittsburgh. The point of the line is to show Gary was actually listening to her and was caught up in her.

Patricia Kalember: Susannah was the one person who didn't want anything to do with Gary, so Gary was there. Isn't that always the way? It's the one that they can't get that they always want. Particularly with men that can't settle. I don't know what that is but it is so typical. The idea of actually conquering someone that doesn't want you is appealing to certain guys.

Peter Horton: Gary was a Peter Pan jazzy guy. I think unconsciously Susannah was solid and safe and Gary needed that. She was unreachable, cut off emotionally. Gary thought he could crack that silo. Gary was a saver.

Patricia Kalember: We just actually liked playing off each other. It is interesting that people see it as sexual chemistry, but I think it is the neurons flying between two actors when they are cooking. A lot of it has to do with the willingness to play and not an attraction. It is the ability to see someone, be open and play. I have worked with actors who don't like to play and you have to do all the work. It is a treat when you are with another actor that is game.

Susan Shilliday: We used to play games of pushing Standards and Practices by trying to get in as much stuff as we could. My favorite line in this one was when Gary and Susannah go to Hope and Michael's for dinner. Susannah says, "I bet you think I never cum and you can make me." They would absolutely not let us get away with that at all.

Marshall Herskovitz: They cut our picture when it aired the first time. They didn't just bleep it, the entire scene was taken out. We went insane. We were so furious about it we didn't speak to Standards and Practices for four episodes.

Patricia Kalember: I don't remember what they changed it to. I do remember the scene. For 1989 it was very dirty. I might have said cum.

Susan Shilliday: Now nobody would even think about it. I was determined to get that line in there. They made us change it to climax.

Peter Horton: It was such a different time in television. Now you see someone climax with full nudity. It is kind of sanctioned porn. I vaguely remember them having a fight with ABC. I remember hearing we may not be able to say it and getting irate about it. I am now a father of two girls and I think, "How dare you?"

Susan Shilliday: The politics in the episode was just real life. It is constant compromising, constant juggling and self justification. Where do you make your stand? We grew up in the sixties where there was one ideal and then discovered the world is a really different place. It is part of everyone's experience. How do you balance all of this?

Ed Zwick: We came out of a time where there was some belief that the artist should participate in the dialogue of the day. That was a sixties feeling that we both shared. The notion of there being some kind of deeper politics in *thirtysomething* was very important. Those deeper politics are subtle, but they were very important to us.

Marshall Herskovitz: This is actually deeply political. If you look at the United States, what do you see? You see a lot of interpersonal trauma. You see child abuse. You see people dealing with drugs. You see a lot of things in America that cut across demographics and economic lines that take a toll on relationships. It is very important to talk about how people communicate with each other. How people resolve conflicts with the people they love. To me this has political ramifications in the real world that we don't talk about as a country. It is very political what we were trying to do.

"Success"

Directed by Ron Lagomarsino

Written by Edward Zwick and Marshall Herskovitz

January 31, 1989

Scott Winant (*Producer*): I was approached by artists all the time. They wanted to be part of the show. They were fans of the show. I actually put my neck out so many times because in those days using music wasn't really done that way. I got a call from a singer. I am ashamed to say, I didn't think she was a good fit for the show. A brand new singer named Mariah Carey. She wanted to be on the show as well as use her music. I turned

Ron Lagomarsino directs singer Carly Simon, Melanie Mayron and David Marshall Grant in an episode where Melissa's success rises as Michael's falls. Melissa gets to photograph a Carly Simon album cover. Courtesy of Kenneth Zunder.

her down. We used artists like Ray Charles, Van Morrison, Joni Mitchell and others. We actually had Carly Simon as herself which was great.

Ron Lagomarsino (*Director*): Recently I went to a Carly Simon book signing, I wasn't sure she would remember me. She did. She was very sweet. It was one day of shooting. They were enormous scenes that we shot in a restaurant somewhere in West Hollywood. Carly isn't an actress so it was really about keeping her loose.

David Marshall Grant (*Russell*): It was a little bit of fantasy land. It was like going to the party you always wanted to go to. It was a parallel universe that was so much hipper than the one I lived in.

Ron Lagomarsino: It was basically just talking and chatting. It was all the quick cuts where Melissa was trying to make a good impression and all of her friends were embarrassing her.

Marshall Herskovitz: Melissa got this job and was embarrassed to be seen with the people that she loved because of how she saw herself with them. It was about her coming to understand and admit that she was embarrassed to be seen with them. It was not because of any problem with them but because she saw herself as diminished with them.

Ron Lagomarsino: Ken and Tim had such different energies, but when they worked together it was a great blend. Tim's Elliot was so combustible. Ken's Michael was always more contained. It made it more crushing when Michael breaks down.

Ken Olin: Rather than figuring out a way for Michael to be masculine in his own way in the pilot, he had to be less realized than Elliot. Elliot could screw around and Michael would be more naive. It felt like that wasn't necessary. In the second season, they could be fully masculine in their own way. They had different ways of dealing with the loss of their business.

Tim Busfield: Elliot had the ability of emotionally detaching himself from a lot of things because of the boy in him. Michael was struggling to be a man and he couldn't put those things away quite so easily as a boy could. Elliot might fail, but then moves on. Whereas Michael might fail in his dad's eyes or in his religion's eyes. He had that crap and they never gave that to Elliot. Elliot couldn't care less.

Ken Olin: I remember thinking the business part of the show was really cool and it was working. They just decided to get rid of all that. I didn't fear playing a character on television that failed. It was more for me what is going to happen now? I don't know how much of that was integrating the characters fears and how much of it was me worrying that we were giving up a really good part of the show. Part of it was getting into uncharted territory. I remember feeling unsteady about it. I thought, "Wait a minute, why are they doing this?" It wasn't so different from Michael thinking, "What will I do now?"

Marshall Herskovitz: One of the first decisions we made before we even pitched the show was that the Michael and Elliot Company would fail. It was so important to show that this is a part of life. Shame and failure are things that men deal with. I am not excluding women, but in those days there was something particularly male about this drive to succeed. The definition of yourself of being successful in business and if you fail, you are worthless. We wanted them to go through that.

Ken Olin: There was an insecurity in that we were doing this in the second year. I loved having all those scenes with Tim. It was a real loss. I learned a lot and I got comfortable with the comedy in those scenes. We would do three minutes of improvisation. This was our world, a third of our show, and it was ending.

Ron Lagomarsino: They were so good with each other. I remember that vividly. The scene in the bleachers of Michael and Elliot breaking down was an example of what the show did best. It just let a moment breathe and it didn't need dialogue. You saw these guys walking off into the abyss. They are in the prime of their life and they should be successful. And yet, they have no idea what is coming next.

Ken Olin: Tim is incredible to work with. That was just how Tim and I were. We are still really good friends. We just brought that chemistry to it.

Ron Lagomarsino: Michael and Elliot present opposing views. Michael had a more realistic view of dread of how things were going. Elliot was

This is the original model created by Brandy Alexander for the set of DAA. The push pins are places where the walls can be removed to fit the camera in the set. This model was used for directors to plan their shots. Courtesy of Brandy Alexander.

not going to go into this lightly. He is drinking a lot in this episode and really hated the fact that Miles Drentell had the upper hand. They kind of grow up in a certain way. Their business is tanking and they are trying desperately to save it. The alternative is having to go work for Drentell.

Ken Olin: The show was a very intimate group of people. It was insular in a lot of ways and now we are bringing in David Clennon (*Miles Drentell*). The first time we worked with David, it couldn't have been easy for him, especially with Timmy and I. It was a very exclusive club in terms of Tim and I get it and no one else does.

Marshall Herskovitz: We wanted to create the boss from hell. We had someone in mind who I had been employed by, who I don't want to use their name even though they are now dead. He was a producer of a show and basically a total shithead. He was a fast talker, kind of a mixture of charm and stab you in the back. He was a mercurial character. You never knew who you were dealing with. We had worked with David Clennon before. He is a brilliant actor, but a terrible auditioner. I see that as a plus. It has to do with his authenticity. He has to really live the part in order to do it. He came in for Miles Drentell. He didn't audition well, but it didn't matter to us because we wanted him in the part. We went to shoot it and we found that it just wasn't him. He was trying to do the thing we wrote, but it wasn't working. It didn't come off as menacing. It didn't suit him.

Ken Olin: The first time we worked with David he kept eating tons of nuts and could barely talk. Tim and I couldn't stop laughing. David was great and came back and filmed it again. But that first time we were just laughing. I think part of it was us feeling that this was our show and we were being put in the position to be in other people's world. It was David's world of DAA even though it was our show.

David Clennon joins the series as Michael and Elliot's business nemesis, Miles Drentell. David played Miles completely differently the first day of shooting, luckily Marshall went back and reshot the scene. Courtesy ABC Photography Archives.

Ron Lagomarsino: The genius of Ed and Marshall was they knew Miles was going to be a major character. It was really a question of tone.

David Clennon (*Played Miles Drentell*): The DVD box of the the second season of *thirtysomething* has an interesting documentary on the bonus disc "Mad Ad Man: Miles Drentell" and a mini-documentary in which I tell how I almost destroyed the character in my first day of shooting.

Marshall Herskovitz: It was one of those moments. When you are doing a television show, you have to make decisions quickly and usually that is a good thing because you have to go with your gut feeling. We had to choose between the actor or the character. We chose the actor. Clennon is great and we gave him the wrong thing to do. We saw in the footage we shot that he had this icey thing happening. We saw it and thought we have to play to that.

Ron Lagomarsino: Miles was a prickly prick. Very manipulative and smart as a whip. He knew he held all the aces, but he also knew that Michael and Elliot would be good for him but on his terms. There was a tonal thing with how broadly David should play it. He was written as kind of an out there character. The way he talked and behaved was sort of Machiavellian. It was important that he not become a caricature. There were times when it was too delicious to not have him do a line reading in a certain way, but you want to be sure he is real person.

Marshall Herskovitz: Miles emerged as an unspoken collaboration between Clennon and us. It was a much better character than the one we had in mind. We decided to reshoot those scenes and over the course of one or two episodes we hit the sweet spot of who this guy was.

Brandy Alexander (*Production Designer*): Marshall was directing the reshoot and he called for me. I thought, "Oh shit, I am in big trouble." He said, "I love this set of DAA. You did an amazing job and I am going to put you in this scene." I show Miles an art board that he signs off on it. I give a nod and walk away. That was not in the script. That was something Marshall added because he was so happy with the set. I was shocked and very grateful. Ed and Marshall were two of the most amazing men to work for. They really did acknowledge people's work.

Brandy Alexander has a small cameo in this episode, as she hands Miles Drentell artwork to sign off on. She also designed his office, shown here. Courtesy of Brandy Alexander.

Ron Lagomarsino: I always thought Ken was very underrated. I think because he was so good looking when the awards came around they dismissed him. Ken had a remarkable reserve. An actor like Tim has sort of a kaleidoscope of colors. Ken's spectrum is a little tighter, but no less deep. Ken also has a darkness about him that made him play a scene more subdued.

Marshall Herskovitz: It was so important to what we were trying to say about what it means to be human that people fail. Shame is inevitable. You have to figure it out. You have to live through it, you have to survive it. That was engineered from the very beginning, that that business was going to fail.

Episode 29

"First Day/Last Day"

Directed by Peter Horton

Written by Joseph Dougherty

February 7, 1989

Joe Dougherty (*Writer*): "First Day/Last Day" is actually kind of linear the way it exists now. It was originally meant to be out of order. It was all about going back and forth and picking up pieces of information at different points. When it was cut together, it was impossible to follow. The fact that it had act breaks in it made it even crazier. We had to go back and put things in order. After that, brand new transitions appeared. It was almost like the script always knew how it wanted to be played.

Tim Busfield: I don't know how Peter Horton didn't win a directing Emmy for that one. All of his episodes were great. He let masters play out and brought a long lens element to the show. Ed and Marshall's respect for Peter's vision was really strong.

Ken Olin: Working with Peter was great. That was a long intense day and it was the three of us all day. It was emotional. I remember being in that empty office and it being sad. As an actor, everything is there for you to draw upon. One of the things I really learned from that experience is why work harder than you have to work? Everything was right there. Use your two years of a relationship with Tim and all that history. Acting is already hard enough, use your life.

Joe Dougherty: We were writing the backstory of Michael and Elliot. We wanted to do a clip show where we hadn't ever seen the clips. How did they come together? Elliot brought more to the partnership than Michael did in a lot of ways. It may not be the healthiest stuff that he brought, but he did get Michael to be more of a mensch.

Tim Busfield: As much as it played out well for the audience, I think the stuff that we liked playing more were the small jealousies. What is the impact of an affair? Not the affair itself but the impact of the affair. So many shows would have played out the affair in its grandness. The actual time spent on the actual affair that Elliot had was itty bitty flashbacks to the copy room. It was the line where Elliot says, "The hard part is this abyss that happens and you don't know how you're ever going to cross it." What can happen when you lie to each other in a marriage? I really loved when the show was about that.

It was always in the plan that the Michael and Elliot company would fail. "First Day/ Last Day" looks at the beginning and the end of their business. Courtesy of Carol Gepper's TV Guide Collection.

Ann Lewis Hamilton: I think Elliot was still a little child and needed to grow up. I had sort of forgotten that Elliot had the affair.

Joe Dougherty: I actually think there was a mistake in the episode. I think there was a continuity error. There was a cut where the window was broken in the wrong shot. There was only one optical in that episode.

Peter Horton: We were so limited back then that the magic tricks really were magic tricks. For example, the shot where we are in the present with Elliot and he throws the beer can at the window, it cracks, tilts down, they are in the past and it's their first day. That is all one shot with a lock off. We had to do it practically. It is a good thing Tim is a baseball player because he had to hit that little square window with the beer can. You lock it off and draw it up on the monitor to make sure you knew the shot. If you had to do take two, we would have to go up and exactly match that for the lock offs to work. Now with special effects these days for a viewer it is probably more satisfying because it is more convincing but for a filmmaker it was much more fun then.

In order to show the first day and the last day at the same time, Ken Olin and Tim Busfield acted with body doubles to make it appear that all four people were in the office at the same time. This was years before computers could have achieved this easily. Joe Dougherty won an Emmy for his ambitious script. Courtesy ABC Photography Archives.

Joe Dougherty: Ken and Tim were not acting with each other. It is all done with photo doubles.

Peter Horton: The choreography of that fight scene was so intricate. It was really a kind of fugue. I had these doubles going from Michael walking one direction in the past and passing someone who looks like Michael with Elliot from behind. That was a double, it wasn't a trick shot.

Ken Olin: I remember being surprised by the ending of the Michael and Elliot Company. I was not part of that evolution at all. It was very unsettling. What was going to happen to Michael and Elliot's relationship?

Joe Dougherty: How bad can we make it? It was an origin story. Let's talk about how people fell in love and how things fell apart. We were deep enough into the series at that time that people wanted to see where they started.

Peter Horton: They would come into the office, walk off camera and there would be an empty frame sitting there as you hear them talking. They would come back at a certain moment. You had such a great tool box to play with the scripts and the cast.

Ken Olin: Those scenes weren't hard to act, they were fun. That doesn't get personal in any weird way. We knew that our daily working together was coming to an end and it was sad. For the three of us to do that was really cool. There was some closure in that scene. It really affected everything. We introduced new characters, we didn't dress the same, and had new sets. It changed the show forever.

Peter Horton: You just had these guys who, when they got going, were so good. The dialogue was wonderfully non-subtext. All the subtext got to be in the action and tone instead of the words. We set up the scenes, shots, transitions and then let these guys do their thing. Take the marks off the floor, so if they wanna move somewhere else they can and let them go where they want. If the camera misses a piece, use it. The real fuel of that show was intimacy and what is personal between us all. The closer you could get to that the more the show would take flight.

Ken Zunder (*Director Of Photography*): Traditional television is you shoot a master, over the shoulder, and a close up. We wouldn't do that. We let people go off camera. They'd have dialogue in another room and then they come back. Marshall, Ed and Scott were very interested in telling stories for television in nontraditional ways. Michael and Elliot wouldn't necessarily sit in a chair. They might lay on the floor of their office. They had freedom to go wherever they wanted.

Joe Dougherty: People were really knocked out that the two guys were fighting at the end, really fighting. Actually, there was some press about it because at that point no one had seen the two lead characters of a television show mix it up like that and it was scary. It was like watching your parents fight. ABC would not let us say, "Son of a bitch." We could say bastard but couldn't say son of a bitch. It was just let us make this scary. Let's end it ugly. It's bad and it's recrimination and it's emasculating and it's making cracks about people's wives. Then the last beat is you are my friend and you complete me and I can't remember our beginning. It's the two of them forgetting what the first day was.

Episode 30

"About Last Night"

Directed by Gary Sinise

Written by Ann Lewis Hamilton, Story by Tammy Ader

February 14, 1989

Patricia Kalember: I think I was hired for a couple of episodes. I didn't know if it would go beyond that season. I was pregnant at the time and they decided to work it into the story line.

Peter Horton: Patricia was pregnant for real at the time. We thought that would be fun to go that way. Let's have Gary get pregnant right away. What we didn't think through was that her actual pregnancy didn't co-incide with the story pregnancy. She was showing when she shouldn't be so we had to have her sitting down or blankets over her stomach.

Patricia Kalember: They had to hide my pregnancy at first and then when they were ready to write about the pregnancy, I had given birth and I had to wear a fat suit.

Gary and Susannah contemplate an abortion but decide to keep the baby. The pregnancy was written in due to Patricia Kalember's actual pregnancy. Courtesy ABC Photography Archives.

Peter Horton: We were having scenes with us being romantic together and she has this baby in her belly and it is poking me while I am trying to kiss her. It became really funny.

Patricia Kalember: I was pregnant and Peter knew that. He was very careful with me.

Susan Shilliday: Life doesn't always go the way you think it is going to go. Things happen like someone gets pregnant and wants to keep the baby.

Patricia Kalember: Once again she assumes Gary was going to pull away and was very insecure. Her reaction to telling Gary she was pregnant was to take the smart route. I am done. I don't have emotions and it is not true. It is a way of keeping people at arm's length and keeping control.

Ann Lewis Hamilton (*Writer*): That is an episode I have not read again. Gary Sinise directed it. He was great. I found letters saying, "How dare you talk about abortion?" All the female characters talk about abortion in the kitchen. We were all so afraid of that scene that it kept getting cut shorter. So, my memory of it is that it comes off as way too casual when it really shouldn't have been. It was probably written longer and then maybe I took it out.

Patricia Kalember: I never saw Susannah as unlikeable, but that is what people told me. I either got she was annoying or people really appreciated her. She was a nice antidote to everybody else.

Ann Lewis Hamilton: It was an impossible situation to come into. Those characters always think they know what is best for everyone else. Jumping into that group would be impossible.

Patricia Kalember: I think there might have been a little bit of that because the cast bonded very closely that first season. It takes a while for a new cast member to kind of ease their way in. I mean everyone was perfectly sweet and charming. A lot of times it is how you feel, not how they are responding.

Episode 31

"Elliot's Dad"

Directed by Dan Lerner

Written by Joseph Dougherty

February 28, 1989

Tim Busfield: We had a great time with Eddie Albert, who played my father. I remember telling him how much I loved him on *Green Acres* (1965). I asked him how it was to work with her and he said, "Eva Gabor or the pig?" He was just so funny. The reason they hired him was that Marshall and his daughter were watching television and *Roman Holiday* was on. His daughter said, "Is that Timmy?" Susan Shilliday looked at the TV and saw Eddie Albert. We looked so much alike.

Joe Dougherty (*Writer*): Patty Wettig read the script and there was something that didn't make any sense to her. I wrote a strange stage direction when Elliot goes to the hospital at the end to see Ethan, who just got his eye injured by shooting off a rocket. It doesn't have an impact on the viewer, only on the actor. I like doing that. Elliot was talking to Ethan, the camera pulled back and Nancy is seen listening to Elliot's speech about responsibility. The stage direction was meaningless. It said, "We will never know how long Nancy has been standing there. We don't know how much she heard." I wrote it because it changes depending on when she got there and what she heard. I like to think Nancy heard the whole thing.

Tim Busfield: I like the scene in the hospital room a lot, but really Elliot should have just punished Ethan and told his wife, "It's not my fault he played with that thing. I didn't buy him the rocket. It wasn't my fault. I wasn't there."

Joe Dougherty: Who could have stopped the accident earlier? Elliot. Who could have said, "Don't buy him this thing?" He was not a suffi-

Eddie Albert (Charlie Westin) poses with Patty and Tim. Grandpa Westin buys Ethan a rocket that injures Ethan's eye. This event makes Elliot confront what kind of father he has and what kind of father he is. Courtesy of Kenneth Zunder.

cient dad to stop it. I am not ready to blame Nancy. The place where you could have stopped the accident from happening was Elliot.

Patty Wettig: I don't remember that scene. I can't comment on this because I don't remember it at all. I don't even remember filming it. What did Tim say? That it was my fault?

Tim Busfield: If Patty was here I would say, "Nancy was a controlling bitch," and she would smile and nod because she knew that was her job.

Joe Dougherty: Elliot setup Nancy by being the bad parent, by putting it on her to take the rocket away which she wasn't prepared to do. Ethan shouldn't have been given the rocket.

Tim Busfield: Everyone get off my ass. You can see Hope and everyone looking at Elliot. I didn't buy him the rocket. I wasn't even home, so shut up.

Patty Wettig: We used to fight like that all the time. I have zero memory of that scene. There are some things I remember exactly and others if I watched it, I probably still wouldn't remember.

Tim Busfield: Our demographic was mostly women. My job was not to be the hero on that show. It was to make sure I was a bad husband. My only saving grace was being a good father. It gave me the moment with Ethan in the hospital. I would always ask for the kids in scenes because I knew if I loved the kids, the viewers would be torn. For most women if he's a bad husband and a bad dad, he is gone.

Joe Dougherty: Elliot wasn't the worst husband. He was struggling to not be the worst husband.

Tim Busfield: I told the writers that I had a distant relationship with my dad. I told them it was fractured and that he would say things like this. Then there was Eddie Albert saying all the things I told them my dad would say. I was like "You guys. What the hell. Knock it off. I'm not answering any more stories about my personal life."

Episode

32

"Payment Due"

Directed by Ron Lagomarsino

Written by Cynthia Saunders

March 7, 1989

Polly Draper: My character went through an ulcer, but it was basically a nervous breakdown. She was a horrible bitch to Hope in the second season.

Mel Harris: Hope and Ellyn were reflective of what happens to two women who became friends when they were single. Then one gets married and it doesn't change much, but when you add a child to that friendship of two women, it really goes in one of two ways. It either continues to move along and the friend comes in, or she feels replaced by the child.

Polly Draper: They were like sisters. They loved each other. There was no question ever. They were friends to the end. We were able to be awful to each other and still have that love. Just like with sisters. You gossip about them, you get furious with them, but you end up loving them. Neither one of the characters had sisters, so we became sisters.

Mel Harris: Neither one of them understood each other. I think the first year of having a young baby is really hard. The sleep deprivation alone is mind boggling.

Polly Draper: I think what came between us happens in the pilot: the baby. The fact that I was kind of like Hope's project. Then she just stopped having time to solve my problems and as a narcissistic person, I was a little jealous of that. I think the way that Melissa and Ellyn bonded was on the single women thing of not having kids.

"Deliverance"

Directed by Peter Horton

Written by Ann Lewis Hamilton

March 21, 1989

Ann Lewis Hamilton: Melanie Mayron sat me down with an early script and said to me, "You don't need to write this dialogue, I can play it." I have been a super minimalist in writing because of Melanie telling me she can play a moment. Ellyn was such a mess in this episode. She was a mess in the beginning and then kind of gets her act together.

Polly Draper: My Father was annoyed with Ellyn because she was such a narcissist. He would say, "I didn't raise you this way." I would say,

The female characters take a trip into the woods. This behind the scenes photo shows them getting ready for the hike. Courtesy of Kenneth Zunder.

"Dad, these are the most interesting characters to play. The ones that are all fine and there is nothing wrong with them aren't fun to play. Just be excited for me that I get to do all these interesting things. Don't be judging me."

Episode 34

"Michael Writes a Story"

Directed by Tom Moore

Written by Joseph Dougherty

April 4, 1989

Ellen Pressman (*Producer*): Scott would be the first one to get the scripts and there were a lot of times when the scripts were too ambitious. We would have to re-conceptualize certain things to make it work for television. We didn't cut things. Scott was very respectful to the writers. It was about reconceptualizing it in a way that was doable. The episode about writing a story directed by Tom Moore was a very ambitious script because Michael kept changing the story. I think if you went to the original script and compared with what was shot it would be very different.

Joe Dougherty: We know Michael was a better writer than he appeared in the class. He was just trying to be the whiz kid. My favorite part was when Gary said, "I am reading a newspaper with nothing written in it." There were all the judgmental voices. I am very pleased with the character of Ivy Dunbar (*Lorinne Vozoff*). I am more Ivy than anybody else. I have been confronted with too many people who have looked me in the eye and said, "How long should I try at this before I know I am no good at it?" My response is, "You should stop now." Michael was trying to use writing to fix things that writing can't fix.

Winnie Holzman: I could relate to a lot of that episode because I certainly had been in a lot of writing classes. I think being a writer demands a questioning of yourself. What am I doing? Am I even doing anything? There is a way in which you ask yourself these really hard questions.

Joe Dougherty: I wanted to talk specifically to people like Michael who think, "If I can write, everything will be ok. If I can figure out a way to get published or get produced, somehow that validation will fix every-

In a fantasy sequence, Ken Olin and Patty Wettig share their one on screen kiss in the series during one of the versions of the story that Michael writes. Courtesy of Kenneth Zunder.

thing." Well that validation doesn't fix everything and even at that time I was still learning that lesson. Maybe that lesson was very close to the front of my head. Marshall wanted something that was a little bit more about the writing process, but I kept saying the writing process isn't interesting to dramatize. It is more interesting to take a look at why you do things. I'd actually like to publicly apologize to Michael Steadman. He was not that bad of a writer. Wherever he is right now, he is probably a much better writer than he was there. He had figured out what the writing was supposed to do. It is not supposed to get you praised. It is not supposed to make you the smartest kid in the class.

Winnie Holzman: Fear is a kind of familiar companion for a writer. I experience it a lot. That isn't my motivation anymore. I am so used to fear that I don't consider it an emergency situation. Back then, I really wanted to prove myself. You want to prove yourself to those who you admire, but you also want to prove yourself to yourself. Can I face this? Can I face this fear? Now, I have logged a lot of hours facing fear.

Joe Dougherty: When I wrote that episode I had gone through what Michael had gone through. I was a struggling guy on Long Island, married to my first wife who supported me on the other side of college. Damage was done to our relationship because of expectations I had which was simply, "Sorry, I am a writer." Through a set of really strange unexpected avenues, I did get a play in New York. I did get representation, then absolutely nothing changed. I was still the same person. My problems didn't go away. I was now acknowledged in public as the person I thought I had always been. I was sitting in an apartment waiting for the three wise men to come and knock on the door and say, "We got off on the wrong foot, but we are here now to tell you that you are a writer and you will be acknowledged as such." I had finally gotten that, but nothing changed. Life actually became more complicated. Eventually, my wife and I separated. I wanted Michael to learn a lesson that it wasn't going

Michael has to confront his writing teacher and Miles Drentell in an episode that focuses on the joys and pains of writing as well as starts the next chapter of the series: Michael and Elliot working for Miles Drentell. Courtesy ABC Photography Archives.

to change anything. Ann Hamilton and I would say, "All you've got is the writing. Once you hand it to somebody else, it is going to be something else." Your pleasure that comes from art, comes from what you did alone in a room.

Ken Zunder (*Director of Photography*): In "Michael Writes A Story," Joe wrote in the script that Michael is sitting in the den at the base of a damn fine shaft of light. He would always put a little fun line in the scripts for my benefit. I created the light as if it came through the window.

Joe Dougherty: One of my great indulgences is that there is an Ivy Dunbar book floating around in *Pretty Little Liars*. She wrote a book called *On Writing*. Aria (*Lucy Hale*) and her teacher (*Ezra Fitz*) traded this book back-and-forth a few times. It actually appeared on screen. I love it because it is a joke that nobody gets. She does say, "I've got that Ivy Dunbar book." Props made it up for me.

Pretty Little Liars *star, Lucy Hale, holds up a mock copy of* On Writing *by Ivy Dunbar. Joe Dougherty created this character on* thirtysomething *and carried it over to* Pretty Little Liars. *Joe shares his philosophy about writing through the character of Ivy. Courtesy of Joseph Dougherty.*

Scott Winant: Ed and Marshall's worst nightmare would be to lose their business and be forced to work under somebody they didn't respect. That was where Miles Drentell came from. That is why the Michael and Elliot Company went out of business because that is Ed and Marshall's nightmare.

Ken Olin: There was that tone and language that Tim and I had. We had the sound. We were used to improvising in those business scenes and now all that was done. I think that was the point of the plot change. It was like they made us graduate to middle school. David Clennon got his feet under him and was just wonderful. Tim and I realized we couldn't laugh and fool around anymore.

David Clennon (*Miles Drentell*): I think Ed and Marshall created a prototype of Miles Drentell and they knew where they wanted to take him for at least three episodes. It was full of potential and possibility. Then the other writers took that prototype and they refined it under the lash of Marshall and Ed.

Joe Dougherty: This was the first time you saw the dynamic between Miles and Michael. What happened to Elliot was that he was going from being completely irresponsible to figuring out how to be self-authorized. Michael hadn't figured out how to do it. Elliot started to realize that Michael wasn't seeing what he was doing there.

Mel Harris: Once again, this goes back to Hope's belief in liking and loving Michael. When he believed he was going to turn out like Miles, she didn't believe him. He was just saying that. There was something about doing things that you may not want to do to support your family and child. In retrospect, maybe she wished it didn't happen. That would be a different show.

Joe Dougherty: It's a pip of an episode. It was the one that went into the book of scripts. It is not the one that they wanted. I said, "I think this is a book for writers and this script should be in there."

Episode 35

"New Job"

Directed by Joshua Brand

Written by Ann Lewis Hamilton

April 11, 1989

Polly Draper: There was nothing they wrote that made me feel like it was counter to what my character would do. There was once when they were going to have me have the clap and I said, "Didn't I just have an ulcer last year? Do I have to have the clap?" They said, "You are right." When the idea that Ellyn had an abortion years ago came up, I did not feel like it was something that wouldn't happen. I thought that plot made total sense with what had preceded it. It fit with her not wanting to be around babies with the guilt of the abortion. She had a past.

Ann Lewis Hamilton (*Writer*): At the end of the first season I had a miscarriage. Ed and Marshall called to say they were sorry. We talked about how a writer can write about bad things that happen to them. Ed said, "Who knows we may have to write a miscarriage on the show and you might end up writing that episode." A couple of months later, Hope was pregnant on the show. Mel Harris had married again and she said, "I am not going to have a baby right away but probably we are going to have a baby next year." So, we decided it would be better to have Hope pregnant in season three. But they made Hope pregnant in "Mike Van Dyke." They said, "We have to give Hope a miscarriage. Would you like to write it? If you don't want to, you don't have to. We understand." I said, "I want to write it more than anything." I was the first of my friends who had a miscarriage. I didn't know anyone else who this had happened to and it was horrible. I thought that maybe writing about it might help other women who had been through the experience. So, I wrote the miscarriage episode.

This original illustration of the DAA set was drawn by Tom Lay for the Emmy telecast in 1989. It is hanging in Brandy Alexander's home. Courtesy of Brandy Alexander.

Susan Shilliday: Even though we were pulling from our life it was everyone's life. When Ann was writing about miscarriages, so many people go through that. It is so common and here was a chance to talk about how it tears up a marriage. Most of the time it just gets brushed aside.

Ann Lewis Hamilton: When I had my miscarriage my husband was doing a movie. He asked if he should stay home with me or go to work and I said, "Go to work." Thinking, "Damn you, stay home. I need you." It was just like Michael going back to DAA. The big scene at the end really was the fight my husband and I had later on. Michael says to Hope, "You should have told me to stay." Hope says, "You should have known what I was thinking." That is such a great male and female thing. I totally expected my husband to stay with me even though I told him to go to work. I was so mad at him. I can laugh about it now, but at the time I was really pissed. Why didn't I just say, "I don't want you to go to work. I need you to stay with me because I am sad."

Susan Shilliday: These issues were the small issues of everybody's marriage so that made it less scary to share with the world because everyone was going through it. It just wasn't being shown on dramatic television. Everyone was going through it and that is why the show was so recognizable to so many people.

Ann Lewis Hamilton: I remember going to the set when they were shooting it. People told me to stay away because by then I was pregnant again. I was on set watching a scene about my miscarriage. My husband didn't see any of the dailies. The episode airs on the screen for millions to see and there is the fight scene at the end. My husband says, "Oh my God, I can't believe you wrote this." When he would go to work everyone would say, "Wow, you and Ann had a big fight about that." Usually when my episodes aired friends would call at 11:00 and say, "Ann, that was a great episode." Nobody called because my friends knew it was about my miscarriage and knew I was pregnant. We went to bed. I woke up an hour later and went to the bathroom and my water broke. I went to the hospital. I was kind of insane and I kept telling nurses, "This is so weird. I don't know if you watch *thirtysomething* but the episode tonight was about my miscarriage and now I am having a baby." The episode aired on Tuesday and my son was born on Wednesday.

Scott Winant: The hardest thing I had to do was fight the studio for money. It is true that I exceeded the budget on "We'll Meet Again" but I used to do that on a daily basis. Anything Ed and Marshall wanted I got them. They weren't going to use The Michael and Elliot Company set anymore. They wanted us to build a new company that was five times as big as that. The studio sure as hell didn't know this was going to happen.

Scott Winant had to plan and scheme like he was Miles Drentell to get the set of DAA built. Brandy Alexander was nominated for an Emmy for her design of DAA. Courtesy of the Brandy Alexander Collection.

I had to go to MGM and say, "You know that beautiful set that we spent all that money building? I am going to get rid of it. We are not going to use it anymore. I need to build the new set on one of the stages even though you guys haven't given us permission to build this set." They got so angry at me. This was after I knew that I was going to do it anyway. The production executive was so beaten down by this point. He said, "Look, I don't want to see this on any of the production reports." So my unit production manager and I would take money from the set decorating budget and I would put it towards building DAA.

Brandy Alexander (*Production Designer*): I based the set of DAA on the architect Frank Furness. He created a very interesting building in Philadelphia. The interior was based on IMK Architects who did structures inside of structures. That is how I came up with their cubicles made of glass windows. I wanted them to be in their office but not in a small box. They had windows to see all the life outside. I got two Emmy nominations because of the Miles/DAA sets.

Scott Winant: If I had a scene that needed a doctor's office, I would make one of the walls become part of Mile's office after we finish filming the doctor's scene. I had to take it apart and use it for something else then bring it back, paint it and make it part of DAA. Throughout the season I had constructed all of DAA by building it in pieces as we went along. When DAA is first seen it's not even there. I had cutting pieces that weren't backed. There was depth but if you went along the side there was nothing there. The studio never saw the money that was spent and that is how we ended up building that set. We were really loose cannons I have to say.

Episode 36

"Be a Good Girl"

Directed by Richard Kramer

Written by Richard Kramer

April 25, 1989

Melanie Mayron: That was a great episode with Phyllis Newman (*Melissa's Mom, Elaine Steadman*) and Sylvia Sidney (*Melissa's Grandmother, Rose Waldman*). I very much wanted to make sure the writers didn't make Melissa boy crazy. You are boy crazy when you're a teenager. When you are in your late thirties, you are survival crazy. You are just trying to live and pay your bills. You want to be in love, but it is not number one anymore. I always wanted to make sure that Melissa was a survivor and wasn't going to compromise her dreams. Ellyn and Melissa were the single woman. Ellyn was more the corporate life. Melissa represented the artist. So, at least there was somebody representing everyone.

Richard Kramer *(Director, his directorial debut)*: I was very concerned at what the grandmother's bedroom looked like. I wanted it to look like you were lost in the woods in it. Sylvia Sidney took to Melanie Mayron. She thought Melanie was the best young actress she had ever worked with. She didn't have to say that. She already had the job.

Episode

37

"Courting Nancy"

Directed by Ken Olin

Written by Susan Shilliday

May 2, 1989

Susan Shilliday: It absolutely felt great to make Nancy feel hot and sexy. Ken, as the director of the episode, gets to show everyone what he sees in his own wife.

Ken Olin: I felt really good about the second episode I directed. I found it a lot easier to direct the scenes with Patty and other men over not directing those scenes. I felt, in a way, that I was controlling how everyone was touching and being with her. I remember Timothy Carhart (*Played Nancy's love interest, Matthew Enwright*) lifting her up and putting his hands on her butt. I would not have liked that if I was not directing. But as the director I thought, "Hey that looks good." If someone else was directing it and I had no control, I might think, "Patty, why did you let them do that?" It was tougher for me when my imagination got away with me.

Patty Wettig: I think it made it easier because Ken sees me as beautiful. He doesn't see me as disparaging and sad. I would hope. The love, joy and beauty is easier to radiate. We had that great song, "She Drives Me Crazy." (*Sings the song)* I think we liked it at the time. It had such a fun beat and energy. When Ken chose it, I remember feeling it gave the dating montage a great drive.

Ken Olin: Fine Young Cannibals was mine. I chose the song. The montage was scripted. Susan was very sweet about it. She said, "This was just how I imaged it would look." Everyone was really happy with it.

"Courting Nancy" has two men vying for Nancy's affections. Despite all the attention, Patty Wettig was hoping for something darker for her character. Just wait till next season, Patty. Courtesy of Carol Gepper's TV Guide Collection.

Richard Kramer: Nancy goes from plain to beautiful as she retained her radiance. She was squashed by her marriage in the first season. Patty and Timmy were genius and it was our luck to come in and work with them. They not only became the characters but they became the characters in relation to the other characters in the series.

Patty Wettig: Hope doesn't think I should get back together with Elliot. They get back together because she loves him. If there had not been kids involved maybe the chances of the marriage surviving were less because you don't fight for the marriage. I think she was still in love with him. They were in love with each other. Susan writes from a very deep place.

Susan Shilliday: To me the key line is when Nancy says, "There is something about the way his mind works." That is what was going to bring them back together. There was some deep connection that really defies any explanation. Nancy recognized that about Elliot and other people may not.

Patty Wettig: Women judge other women more in a negative way for staying with men instead of leaving men. They like to imagine the heroic act of leaving. Is that always the best thing? I think what Nancy was saying to Hope was a truthful thing. When you are in a young marriage, you don't think any bad things will come to your marriage.

Ken Olin directs an episode that focuses on the beauty and sexuality of his real life wife, Patty Wettig. Ken felt it was easier to direct episodes with Patty as opposed to wondering what another director would do. Courtesy of the Dan Steadman Collection. TV Guide

Susan Shilliday: It wasn't from knowing what was in store for Michael and Hope. It was from knowing marriage. It is the way it is. I believe Nancy's speech. By this time, I was the automatic go to person for Nancy stories just like Joe Dougherty was for DAA stories. That was my specialty.

Joe Dougherty: I don't know if anybody was really in charge of any particular story line. I became very possessive of Miles. If anyone else wrote him I would give them a dirty look.

Patty Wettig: Finally, in the second year, Nancy got it together. She was dating and feeling better about herself. For me as an actress, the work became a little boring. I was looking nice, feeling better, but the work wasn't challenging. Marshall and Ed thought I would like it because I got to be prettier and all the boys liked me. I went into their office at the end of the second year and said, "I don't mean to complain, but I really would like to have something grittier or interesting next year. I would like to get my teeth into something. I don't know what, but I don't like just being happy."

"Best of Enemies"

Directed by Joseph Dougherty

Written by Joseph Dougherty

May 16, 1989

End of Season 2

Patricia Kalember: Susannah was jealous of Hope. Hope probably was a cheerleader. Susannah took herself out of that competition by being intellectually superior, but deep down was jealous of the cheerleader.

Ann Lewis Hamilton: People didn't like Susannah. They didn't like that character because she was tough. I think some of that is that women who watched the show were madly in love with Peter Horton. Way back then he was like Prince Charles. Everyone wanted to marry Prince Charles. He was gonna be the most perfect husband ever. Which turned out not to be true.

Joe Dougherty *(Director, his directorial debut)*: Patricia Kalember had that great line, "Not an evil bone in Gary's body, but look out for his good intentions."

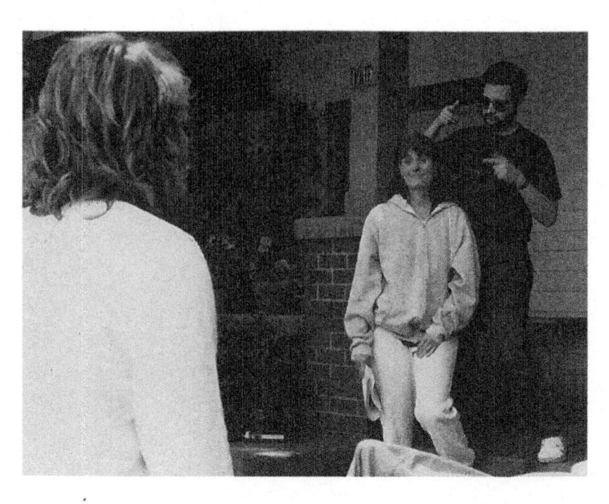

Actress Mel Harris (Hope) is directed by Joseph Dougherty in his directorial debut "Best of Enemies." Many of the writing staff, as well as the cast, directed episodes. Courtesy Joe Dougherty.

Ann Lewis Hamilton: Plus why wasn't he with Melissa? Poor Susannah. It was stacked against her because people thought Gary deserved the best. Patricia Kalember is the sweetest person in the world. Just like David Clennon, because people are like, "Oh, Miles is the worst." But David Clennon is the sweetest man on the planet.

Joe Dougherty: This was my directorial debut and it has the fewest set ups of any episode in the series. The script supervisor told me it only had eighty-five set ups.

Ken Zunder (*Director Of Photography*): We named a lens after Joe Dougherty. The 29mm lens. We called it "GI Joe" in honor of him because he would always pick that lens to do his masters in.

Joe Dougherty: The first thing I shot was Patricia Kalember opening the door with Mel Harris on the other side. I looked ahead and saw that Mel was standing in front of a blank wall. I looked behind me and there were sixty-eight people with heavy equipment waiting for me to say something. I immediately turned back to the blank wall. Directing is very grown-up. I am better at it now than I was then.

The Samurai School of Directing

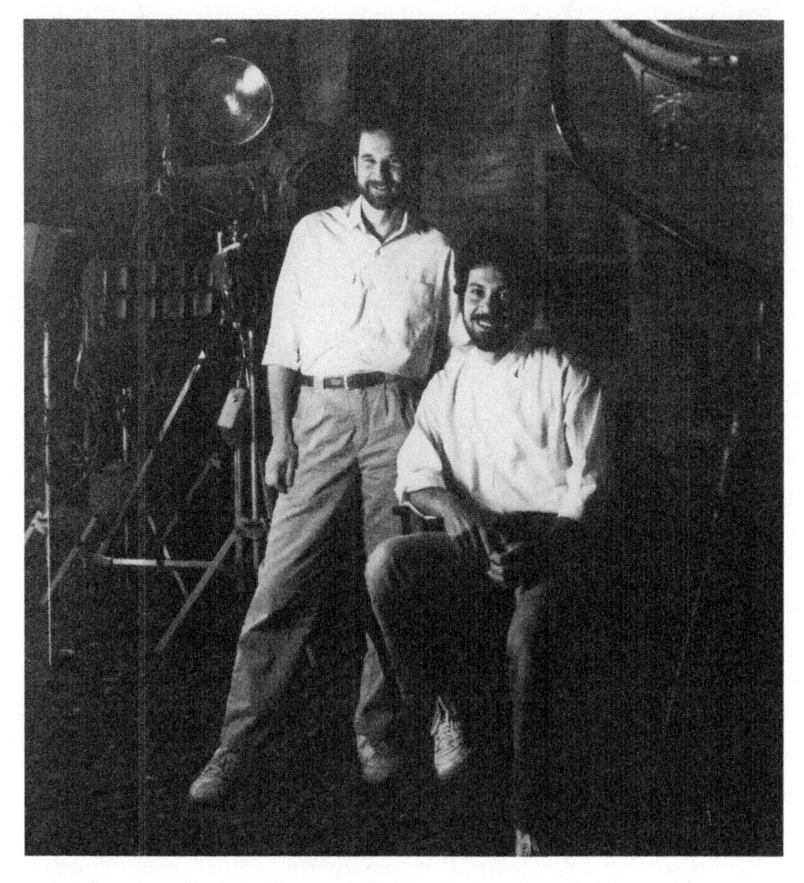

Creators/Directors/Writers Marshall Herskovitz and Ed Zwick started a school for directing on thirtysomething. This section focuses on directing the series. Courtesy ABC Photography Archives.

Marshall Herskovitz: We used something close to forty first-time directors over the four years. Back in those days, television was still the vast wasteland. Experienced television directors were basically shop foreman. They were doing it the quickest way possible. They bring people into a room and shoot it with a master shot. They would shoot coverage over the shoulders. There was no cinematic sensibility in television at all.

Ed Zwick: From the very beginning we thought that it would be much better to have people who had no habits rather than people who had developed bad habits. Marshall and I had a very specific vision of how the show should feel directorally. We had each worked in episodic television before and seen guys come in whose biggest goal was getting the crew home by 5:30. They did what was needed to be done and not a bit more. They didn't approach it with the belief that you could personally invest your own point of view and meaning into directing.

Marshall Herskovitz: People who were experienced television directors would do a horrible job on our show.

Ken Zunder (*Director Of Photography*): It was one of the few shows that truly cared what it looked like. We tried to make it look natural instead of Hollywood. We tried to light it as if the light came through windows. That was part of Ed and Marshall's idea of not hiring television directors. They also didn't hire television DP's (*Director Of Photography*) hoping it would look different.

Ed Zwick: We took it upon ourselves to encourage a kind of a laboratory where directing was as important to the show as the writing.

Joe Dougherty sits in the Director's chair even though his main job was a writer on the show. Stylized directing was an important principle that Ed Zwick and Marshall Herskovitz demanded from all the show's Directors. Courtesy of Joe Dougherty.

Peter Horton: What you hear from directors all the time is that there isn't an apprenticeship program for directing. You kind of get thrown out onto the floor and you either sink or swim.

Ed Zwick: I believed to somehow throw them into the deep end of the pool and be challenged as a first time director would unleashed something ineffable between them and the entire company.

Peter Horton: It was the perfect place to learn because Ed and Marshall were both directors. We used to call it "The Ed Zwick Samurai School of Directing."

Joe Dougherty: I went to the kinder gentler Marshall Herskovitz school, many portions of which I still use today. He gave certain axioms: watch your transitions, everything cuts from one thing to another, get in as late as you can in a scene and get out as quickly as you can and wear good shoes.

Marshall Herskovitz: We essentially started a school and taught people how to direct. Ed took more of that burden than I did. He did a tutorial that lasted several days. They would shadow us on the set. We would talk about the principles of directing. Then we would sit with them while they directed to make sure they were getting it.

Ellen Pressman: Because there were so many first time directors Ed took it upon himself to do seminars. At the beginning of the season, he would put together different clips from movies and wrote out his ideas about film making.

Marshall Herskovitz set the directing tone for the series by helming the pilot episode. He also directed the pilot for Once And Again in 1999. This series used many of the same directors who got their start on thirtysomething. Photo Courtesy of Marshall's Twitter account.

Melanie Mayron made her directorial debut on the show, as did four other cast members. Courtesy of the Dan Steadman Collection. Tv Guide.

Richard Kramer: Ed liked to show the wedding scene from *The Best Years of Our Lives* (1946). He loved that movie. They probably showed something from *It's A Wonderful Life* (1946) as well.

Melanie Mayron: I remember going to Ed's office and he would screen classic films and he would teach from them. I had always done still photography and what makes a good photo is a flat background where subjects are standing against a wall. Ed explained that when you are photographing people in film you don't want to put actors in front of a flat surface. You want to look for the depth in the frame. How far in the distance can you see behind them? He was really right about that. In film, there is always space behind the actors. That is something I still think about today when I am directing. *thirtysomething* was my in the field film school.

Ed Zwick: I do relish teaching and I have continued to do that since then. For better or worse, we had a point of view that we believed to be part of a tradition that was in disrepair. Is the purpose of teaching to encourage the individual to express themselves in whatever way they want to? Inevitably, a teacher does have a point of view.

Scott Winant: We rarely hired television directors. I had commercial directors, theater directors and our cast directed. We did this on purpose because we didn't want anyone to bring television habits to the show. Sometimes it was a strain on me for sure, but I think overall it was better.

Ken Zunder (*Director Of Photography*): Having first time directors was great for me. It made me that much more involved in the story telling. It wasn't like they came to me and said I want this shot and I would just go do it as a technician. They involved me. My job is art and craft and they gave me a lot more art because I was involved with the directors in how to block it. So much of *thirtysomething* was in the staging as opposed to just get a bunch of coverage and we will make the performance in the editing room.

Ed Zwick: I grew up in Chicago and a bunch of the folks from Steppenwolf are my friends. It is not a surprise that Terry Kinney and Gary Sinise were a part of the show. They come from a tradition that created a vision of a theater company. I just felt that somehow internally that we would be able to push each other and enlarge upon whatever vision that we had. Everyone would add to that vision with their own passion.

Peter Horton: Ed was a harsh task master, but it was a great place to learn your craft with great material, a really good cast and intimate subject matter.

Ed Zwick: Peter is being a little bit coy by describing himself as a novice because he wanted to be a director for a very long time. Nobody was more avid of this process than he was. The same with Kenny, Timmy, and Melanie. I did believe the learn as you earn school was the best way.

Ken Olin: Ed was a great teacher. I didn't go to film school. I studied acting. Both Ed and Marshall are affiliated with AFI (*American Film Institute)* and are very serious film makers. Ed was generous and enjoyed mentoring. He mentored me throughout those years. They were arrogant about what they wanted to do on that show. He could be really tough on me.

Tim Busfield: You didn't want to sit between Ed and Marshall during dailies. We had them every day which no television show does that. They had lunch everyday. They had it up in the dailies room and anyone could go watch.

Scott Winant: I didn't think twice about it back then but every day at lunch Ed, Marshall, myself, the writers and whoever was directing that day would go to a room and watch dailies like they used to in the 1930s. We all collectively watched them together. It was frightening. It was terrifying.

The show never released Ed or Marshall's tips for directing but they did release the best scripts written over the first three seasons. This is one of two official products the show released. Each writer picked a favorite episode and wrote a new essay explaining why. The series expected high quality from writing and directing. Courtesy of Scott Ryan's Collection.

Ellen Pressman: Ed and Marshall were there at dailies and it was an opportunity to critique the director's work. I wasn't used to being critiqued in public. We were all sort of scared of the public experience. I remember Ed getting upset at me and saying, "Why did you do that? It was an unmotivated camera move." He was right. It was embarrassing, but he was right.

Tim Busfield: When you directed, you had to sit between Ed and Marshall. They would stop the dailies and sigh. They would rub their face in their palms. You would feel like you were gonna shit yourself. Kenny and Peter would be smiling behind you because they were not sitting in the hot seat. I would be sweating, but learning so much. Two great filmmakers talking you through the process. It was made available because Peter and Kenny let the door open.

Ron Lagomarsino: I don't remember having to sit between them literally that would have been scary. They were very honest. If something wasn't working they would point it out.

Brandy Alexander: Ed and Marshall mentored all the directors by sitting at the table in the front of the screening room where a director would get a lesson. It was a positive environment. There wasn't any back stabbing like I have seen on other series.

Marshall Herskovitz: Every day at dailies we would sit there with the director and we would critique what they did. Not in a mean way, but in a way that was constructive. "See you did this, where you could have done that in one shot. Had you been willing to move them around, you could have choreographed it in another way." We were trying to impart the esthetics of how you can do a television show and make it feel more like a movie.

Brandy Alexander: Today, only the executive producers get dailies on shows. But we would have lunch every day together and watch dailies. Every once in awhile I would get a compliment from Ed or Marshall, "Brandy, I really like that piece of set dressing in the corner. It really tells the story." It wasn't just notes for the director or actors. They would compliment the Costume Designer. It wasn't only insults or negative comments. When you get a compliment you work harder.

Ron Lagomarsino: My first day of shooting I was so prepared because I was nervous. I was so on fire that we finished at 4:00, which was unheard of. The second day I was shooting on location in a camera store, so I couldn't watch dailies with them because they were back at the studio. Right in the middle of a rehearsal in walked Ed, Marshall and Scott. I thought, "Oh, no. How bad were my dailies? They left the studio to come fire me." They walked right up to me. They hugged me. I could see in their faces that they loved what they saw. That was my second day of shooting single camera in my career. It says something about them that they bothered to get in the car and come to the set. It was very classy of them.

Ed Zwick had directed the feature film About Last Night before he directed on thirtysomething. Courtesy Lisa Mercado Ferrnandez.

Patty Wettig: We would all sit and watch the dailies together. I have never done that since. Producers, actors, writers, editors all in the room together watching the dailies and having feelings about it. You get to know all your takes. Everyone is trying to come up with what is the best episode we can make. Maybe it is silly now. We took it extremely serious at the time. It was almost ridiculously self-involved. The investment was intense.

Ellen Pressman: They wanted the directors to bring their own visions and they didn't want every episode to be the same. In television today there is a "style." You come in and you are there to facilitate the "style."

Peter Horton: The other thing as a director that was important was that they encouraged directors to come in and experiment. Unlike television now that has a directing producer to make sure that everything is the same. Back then, it was come in and make it your own. You could really stretch.

Ed Zwick: The fabric of the series was elastic enough to contain different sensibilities. Nobody's sensibilities could be more different than Joe's and Richard's. The world view is expanded by having the fabric stretched that far. So we could bring in someone like Rob Cohen or Peter Horton to direct. This way, the episodes wouldn't have that horrible predictable, metronomic television thing. Where at any given minute of the hour you know exactly what the camera is going to do and where the story is going to go and you could beat it out with your eyes closed and say, "Here is the moment." The idea that we could have a commonality of intention with the philosophy of a story that seemed to be about one thing, but then would reveal itself to be another. The direction of it would only enliven the experience because then you wouldn't fall into that hateful redundancy. The actors were the same, the sets were the same.The dissimilarity of each director's work was mitigated by the subject.

Marshall Herskovitz: When you try to do a filmmaking sensibility in eight days, it is hard. We hired people like Rob Lieberman. He had done commercials that were interesting as an artist. Rob Cohen was another great one for us. We looked for people who had been film directors like Claudia Weill or people who were theater directors like Ron Lagomarsino.

Patrick Norris, atop the ladder, was the Costume Designer on the show that shaped the look of fashion in the late 1980s. He went on to direct an episode of My So-Called Life for Ed and Marshall. Courtesy of the Dan Steadman Collection.

Ken Zunder: It was one of the first shows to shoot eight days an episode. Up until then shows were twelve hours a day, seven days an episode. Marshall and Ed wanted to shoot eight days but ten hours a day. That is less hours but more days, figuring you would do the bulk of your good work in the morning and you do catch up in the afternoon. There is phrase we old timers use, you shoot *Sound of Music* in the morning and *Highway Patrol* in the afternoon. They figured let's have eight *Sounds of Music's* per episode.

Marshall Herskovitz: Over time people on the show wanted to direct. I think five of the seven actors ended up directing. Patty and Polly didn't want to direct. On *My So-called Life,* even our costume designer, Patrick

Norris, came to us and said he wanted to direct. We instantly said he could, even though there was no reason to believe that he could and he turned out great. He is still a working director today.

Ed Zwick: I felt that the more people knew the series the better that they would be at trying to carry forth its intentions rather than someone coming from the outside. Who knew the show better than these actors?

Melanie Mayron: *thirtysomething* was not a cop show or a medical show. It was just about people and relationships. Those small moments and stories are big and worth telling. It's those moments I like to mine. Those are the moments people take away and it is an honor to give time to real moments. I didn't go to film school, so I was doing it on the fly.

Polly Draper: I wish I had directed an episode of *thirtysomething* because I would have received great instruction from two great directors. It would have been a wonderful way to break myself in. Later, I directed *The Naked Brothers Band: the Movie* (2005), the *thirtysomething* cast was in the movie. I hired Melanie to direct an episode of the series on Nickelodeon as well.

Brandy Alexander: It was a well oiled machine. You could put almost anyone in there and it would come together. I am sure some shows would have been better if the director was Ed or Marshall but they were all such excellent scripts that it all came from that. The scripts were so good I would read them in traffic while I drove home from work on the freeway.

Ken Zunder: It was truly a family with good natured competition. Every afternoon you get a snack around 3:00. I don't know how it started, but the actor who directed would buy the crew a snack. We ended up going from hot dogs all the way to sushi chefs on stage. Just to see who could buy the best food for the crew.

Joe Dougherty: To this day I can hear Marshall say, "Prioritize in a script, in a scene, in a take. There is no perfect take." I have seen first time directors look for a perfect take and the odds of getting it are pretty slim. He also said, "There is no such thing as we're going to try for one more take." You should prepare for it to turn into three more takes.

Ron Lagomarsino: They gave a sheet of paper that had directorial tips. It had camera movements and pass offs. The camera following one actor in, then someone walks in and you follow them. Marshall saying, "If the scene feels like it is the right pace make it faster because it is probably slow." I didn't get that until I got it. When you see it, then you realize, I should have shot that quicker. Ed and Marshall always talked about the breathe of life. Having an activity or gesture have a real sense of life.

Peter Horton: Ed would say things like, "Filmmaking is towards the camera and away from the camera; it is not a proscenium. Lenses are supposed to tell a story. They not there to record a scene." It would really challenge you.

Ken Olin: When I was stuck with my first script, Scott Winant said one sentence to me that changed my life. He said, "When you read a scene and you get an image in your mind, you stick with that image. You keep that central image." That is the most beautiful and articulate distillation of a place to begin. Work from that image backwards and forwards. So now I read a scene, an image comes to mind. So the image might be

Writers Ann Lewis Hamilton and Joe Dougherty both had their directorial debuts on the show. Writers and actors got a shot at directing, as long as they followed the Samurai School Rules. Courtesy of Ann Lewis Hamilton.

Hope sitting in the corner with her knees to her chest. How do I get to that? Is it the beginning of the scene or end? It just helps you stage the scene. It was such a clear place to begin for me. I still do that today.

Scott Winant: I actually remember that moment very clearly. I too was figuring out what my process was and how to prepare. I was responsible for all the directors, most being neophytes, so I had to find effective ways to articulate the process and respect each director's individual approach. I was not a fan of the formulas set down by series television. I encouraged each of my directors to express themselves artistically within the rules of cinema and continuity of motion.

Ellen Pressman: I was really lucky to work with Ed, Marshall and Scott as my mentors. Those were the first four episodes I ever directed. I was just learning. I was lucky to get to sit in the room and listen, watch and learn and see the mistakes. They let us make mistakes. At other places you might get fired for making mistakes.

Ed Zwick: We showed dailies at lunch to be part of the conversation about what we were trying to do. What we succeeded at and what we failed at and why.

Scott Winant: I am more lyrical in storytelling and I feel that sometimes visually we want to link our story to make sure that we understand that these are not module ideas in a script. As these events are happening, something separate is happening but completely connected to the same story. I like the continuity of motion in film. If an object is moving left to right, and you cut, it should continue in that motion. Whether the audience is aware of it or not it is pleasing and makes you feel like a story is being told. They used to call them "Winant Wipes." I would go to the art department and say, "I need you to build me a pillar and it has to be one color on the right side and another color on the left side." All these transitions are done with no effects. I do them with eight frame dissolves.

Ed Zwick: Scott, as a director, was extraordinary in his stylistic flourishes that he found himself capable of and began to explore more and more. Everyone brought something very different to that process.

Ed Zwick directed Glory with Denzel Washington during the second season of thirtysomething. *Courtesy TriStar Pictures.*

Richard Kramer: Ed was making *Glory* (1989) when I directed "Be A Good Girl" so he wasn't around much. I did attend his seminars with other people before I directed. Ed got angry with me before we started shooting because I was focused on what the sets were going to look like. He said, "Stop decorating and start directing." In my anxiety, I was micro-focusing on some of the lesser things. I don't want to say he was right, but he wasn't wrong.

Brandy Alexander: Ed had been off shooting *Glory* and he had been gone for months. They start the dailies for lunch and up comes Denzel Washington in a soldier's outfit. Everyone starts looking around asking, "What is this?" Ed came around the corner and said, "How do you like my film?" We were totally surprised that he was back from the shoot. There were lots of hugs. That sense of family isn't how it is on most sets.

Patty Wettig: This was a very unusual working situation. I have never found it since. We were all so involved with the making of the show. Yes, Marshall and Ed were the head dudes. No one questioned that. They had the authority. Everyone's contribution to it was about being all in. That is just unusual. If we had things to say, we were listened to. If someone was directing they were in the inside of it.

Richard Kramer: There was no hierarchy because Ed and Marshall were not going to be toppled. There was no way they were gonna be removed. The lack of the ability to stab someone in the back made the work better. It wasn't *Julius Caesar*. They made it clear from the first minute that they were in charge and everyone thrived knowing it.

Winnie Holzman: For me it was like going to film school, but getting paid. The show meant so much to us when we were creating it. We poured everything we had into it, the cast and behind the scenes.

Mel Harris: I knew a lot about lighting from the modeling world. I would have the camera operators explain to me what they do. It was all interesting to me. So to be able to get to direct and put it all together was very interesting.

The series soundtrack is the other official product that the show released. The track list of song titles is a major spoiler alert. Never look at the soundtrack unless you know what happens in Season 4. Pictured here is the vinyl record released only in Europe. Courtesy of Scott Ryan's Collection.

Joe Dougherty: I learned something crucial from Marty, my editor. He came down when I was directing and said, "Stuff looks great, but you are saying cut when you want me to cut the scene. You have to let it roll for three more feet. When you are ready to say cut, count to three." That was helpful.

Marshall Herskovitz: There is a theory we learned from our teachers that images die after awhile. You can't just stay on the same image. You have to keep changing the angle, or what is happening on screen. So doing a oner, a long take that does not have an edit in it, meant you had to choreograph the camera to the people. There are moments you need to indicate being in one character's head and then another. Normally that is done with cutting to a reaction shot.

Ken Zunder: A oner doesn't mean the camera just sits there in a wide shoot. It moves in and moves out. The camera moves with, around, through and behind the actors. We would do a lot of takes of the oner and maybe rehearse it for forty minutes instead of twenty. You don't have to do the close ups because we knew it would play in one. If you have to do coverage you might have fifty set ups a day where on *thirtysomething* we might have fifteen. It was elaborate. It was intricate and when it worked it worked great.

Marshall Herskovitz: It is complicated and it has to relate to the meaning of the scene. I would say to them, in this moment this has to be a close up of you Mel, then Kenny you walk in. Kenny would say, "I know what to do. I will move back then." Everybody was working to the same end because they understood the same end.

Ron Lagomarsino: The rehearsal for *thirtysomething* happened on the set before you shoot the scene. It was always about making it feel like life which meant people were constantly moving and doing things. We would sometimes shoot a three or four page scene in Michael and Hope's kitchen. We would shoot it all as one long tracking shot, which means a long rehearsal of camera movements with the actors. If you are shooting a long tracking shot it has to be perfect because there is no coverage to cut to.

Marshall Herskovitz: It is a way to save time because in those days lighting took a long time. If you had a two page scene and you were going to cover it, then you were going to have to do five set ups. It could be quicker to choreograph the people in such a way that you could get everything you needed in one shot. Which meant they would bring themselves into their own close-ups. It was like a dance. We grew to love the challenge of it.

Ellen Pressman: It takes a lot of work. It is not easy for the actors to constantly be moving. It is one thing to do a walk and talk, but another thing to do behavior. The camera had to move because of behavior. You didn't impose it on the scene you found it in the scene.

Ken Zunder: You tell the story by how you stage the actors and how you move the camera. In any given moment you think what do you want the audience to see and what is the most important part of the story? Do you want to see the person who is talking or who is listening? We tried to tell the story through the camera without manipulating the audience. With cutting, you are basically telling the audience what they have to look at.

Ron Lagomarsino: There might be shows that do oners today but I doubt they would be on network anymore. That is the trick, if you don't shoot the coverage there is nowhere to run and hide. Also if a show is running long you can't trim a long one shot if you don't have any coverage.

Peter Horton: I really didn't shoot coverage on the one shots in the episodes because that was the tone of the show. They were like push it, try it, go for it. We were all students of Coppola, Scorsese or Woody Allen. Woody was the guy who would inspired us to have people talk in a master shot and have them walk out of the room and keep the camera there. Let them talk outside and walk back into frame. We were all were schooled in a time when film was experimental. Commerce and art came together in the eighties. We had been born and raised in that era. It wasn't quite as so sanitized and controlled as it became afterwards by the tentacles of corporate networks.

Melanie Mayron: Everything is so fast paced now with forty-two minutes of air time. We don't sit on things very long. You can sit, you can stay, you can hold, you can move in and you can let the moment live. You can let the actor do what they are doing and we can feel it. That is what I have taken away from directing the series the most.

Joe Dougherty: Marshall knew more than I did about directing when I turned in my first cut of my directorial debut, "Best Of Enemies." So he went in and attacked it. He got his fingers into it which was intimidat-

Peter Horton was the first cast member to direct on thirtysomething. The majority of his episodes focused on Nancy and Elliot. Courtesy of Kenneth Zunder.

ing to me. I thought I saw him pull it apart when he was actually finding what it was. I didn't understand because I had not directed on that level. I remember walking out of the room because I was upset. Marshall said, "You can't walk out. You can't give up. You have to stay in the room. You aren't going to get anything you want if you leave the room."

Scott: One of my biggest jobs was going back to the set after dailies and re-encouraging a director to go forward after being confronted by Ed and Marshall at dailies. They were tough and they demanded that you knew what you were doing. It was tougher on some than others. It was tough on me, I have to admit.

Ed Zwick: We had no idea of how lucky we were. We didn't take the time to look around and wonder why we were given this privilege to do this. We were so focused and absorbed. The idea that we could have this moment where we could grow and experiment was so extraordinary. Why would we hire a newbie like Peter over someone who had a ton of hours of directing logged? It just seemed like the organic thing to do. It was another piece of what we were trying to attempt.

The storyline that thirtysomething *is most famous for takes shape in "Another Country" in Season 3. The series takes bold leaps with each of the characters. Keep reading to learn how they managed it. Courtesy ABC Photography Archives.*

Season 3
(1989–90)

"Nancy's Mom"

Directed by Ron Lagomarsino

Written by Ann Lewis Hamilton

September 19, 1989

Patty Wettig: It wasn't conceived to be a series where Nancy would be the center of things. I was the seventh cast person on the sheet originally. It evolved in the running of the show. I got great material to do. It was not in the original idea of the show.

Ann Lewis Hamilton: I had really forgotten this episode. I was very surprised how much I liked it. I enjoy the episodes that are more simple and emotionally grounded. I loved the scene where Elliot and Nancy were getting back together and he snuck into the house while Nancy's mom was there.

Tim Busfield: The getting back together seemed perfect. I think in the social media world we have today it would have happened sooner. They would have known people wanted it, but we didn't have that. I can only imagine what the show would be like now with tweeting and the influence of the audience.

Ann Lewis Hamilton: I wrote "Nancy's Mom" and I remember being in the hospital when Marshall and Ed called to say it needed a polish. I said, "I'll do it from the hospital." I had a C-section and was on all kinds of drugs. I said, "Send the pages." They were like, "No, that's okay. We'll get someone to do it. Relax." I think Susan Shilliday did a polish on "Nancy's Mom."

Susan Shilliday: I sort of jumped in and finished whatever was going on.

Ken Zunder (*Director Of Photography*): As the camera man you are always worried about things being too bright. Tim Busfield was in bed and was covered up with some white sheets. My eye was going away from his

Season 3 started with an episode about Nancy and Elliot moving back in with each other. Nancy's Mom and Elliot have to repair their relationship as well. Courtesy of Carol Gepper's TV Guide Collection.

Fellow redheads Ken Zunder and Tim Busfield had fun on the set filming "Nancy's Mom." Courtesy of Kenneth Zunder.

face because all I could see were these bright white sheets. I said, "Tim, would you mind pushing the sheets down?" He pushed them down. I said, "Put them back up. Your legs are more white than the sheets." He and I ended up doing a mini-series in Arizona years later. We both were redheads with very fair skin.

Tim Busfield: We laughed right up till we rolled the camera. I often cracked up with Patty in scenes that were too intense. I would start giggling and she would get mad. I dropped the IQ so low. Patty would actually get annoyed with me that I would laugh.

Episode 40

"Love and Sex"

Directed by Marshall Herskovitz

Written by Liberty Godshall

October 3, 1989

Liberty Godshall: Marshall always subscribed to the idea that men and women were from different planets long before that book came out. We argued constantly as to how these people looked at sex, parenthood, and the stress of trying to get pregnant and what that can do to a marriage.

Ed Zwick: I was in Atlanta directing *Glory* (1989). Liberty was writing the episode and was communicating with Marshall by phone. It was about Michael and Hope having stress on their sex life. Liberty and Marshall really got into it. He was tough on her, he was trying to force her to make changes in her script that she didn't want to do. Finally Marshall pulled rank and said, "Look, I am just going to give this to Susan to do a rewrite." He gave it to Susan, she looked at it and said, "No, I won't do it. I agree with Liberty."

Marshall Herskovitz: There was a scene between Michael and Hope on the steps and it was a four and a half page scene. It was hard to shoot on steps because of the banister and the wall, it was hard to cover. I said to Ken and Mel, "Let's see if we can do four and a half pages in one shot." They said, "Yes!" We just went for it. We had so much fun and it worked.

Mel Harris: We met Michael and Hope as loving and carefree. We watched them go through real life things. If you look at some of the early episodes about raising the baby and what Hope was feeling about it, all those stresses, good or bad, impacted the relationship. There were work problems and stresses on Michael that clearly impacted Hope, the relationship, and the family.

Liberty Godshall: Growing into an adult is a series of mini deaths. It is not just one part of your life. As you adjust to huge career failures and medical issues you have to keep shifting. There is a mourning period where you lose some of your innocence. That is what happened to Hope. There is nothing more depressing than planning out sex and then to put on top of that, that it isn't working. It just changes everything. The whole thing about *thirtysomething* is some people would say, "Just get over it. Is it such a big deal?" Well yes, I think it is.

Ellen Pressman: I remember being up in the office and someone coming up from the set and saying, "Oh my God, the most gorgeous man is down there on the set and you have to come look." Brad Pitt was an extra on the show. I don't even think he had a line. Maybe he had a word.

Liberty Godshall: How fun is it that Brad Pitt is in it? From the moment he was cast it spread around the office. When that little scene of him kissing the babysitter on the motorcycle was shot, every woman came out of the office to watch. He had some magnetic pull.

Brad Pitt had a small part as Hope's babysitter's boyfriend in only one episode. Later he would be directed by Ed Zwick in Legends of the Fall. *Courtesy ABC Photography Archives.*

Marshall Herskovitz: It really is funny that I never do a close up of Brad in the episode. What can I say? It was just one of those things. Brad was a complete unknown. The entire production office emptied of women. There was not one woman left in that building. They all were watching him film. It was so obvious that he was going to be something special. Nothing like that happened before or since. Then, it turned out he actually had talent. People went nuts over him. When we did *Legends of the Fall* (1994) he remembered it and laughed about it. He's a good guy.

Liberty Godshall: Hope took the ride in a convertible with the babysitter to go back in time. I loved putting the very thing Hope felt she lost and was never gonna get back, right in her face. She wanted to do something that was mini irresponsible to feel the feelings she was not feeling in her marriage. I loved that it just doesn't work. My favorite thing was when Hope and Michael met at the restaurant. She was so excited and Michael was looking at her like he had no idea what she meant. She realized she couldn't transmit what she felt.

"Mr. Right"

Directed by Scott Winant

Written by Jill Gordon

October 10, 1989

Scott Winant: My wife, Jill Gordon, wrote that episode. I directed it with my friends. Working with Polly and Melanie was a joy. I had short cuts with each of the actors. I loved Polly because she is such a talented actor but she was so goofy. I used to refer to her movements as Polly Pops. If I got her worked up enough she would always do something funny. You would ask her to pull a kitchen drawer open and sure enough it would come out and all the silverware would fall on the ground or she would take out a chair. She was very funny.

Melanie Mayron: Polly and I had so much fun doing that episode. Our characters had the most scenes with each other that we ever did.

"Mr. Right" took a page from Cinderella and had Melissa find her Prince Charming through video dating. This episode was the first of three episodes written by Director Scott Winant's wife, Jill Gordon. The series had multiple married couples working in front of and behind the camera. Courtesy of Carol Gepper's TV Guide Collection.

Jill Gordon (*Writer*): I believe the only reason I was hired to write "Mr. Right" was because ABC suddenly tagged an episode onto their season and they were simply too exhausted to write another script. So my husband, who was the associate producer at the time, said I would. I wanted to write an episode that was a little bit different in tone for them, possibly a funny *thirtysomething*. The brilliantly comedic Winnie Holzman had not come onto the staff yet.

Scott Winant: This was early on during the video dating phenomena and one of our crew members did it. She would tell us while we were on location scouts how it was going. I shared that with Jill. Many of our episodes were just things that happened to one of us.

Brandy Alexander (*Production Designer*): I gave them the storyline for "Mr. Right" where Melissa and Ellyn go video dating. I took the entire shooting company to the place where I actually video dated. It was called Great Expectations. I then had to build the set for our show. I met my husband on a video date from there and we are still married twenty-six years later.

Jill Gordon: I also interviewed a lot of women who were dating through video dating services. One woman in particular was extremely open with me, Brandy Alexander. She was actively video dating and a wonderful source of insight.

Polly Draper: I loved when I tried to talk to the camera for my video dating interview. I was trying to do it right and I kept getting lipstick on my teeth and my hair was sticking up. That was all just good writing. It had nothing to do with my acting.

Jill Gordon: Having never done video dating, I actually went to a video dating service and asked them to put me through the process. It was fairly mortifying and when I went to sit on a chair and speak to the camera, I couldn't stop laughing. I felt so self-conscious. That's how I came up with the scene where Polly and Melanie can't stop laughing.

Melanie Mayron: A lot of people look back at it as such a dramatic show and the drama was amazing, but there was so much comedy and light moments. It had a bit of everything.

Corey Parker joins the show as Melissa's much younger love interest, Lee Owens. This was a plot suggested to the writers by Melanie Mayron. Courtesy ABC Photography Archives.

Scott Winant: I put 400 feet of film in the magazine and ran the camera. We would do the interviews over and over, improvising so that they would feel natural. I was the guy asking them questions. I tried to keep them loose and put them on the spot. I got Polly to recite Joni Mitchell lyrics from the song "All I Want" (1971). So we had to license it.

Polly Draper: That is my favorite episode. Scott was the one that saw the fun chemistry between Melanie and I. I think it was because of the bonding moment of Melanie and I flying out to audition from New York. We felt a kinship because everyone else was from Los Angeles. I hired her to direct on *Naked Brother Band* (2007) which was my show for Nickelodeon.

Jill Gordon: Ed and Marshall were anxious about me writing a "funny" episode. I had written for a lot of sitcoms. They were anxious I'd put in a lot of jokes. I will never forget what Marshall said to me right before I was sent off to write the script, "I'd rather the script be honest and dull, than slick." I completely understood what he meant and desperately wanted to respect it.

Melanie Mayron: I suggested that Melissa should have a younger boyfriend because at one point I had one. We were coming of age in the mid to late sixties and that was the whole time of the women's movement. Women could have career and family. That is what they were telling all of us. It was easier to say it than to live it, but we all believed it. Which is why so many of my generation had babies later in life and their careers first.

Corey Parker (*Played Lee Owens, Melissa's younger boyfriend*): I was a twenty-three year old New York actor. I wanted to stay as pure as an actor as I

Corey Parker dressed as a painter and even carried in a ladder to win the part of Lee Owens. Could have been that or could have been the chemistry with Melanie Mayron that won him the part. Courtesy of Corey Parker.

could. The way that translated into the casting process was that I knew Lee was a painter. I did something that you are not supposed to do. I brought a six foot ladder and a scraper to the audition. I looked like a guy who had just been painting. Sitting in the waiting room was funny because all the other guys were laughing at me. It was an absurd thing to do. When I got into Ed's office, he smiled when he saw ladder. I climbed to the top of it and started to gently scrape the tile of his ceiling and I read for the part of Lee.

Melanie Mayron: Corey and I had studied with one of the same acting teachers and he came to the audition with props. They had me read with him and we were like two peas in a pod. I was thrilled they cast him. It is why the casting of *thirtysomething* was so great because we all loved each other so much.

Richard Kramer: We saw every young good actor for the part of Lee. David Duchovny even auditioned for the part. Corey was an incredible gift to us. He had such chemistry with Melanie. It was sexy between them. We were committed to making Melissa not neurotic, but making her real.

Corey Parker: Melanie, Scott and I ended up meeting on a Sunday at the set. Scott said to me, "At some point you may have to take your clothes off because there is a love scene. I hope you are okay with that." I translated that into the producer thinks there might be a problem. I just slowly walked behind them. Without them knowing it, I removed all of my clothes. When they realized I wasn't there, they turned around, I had nothing on. So, it was mission accomplished for me. They had a good laugh and told me to put my clothes back on.

Melanie Mayron: It was a great storyline and gave them a lot of material to mine. It was always that men could date younger women, but it wasn't out there that women could date younger men.

Corey Parker: I was actually married to someone who was eleven years older than me at the time. I was totally cool with the age difference. Melanie was so beautiful in so many ways. She has an incredible spirit. I would never tell any of my students to bring a ladder to casting. However, to all those dudes who were laughing at me in the waiting room, "So long, suckers. I got the job."

Episode 42

"New Baby"

Directed by Marshall Herskovitz

Written by Ann Lewis Hamilton

October 24, 1989

Ann Lewis Hamilton: We had to have the birth of Gary and Susannah's baby and we didn't want it to be a boring episode. Joe Dougherty and I loved the Harold Pinter play *Betrayal*. Joe made the joke, "Why don't you do it like *Betrayal* and tell it backwards." It was such a stupid idea, so naturally I loved it. I went to Marshall because he was going to direct it. He said, "Why not do it backwards. That could be really cool." Reading the script again I don't know how I did this. It was really tricky. It was a nice interesting way to tell the story of a birth of a baby that you hadn't seen before. Thank you very much, Harold Pinter.

Patricia Kalember: My husband and I were doing *Betrayal* during this time. Ann Hamilton had her baby the same day as I did. So, it was a weird coincidence.

Ann Lewis Hamilton: I wrote Act 4 first, but I wrote it from beginning to end. Then I wrote Act 3, Act 2, and then Act 1. That was another example of life imitating art because Patricia and I were pregnant at the same time. We all talked about what we did during labor.

Patricia Kalember: I think it is more of an experience watching the episode out of order than filming it out of order because we always tend to shoot film out of sequence. It is like when we did the play, you take it apart and you rehearse the scenes one by one. We filmed it the same year as I gave birth so it was pretty accessible. Honestly, that one

"New Baby" shows the birth of Gary and Susannah's baby told backwards. Each scene takes place after what just happened. It was a creative way to tell the common story of a couple having a baby. Writer Ann Lewis Hamilton and Actress Patricia Kalember, coincidentally, gave birth to their children on the same day, April 12th, 1989. Courtesy ABC Photography Archives.

was a lot of hard work but it was fun. I have not seen it since. I am not good at watching myself. I feel like I am a little too Gloria Swanson if I go back.

Ann Lewis Hamilton: I remember being on the set when Susannah had the baby and they used a real preemie baby. I think now they have fake babies that look real, but back then they had real babies that they cover in grape jelly. Patricia was holding this little baby and it was so amazing. My marriage, my miscarriage, the birth of my child, I got to write about all of it. It was pretty awesome.

Patricia Kalember: Ann was so funny because she said the only difference between the two of us in labor was that I still had cheekbones dur-

Wonder where Ann got the idea for Melissa giving Emma a car? Her friends gave her baby one. This is the actual car that had to be hauled away. Courtesy of Ann Lewis Hamilton.

ing the episode. I think the labor in the show was a combo experience of both our labors because I ended up with an epidural so I didn't gut it out. I think Ann gutted it out.

Ann Lewis Hamilton: At the big hospital in Los Angeles, if you are lucky you get to be in this beautiful room. It has prints on the wall and it is really nice. Sarah Caplan, who worked on the show, was also pregnant at the same time. She had her daughter just before I had my son and she got the super special birthing room. I went in two weeks later and there was no super secret birthing room for me.

Patricia Kalember: Patricia Heaton (*Everybody Loves Raymond, The Middle*) played the ob-gyn. She is a wonderful actress. It is funny how people get pegged.

Ann Lewis Hamilton: The reason I had Melissa give Gary's baby a car was because it happened to me. Two friends, one was a woman who worked on the show, gave my unborn son, who everyone referred to as "Mo," a car at my baby shower. I think they paid $100 for it and they told me I had to keep it for my son to drive when he was old enough. I think we ended up having to pay someone to take it away and junk it because it wouldn't start. That's why it's called the "Mo - bile."

Peter Horton: I think when Gary had the baby he started to grow up. Having a kid changes everything. It is a cellular change. When they got pregnant it started, but when they had the baby he really started to shift.

Melanie Mayron: In the four years that goes by, people do change and it is hard when Gary falls in love with someone else. It was like musical chairs and you were not sitting so close anymore.

Ann Lewis Hamilton: There were baby pictures on the wall in a hallway in one of the scenes. Those babies were all of our children from people on the show. I still have two of the big pictures in my house that were on that set. It was a great job to have while being pregnant and writing about marriage, pregnancy and life. I hadn't thought about this in years, but it was extraordinary.

Episode 43

"Legacy"

Directed by Scott Winant

Written by Joseph Dougherty

October 24, 1989

Joe Dougherty: The second time I was in Ed and Marshall's office I pitched a story. I wanted to put Elliot and Michael in an airplane and then pull the bottom out and see what they did about it. The first season was not a place where the characters were ready to do that. We waited and I repitched it. I think that was Elliot right there. He looked, in his own kind of strange Elliot way, into the abyss and let the abyss take a peek into him. You kind of heard a guy standing there saying, "I think I need to listen for awhile. I have been making too much noise." He said to Nancy, "We fell down in an airplane." That was his voice.

Scott Winant: I directed the episode where Michael and Elliot were in an airplane that loses power and went into a dive. I shot it with a budget that was basically pennies. I had to rig this set and I used the camera to create this impression that the plane was crashing. I was very flattered because Peter Weir's people called me to ask me how we did it. He was directing a movie called *Fearless* (1993). I am sure they used gimbals and lots of special effects and all I did was move the lights.

Marshall Herskovitz: When you rent a plane set, they don't twist and turn. They just sit there. Scott figured out how to build a rig so that all the lights moved and everyone on cue moved in a certain way. That makes it look like the plane had turned. He so understood the perspective of seeing from inside a camera that he knew how to fool the eye.

Ken Zunder (*Director Of Photography*): Outside the window was a day blue. We had an E fan blowing smoke by the window so it looked like clouds were passing and then by raising and lowering the height of the light it looked like the plane was either falling or rising. I would go behind the camera and while it was moving and tilting in conjunction with the lights, I shook the camera as hard as I could. I scared the operator by shaking it so much to give it the feeling of turbulence.

Is Miles Drentell a father figure or a business obstacle? It depends on who you ask. Courtesy of Carol Gepper's TV Guide Collection.

Marshall Herskovitz: When you look at that shot you cannot tell. You believe that plane is diving. They had bags on strings so they could pull them back. It was an entire gag that was done live. It was so amazing that he was able to pull this off. Scott just figured it out. That is who he is. He is an incredibly creative person.

Richard Kramer: Joe Dougherty sort of co-opted the Miles Drentell character because he understood him. Miles was sort of the devil who was corrupting Michael. Michael wasn't very good at picking father figures.

Joe Dougherty: Michael's problem was he was still trying to get his father's approval and he kept picking the wrong dad.

Ken Olin: No, Miles wasn't a father figure. Miles represented more. A father figure seems too pat to me. It is an oversimplification. With the education of Michael Steadman, he had to come up against someone who didn't play by Michael's rules.

Mel Harris: I honestly would say anyone who would look at Miles as a father figure must be nuts. Seriously, I had never heard that before. I don't know if he looked for a father figure as much as he looked for approval. I think Michael searched for who he was.

Joe Dougherty: What's the difference between looking for a father and trying to be the father you thought you wanted? He was someone whose models for fathers were not perfect. Here is something that might sound

The DAA set is where viewers mainly see Miles Dentrell. "Legacy" is one of the few times Miles is seen outside of this set when he visits the Steadman house for a party. Courtesy of Brandy Alexander.

like an insight. Michael hadn't figured out how to be a son yet so he was completely unprepared to be a father. I just made that up and I don't know if it means anything, but it sounds good. Then you get to look at the whole series as people trying to figure out who they are. Sometimes you make a bad choice. I think all of the characters end up making good choices. Michael was very close to booting everything but his intentions were good.

"Strangers"

Directed by Peter O'Fallon

Written by Richard Kramer

November 7, 1989

David Marshall Grant (*Russell*): I had been prepped that controversy was going to happen for this episode. At this point, I figured let's make a splash. If we were gonna do it, let's do it. I was proud to do it.

Richard Kramer: I feel incredibly grateful to have been given the opportunity to write that episode. I was supported by Ed and Marshall at a period when not everybody would have been supported. One of the principles of the show was that we couldn't do an "important" episode. I wasn't trying to write the gay scene. It was very much about something else. It was about the burden of self consciousness and absorbing what other people think of you. Melissa was letting that be an obstacle in her life.

Melanie Mayron: The theme of the episode was how we sabotage relationships. Russell sabotaged his and Melissa sabotaged hers. We get something good and then we stand in the way of it.

Marshall Herskovitz: I got into a huge fight with the head of Standards and Practices from New York. We usually dealt with the people in Los Angeles, but for "Strangers" we got a call from New York. Al Schneider was a very senior executive. He was an old time television guy. He called when they got the script and said, "I am calling you myself. This call is not going to be a negotiation. I am going to tell you what ABC's policy is." He had never talked to us this way before. He said, "ABC is in support of the idea of two gay characters. ABC is in support of two gay characters in bed. But never on this network will two gay characters kiss. That will not happen." In the original script the two men kissed. At which point, (*Laughs*) we went after him and he went after us. Voices were raised. I am not proud of this, but he was Jewish and we were Jewish, and I said to him, "I am really surprised to hear you say this given that you are a Jew." You could hear him on the other side of the line, saying, "What does that have to do with it?" I said, "Who did Hitler go after in 1936 besides the Jews? Gay people?" He just started screaming at me, "That has nothing to do with this. That is extremely irresponsible." Ed was just sitting there laughing at me for saying that, but I was really angry. He said, "If you do the kiss, this will not air." We said, "We are doing the kiss." The phone ended abruptly in a standoff. We didn't really know what to do. We didn't want them to tell us what to do.

David Marshall Grant: It was 1989 and two men had never been under the covers naked on television before. I am not sure if two men had even kissed before on television. We didn't because we were naked under the covers.

Ken Zunder (*Director Of Photography*): I remember Marshall and Ed saying, "They are absolutely going to kiss. There is no way they are not going to kiss."

Peter Frechette and David Marshall Grant made television history as being the first two gay men to be seen in bed together. Per the network, it was "No touching!" Courtesy of the Richard Kramer Collection.

Mel Harris: Ed and Marshall were willing to push envelopes. Having two men in bed together, although they couldn't touch, was pretty revolutionary at the time. It is hard to believe, but it was. I think the advertisers all pulled out. I can't remember what happened, but there was a lot of controversy with that episode.

Marshall Herskovitz: Richard Kramer called us the next morning and said, "I believe seeing two gay men in bed in the most casual way is just as revolutionary as seeing them kiss." On the basis of that, we took the kiss out of the script.

Richard Kramer: Not only were they in bed together, they were post coitally in bed together. This was two guys who had obviously just had sex. Why else would they be there? That scene, which is broken up into two parts, was written as an eight page scene to audition actors with before there was even a story. I wrote it, brought it to Scott and he said, "Let's find a story." We went to Ed and Marshall who said, "Do whatever you want." We skipped past whatever might have been shocking. It really wasn't shocking at all.

David Marshall Grant: Ed and Marshall were on the set that day to be sure that everything ran smoothly. It was their show and they put this on. They approved the storyline. They had a lot of gay friends, so I think they felt they owed an honest storyline to those people. They were nothing but brave and supportive.

Marshall Herskovitz: I don't remember having to be on the set. I don't remember ABC being on the set. I don't think we would have allowed that. It is possible that they came that day, but I don't remember it. We didn't bar them from the set, just from telling us what stories we could tell.

David Marshall Grant: We could be under the covers simulating nakedness, but even our shoulders couldn't have contact. That was the blocking and we just lie there. Someone from the network was on set to be sure we didn't touch or the entire episode couldn't air.

Richard Kramer: I wasn't on the set when they filmed the episode. I was writing my next episode. I think one reason they didn't touch was that it had never happened before. We came at it in a very *thirtysomething* way.

Melanie Mayron had to learn a boxing routine, play multiple characters and have a main storyline with Corey Parker in "Strangers." All for an episode that would only air once and be remembered for the other plot. Courtesy ABC Photography Archives.

There was no question that they had sex but we didn't show anything. There is no such thing as bad controversy for popular entertainment. We weren't going to be fired.

David Marshall Grant: The edict probably came from whomever had a fiduciary responsibility to their parent company. Although one of us definitely smokes, probably it was Peter Frechette. We could kill ourselves with cigarettes, but we couldn't touch.

Ken Olin: David and I had worked together before that episode. We had done a play in New York. We are still friends. I hired him to kill Michael Vaughn on *Alias*. Somehow Vaughn survived eighty bullet wounds shot by David.

David Marshall Grant: I knew Ken from long ago. He was in one of my very first plays I did in New York City. It was very comfortable and he is an amazing actor. We ended up working together a ton on *Brothers and Sisters*. It was a joy.

Melanie Mayron: ABC only aired the episode once. They got so much pressure it was never rerun. It was an incredible episode for my character so that was really heartbreaking. It was a drag.

Richard Kramer: By the time a controversy happens you are already five episodes later and you are already thinking about how you are gonna get through this one. These controversies are very cooked up by those who want them to be controversial. It is used as an example of how the culture is crumbling. It wasn't controversial among any thinking or feeling person. It was controversial to a well organized group that is very good at getting attention.

David Marshall Grant: Many of the affiliates pulled the episode so it never aired in some parts of the country. It was preempted in New York City because of a mayoral race. So, it wasn't aired until one o'clock in the morning in the New York area. There was no immediate knowledge back then, so everything was anecdotal.

Richard Kramer: It isn't like opening a play. It is all in the past and you are solving other problems. No one comes to your office and says, "We hate you." They don't send the horrible letters to you. There was no internet.

David Marshall Grant: It was clearly a dangerous episode for the affiliates. I think it cost ABC lost revenue. To their credit, they made it, they put it on. They are not in control of what their affiliates do. I have always given them credit for that episode. I also do for their content through *Brothers and Sisters*. As a writer they allowed us to do anything with Scotty (*Luke Macfarlane*) and Kevin (*Matthew Rhys*). They deserve huge props for what they have done with that regard.

Richard Kramer: The key scene in that episode was the fight scene with Melissa as a prize fighter. This was Melanie being amazing. It was filmed by a very good director named Peter O'Fallon. Melissa was her own worst enemy. The other day, Liberty reminded me about Lee's line where he says, "Nobody's watching. Nobody cares."

Corey Parker (*Lee*): Melissa cared so much about her friends. What happens when caring about what your friends think actually gets in the way of making you happy? That is what that moment was about for me. Lee loved Melissa and hoped it was possible. Richard Kramer's lines were some of the best writing I have ever done. Those lines were so good you just have to get out of the way. Without Richard, I don't think Lee would be what he was. The writer is where it all starts.

Corey Parker, now an acting teacher in Memphis, delivers the key line in the episode, "Nobody's watching. Nobody cares." Courtesy of Corey Parker.

Melanie Mayron: Melissa has a fight with herself. She also plays the judge and an audience member. So, I had to learn a choreographed boxing match. I had to be both sides of the fight. It was about Melissa judging herself about going out with a younger man.

Richard Kramer: It was exciting for me to write for Melissa because Melanie was so inspiring to me. There is nothing she couldn't do and nothing she wouldn't do. When I was working on a Melissa episode, I would ask Melanie to come in and sit in my office. She would just read. She wouldn't be on her iPhone because there was no such thing. I would look at her and she would just be there. She was an inspiration to me and an incredible piece of luck in my life. She was my muse.

Melanie Mayron: I am thrilled that Richard calls me his muse. We were very collaborative. He would often show me what he was writing. We would change the dialogue so it would roll off my tongue. He was quite collaborative with me. I don't think that happens all the time. Writers in television write and the actors have to say what they write. It was a bit more of a give and take with the creative team and the actors.

David Marshall Grant: I did get letters that were moving. It is hard to single out an incident. As recent as six months ago someone came up to me and told me how much it meant to them that on their small television in Idaho or Alabama that they saw that episode. It gave them hope. That has been enormously gratifying.

Corey Parker: Television is an industry just like any other industry. It doesn't want to lose money. It doesn't want to be boycotted. I understand why these things happened. I just thought all the attention was ridiculous. There are so many aspects of life and our job is to tell the stories and that is what we did.

David Marshall Grant: I think in the long run it helped my career. I had to leave the show because I got a movie called *Bat 21* (1988). I played an extremely butch helicopter pilot. I couldn't do other *thirtysomething* episodes that they were suggesting. I think it opened my eyes to what I could do in this world if I was honest with myself. The fact that I now have success as a writer can be traced back to that episode.

"Pilgrims"

Directed by Ken Olin

Written by Richard Kramer

November 21, 1989

Ken Olin directed the second Thanksgiving episode in the series. It focused on Ethan not wanting to come out of his room. Courtesy of ABC Photography Archives. The Lisa Mercado Fernandez Collection.

Ken Olin: The third episode I directed was the one Richard wrote. I remember Ed was really frustrated with me. He came down and yelled at me, "It is not just enough to point the camera and shoot!" That was not my best work or the best episode of the series.

Episode 46

"The Burning Bush"

Directed by Mary Beth Fielder

Written by Susan Shilliday

November 28, 1989

Polly Draper: The thing about having relationships with married men is that 90% of them don't work out, but when you are in them, you think you are the 10% exception. I think every woman who ever had an affair related strongly to the Jeffrey and Ellyn situation. They also knew it was going to end in doom because that is what usually happens. I think that was the role that Hope played. She knew that Ellyn was losing herself. That he was gonna go back to his wife and it was all gonna suck.

Ann Lewis Hamilton: Those characters always thought they knew what was best for everyone else. Ellyn, you don't want to have an affair with a married man. Melissa, you don't want to be involved with Lee.

Polly Draper: Melissa didn't have the same kind of stake in it, so she was able to give Ellyn the advice to go with her heart. Hope thinks Ellyn is going to crash and burn. She was giving Ellyn very good advice, but you can't tell a person who is madly in love to stop being in love.

Liberty Godshall: Hope was a real pain in the ass in a lot of ways. She was always spouting off about things that were wrong in the world. She became an environmentalist and became very passionate. I was struck by how annoying that came off. I realized how annoying I must be in real life. So that was good.

Susan Shilliday: This is my worst episode. I don't like it. I was trying to dig into the basis of friendship and how it changes over time. Hope

Ellyn and Hope hide their respective secrets from each other. Hope is pregnant, Ellyn is having an affair with a married man. Susan Shilliday wanted to explore the difficulty in sustaining a life long female friendship in "The Burning Bush." Courtesy ABC Photography Archives.

getting married and having kids put a strain on their relationship. That was something I knew more about than anything else. The experience of having kids can really change friendships that you thought were rock solid. I don't think it worked very well.

"New Parents"

Directed by Gary Sinise

Written by Ann Lewis Hamilton

December 5, 1989

Patricia Kalember: Suddenly, Emma was there and Susannah didn't have to worry if there was someone who liked her or not. The baby actually didn't turn away and wasn't manipulative. Emma was probably the first person she had to deal with that didn't have an ulterior motive.

Peter Horton: There was a scene with my mother where I started to talk about an old girlfriend. I actually had an old girlfriend that had broken my heart so I put her name in there. It was all so personal and from our lives. It was cathartic.

Ann Lewis Hamilton: Gary was so strong in a lot of ways and then we saw him want to stay home with his baby. He also struggled with the ghost of his father who said that he wasn't good enough. It was really an interesting struggle.

Patricia Kalember: I thought Gary staying home suited them. My husband did it for the first eleven years. I had Becca and he said to me, "Don't worry I got this." He gave me the freedom to do things which not everyone gets.

Ann Lewis Hamilton: I wrote about my in-laws and reading this script again I thought, "Oh my God." I don't know what their reactions were when they saw it. Gary's mom is named Eileen after my mother-in-law. It is all about Gary never living up to his father's expectations and that was my father-in-law. They are not with us anymore, but they were alive when I wrote that episode. I don't know what I was thinking. They were very nice to me and never said anything to me about it. That was another example of my husband going, "I can't believe you wrote this."

Episode 48

"Michael's Campaign"

Directed by Joseph Dougherty

Written by Joseph Dougherty

December 12, 1989

Episode 49

"Pulling Away"

Directed by Rob Cohen

Written by Joseph Dougherty

January 9, 1990

Joe Dougherty: Since I was directing "Michael's Campaign" it was very hard to finish the writing on "Pulling Away." I think Ann did some rewriting on it. There was a discussion about bringing Steven Hill back as Michael's father, but he was not in Los Angeles and there were scheduling issues. I had a great time with Scott Marlowe (played younger *Leo Steadman*) who was part of my childhood in that he was in two episodes of *Outer Limits* (1963). Patrick Norris, our Costume Designer, went to Scott Marlowe and said, "This is the hat that Steven Hill wore. You will be wearing his hat." Then Patrick walked by me and said, "That is not the same hat." So he lied but it was a beautiful lie.

Mel Harris: I do think that Michael was a good dad. He became conflicted about where his focus lay in terms of job, work and Miles Drentell. It is also very easy for a stay-at-home parent to point out the lack of time or focus the parent who works outside the house isn't paying to the child. It is a tough balance no matter who does it.

Joe Dougherty: We were back with Michael's search for a father and how to be a father. He remembered the childhood mistakes. How he thought his father was asking him to do something he didn't want to do and how it got screwed up. It all lived in the table scene when we go back and forth between old Michael and young Michael and his father's approval of him. Then Michael picked up Janey and started getting wiser. The episode also had the great stuff with Stanley Tucci (*Karl Draconis*). He was just a doll.

Ken Zunder (*Director Of Photography*): Rob Cohen directed Stanley Tucci in that episode. The most amazing thing about Stanley Tucci and David Clennon is that they absolutely controlled the scene by not yelling. They talked softly and made everyone turn their attention to them. All the scenes with Miles, he would talk slow enough that you were forced to turn and look at him. He made himself the center of the scene. Rob Cohen directed a scene where Stanley got very mad at Michael. Instead of yelling at him he quietly and calmly put him in his place. Rob did a great job on that episode.

"Michael's Campaign" and "Pulling Away" are a two part episode about Michael and Elliot's strategy for advertising Oh-My's Pies. The prop department made this box for the invented product. Joe Dougherty kept the prop. Courtesy of Joe Dougherty.

Director Rob Cohen, Ken Olin, Tim Busfield and Ken Zunder on the set of "Pulling Away." Courtesy of Kenneth Zunder.

Joe Dougherty: The fact that I worked with Stanley and saw his process was great. When Michael and Karl stood by the window and he said, "You are trying to gaslight me." You want to spend the entire day there with Ken and Stanley. The two of them are magnificent. The whole world changed when Miles turned a coffee cup.

Ken Olin: When you are trying to succeed in business or the arts, you have to come up against people that are more ruthless and cutthroat than anything Michael and Elliot would have come in contact with in their little company. That is what Miles represented.

Joe Dougherty: There was a scene where Miles was up on the platform and he threw Michael an apple. Michael turned and caught it. I remember David said, "Michael," he waited for Ken to turn and then threw the apple. I told David a couple of times, "You throw the apple before you say his name." He couldn't understand what the difference was. I said, "It is because it is Miles. He just wants to find out if the guy can react fast enough. It is only going to cost him an apple if he can't catch it." In the great tradition of David Clennon you just saw something happen behind the eyes. He just got what was going on. He would actually say in subsequent conversations. "It's just an apple."

Ann Lewis Hamilton: I think one of my favorite relationships in the series is Elliot and Michael. I love watching them. I am thinking about the great Michael and Elliot episodes that Joe wrote. Their arc in the series is so interesting.

Ken Olin: Timmy and I leaned on each other and now we were being separated. That was a big adjustment.

Joe Dougherty: That is the way life is structured. Michael and Elliot are so radically different, they had to be partners to be complete. That doesn't mean they would be successful just that they had to to be together.

Ken Olin: Miles started to empower Michael in a direction of maturity. It was a cool thing for Michael to encounter. David had a completely different sensibility of delivering lines.

Michael (Ken Olin pictured here with DP Ken Zunder) gets promoted over Elliot as he begins his path to a higher level of confrontation with Miles Drentell and leaving Elliot behind. Courtesy of Kenneth Zunder.

Joe Dougherty: David was the negative Christopher Walken, you take out the commas, take out all the punctuation. How is David gonna say this? Let's find out. The level of commitment that he had to Miles Drentell was incredible. He didn't win an Emmy for playing Miles which is a shame. It shows that if you are extremely good at what you are doing, nobody notices.

(*Editor's Note: From here forward there could be spoilers for future episodes.*)

Episode 50

"Another Country"

Directed by Ron Lagomarsino

Written by Richard Kramer

January 6, 1990

Marshall Herskovitz: At the end of Season 2, Patty Wettig was very unhappy and felt she wasn't given enough to do. She sat with us for an hour and basically read us the riot act feeling that she was wasted. We had tried a storyline with her that didn't work and we just felt like we failed her and her character in Season 2. We apologized.

Patty Wettig: I was at the grocery store at the end of the summer. We were going to start back to work in a week on Season 3. I ran into Marshall. He said, "I think we have come up with something." I said, "What is it?" He said, "Not here." I said, "No, tell me." He said, "Cancer." I said, "Yes, I love it!"

Marshall Herskovitz: From the very beginning we knew we wanted to give someone cancer on the show. Finally, after the third season, we figured we could handle a big storyline like that. We still hadn't decided who should get the cancer. I fully understand the irony. To the outside world giving cancer to someone was a terrible thing, but among these actors, they all wanted it because it would be the storyline of the year. To get cancer was the prize. We decided, as a result of how we failed Patty in season 2, we would give her the cancer. People on the outside will think we did it to punish her, but in fact we did it because we wanted to really give her the plum and she got it. She won the Emmy and was incredible. It turned out in many ways to be a defining moment for the show.

Patty Wettig: They said, "The problem is that you might not be alive for the whole series." I said, "I would rather act in something and be challenged by it. If that costs me a year or two on the show, I don't mind." Nancy was going to die. They told me they wanted to explore a contemporary dying that you weren't expecting. That was the pursuit of the cancer story.

Susan Shilliday: In the context of the show it was okay that Nancy got cancer. In the context that Patty could show everything she could do, I was happy with it. Originally, Ed and Marshall wanted to create a crisis to delve into. They had the idea of a child dying. Both Liberty and I said, "Absolutely not. You will not do that. You will never be able to talk about anything else." It would overwhelm everything in the show because that is the worst thing that can happen to a person. So, you ended up with Nancy getting cancer. The show wanted to study the big stuff that happens and still look at it through the *thirtysomething* lenses of small moments.

Patty Wettig and Tim Busfield take on the emotional weight of cancer in "Another Country." Their characters just reunited when the disease hit. Patty would go on to win the Emmy for Best Actress in a drama for this episode. Courtesy of ABC Photography Archives. The Lisa Mercado Fernandez Collection.

Joe Dougherty: There was resistance from the writers from doing the cancer story at all. It was melodramatic and was too much like television. Then Ed and Marshall would look at you and say, "Yes, but you will do it better." There was a debate about whether it should be Nancy that got sick. I remember I said, "If we are really going to do this, shouldn't we just pick someone randomly?" I wouldn't take that stand now. I do remember it was one of the only times all the writers were gathered and we went into their office and said, "Isn't this just TV? Isn't this just soap opera?" It seemed punitive because her marriage just got better and her book was going to be published.

Richard Kramer: I don't remember that at all. We never talked about other people's episodes. I wrote the first cancer episode and wasn't concerned if she was going to live or die. Maybe Ed and Marshall knew the plan but I don't remember there being camps of writers or discussing the episode with anyone. I went to them and told them I had a friend who had AIDS. I said, "Wouldn't it be interesting to do a show about a person who has an illness and has to live their life anyway." They never would have told me they decided to give Nancy cancer. That is my version of it. It probably has some truth to it but not all the truth. It is the Stephen Sondheim song "Someone in a Tree"; everyone has a version of their truth. That is the "Someone in a Tree" of "Another Country."

Ron Lagomarsino (*Director*): I was aware that this was a big episode and a long story arc. There was also a question of if she was going to live or die. I don't think they had an endgame at the time. Patty was so strong on the show and it gave her so many amazing arcs to play. Part of the feel was Richard's script which had a kind of a visual poetry. There was a scene with the kids under a sheet and they had a flashlight. There was this sense of a cocoon and what was to come. Richard's scripts had those elements. There was imagery in some of the dialogue that was different. It was ever so slightly heightened, but beautiful.

Richard Kramer: I talked to two doctors about which cancer she should have. I remember arguing with Susan about it. That really wasn't what that episode is about. It was about living your life anyway even in the face of a catastrophic illness. That was the root of the series as a whole. You could call the series living your life anyway.

The crew created snow in Los Angeles for the scene where Nancy starts to feel ill outside of Ethan's school. Courtesy of Kenneth Zunder.

Ron Lagomarsino: The actress who plays the doctor is Patricia Heaton. I have run into her a couple of times. She certainly remembers the experience.

Ken Zunder (*Director Of Photography*): There were a couple kinds of snow that we used on this episode. They had the dry snow in the buckets. The camera was shooting across the driver so the only snow seen was out the window. We used the dry snow which was a lot easier to deal with. Wet snow was what we put along the ground for the wide shots. (*See photo*)

Richard Kramer: The title of the episode came from Susan Sontag's book *Illness As Metaphor* (1978). It has a famous first line about being ill is another country. Patty was a great collaborator on that episode. I would bounce lines off her while I was writing it. She was fearless. There was a final scene that today we would do because the show would now be on cable. The very final scene when she said to Elliot, "Make love to me."

We rehearsed it as, "Fuck me." We never shot it because the chances of that being aired didn't even exist. Patty would have done it. Timmy would have done it. They would have been thrilled to do it.

Ron Lagomarsino: I recall the scene where Nancy and Elliot were sitting across from the doctor and they just said, "I love you." It originally had more lines and as we got closer to shooting there was an idea that it would be more effective with no dialogue. Tim and Patty together were so rich.

"Post-Op"

Directed by Peter Horton

Written by Susan Shilliday

January 23, 1990

Susan Shilliday: I think this is the best writing I did on the show. I am really proud of that episode. It was hard to write. The key to it was Nancy's sister. (Played by *Tess Harper*) Being able to have so much subtext so that what they were talking about on the surface was the relationship

Nancy's sister comes to visit in the aftermath of Nancy's surgery. The episode captures what it is like to have family around an illness that no one wants to talk about. Courtesy of ABC Photography Archives.

with the mother and all the subtext was what was really going on with Nancy. A look or a word set them giggling with their alliance against the mother. I really felt this episode deeply.

Patty Wettig: I can remember the scene where I have to say goodbye to my sister so well. I loved Tess Harper so much. I just never felt any space between Nancy and I. It is that actor thing. Do you believe in this imaginary circumstance? If you do, it is not just that your brain takes belief in it. It is your nervous system. I don't know why or how, but my blood was engaged with that character. When I shut that door, that was my sister in that moment and it felt like I might not see her again. I didn't have to say anything to show it. It just happened. Part of it is a gift. If all acting was like that, it would be the most phenomenal thing to engage with, but it isn't. When it is, it is a spiritual thing. You are not working that hard. You are just there.

Susan Shilliday: I was probably writing it four to six weeks out from when it was going to be filmed. The writing on this one was more seamless for me. There was no going back and replacing big chunks. I just knew this one.

Tim Busfield: Susan wrote Nancy and Elliot so incredibly well.

Susan Shilliday: Elliot and the sister call each other Jules. That is what Ed and Marshall call each other. It just got translated into Elliot and the sister. Being able to bring in a character and have that easy intimacy between them was the point of the nickname.

Patty Wettig: My favorite scene in the entire series is the mailbox scene. Nancy felt in her body the connection to her children. The sadness that if she died from cancer her daughter wouldn't know her. It is one of the most unbearable things to think about. It is the most female scene written in the deepest way. Peter Horton directed the scene. We tried to rehearse it. I told Peter, "I can't rehearse this. If I say these lines I am gonna cry." We just filmed it once because I so deeply understood those words. I told Peter, "Let Mel Harris and I just do this scene." We both understood it. Susan understood it. I have had women come up and talk to me about that scene ever since. It is because it is a maternal, female feeling.

The scene where Nancy talks to Hope about what it will be like for her daughter to not remember her if she dies was so intense that Patty Wettig couldn't rehearse the scene. Courtesy of ABC Photography Archives. The Lisa Mercado Fernandez Collection.

Susan Shilliday: I wrote that out of my own experience of being a mother of two kids and feeling the anxiety. You don't know what anxiety is until you have children. To be more honest than I should be, I was writing it out of the idea of knowing what deep depression was and translating that into what another kind of more life threatening situation would be. A lot of it just has to do with being a mother and knowing what that feels like.

Patty Wettig: The thing about Susan that is so great is that it was not a labored speech. It was so simply put. It said exactly how and what to say without in anyway sentimentalizing it. It took everything in me to not cry. As opposed to when you have a scene where you think you should be crying at the end so you work hard to cry. This was the opposite. I just tried not to cry. I tried to say those words as clearly as possible. It is my favorite all time scene. She is an incredible writer. So clear, clean and heartfelt.

Polly Draper: I remember getting so much flak from the scene where Ellyn visits Nancy in the hospital. Everybody was mad because I didn't kiss her because I acted like I didn't want to catch "the cancer" from her. Really what was on my mind was that I was afraid of breaking her because she was so fragile. There wasn't really any evil intentions like everyone thought there was. There was so much truth to that moment that everybody has that fear when they go into a hospital seeing a sick person. What do you do? Do you hug them? Sit on their bed? How close do you get to them? I can't remember if it said in the script if I was supposed to kiss her or not. I think it was just something I did in the moment.

"Once a Mermaid"

Directed by Ellen S. Pressman

Written by Ann Lewis Hamilton, Story by Ellen Simon

February 6, 1990

Ann Lewis Hamilton: We would ask the actors what they could do. Polly had been a swimmer so we had talked about her swimming in an episode. We loved the image of her being underwater and being lost in not having a relationship. I mean she was in a relationship, but it wasn't a good one. It was a relationship that had to be lived under the surface like a mermaid. She couldn't reveal Jeffrey (*Richard Gililand*) to anyone since he was married.

Polly Draper: I used to be on a swim team. Ann knew that and wrote the whole episode based around it. I realized when I saw it that it had been awhile since I'd actually swum and was horrified by how bad my form was.

Ellen Pressman (*Director, her directorial debut*): The water element was a really important element in the episode. I think it was the first time that we ever saw Ellyn in love. She was having an affair with a married man, but to me it wasn't about that. It was true love for her. That was the story I was trying to tell.

Ann Lewis Hamilton: I wrote a lot of the water. I think I knew I wanted her to swim throughout and see her underwater. Ellen Pressman added water in just about every scene. We worked on the script together to try to add more water elements. She added a fish tank in a restaurant scene and the big rain scene with Jeffrey.

Ellen Pressman: In the beginning of the episode, her life is languid so we had her swim slowly. When she went through turmoil I wanted her to swim very sternly. We tried to show her naked bottom. I am not sure if that got cut out.

Polly Draper: There was also a big scandal about my naked butt. A lot of advertisers pulled their ads when they saw the episode because of it. I remember Ed and Marshall being really pissed off about that and not wanting to change it. I think in the end they capitulated, however. Still, it was a beautiful, sexy episode and I am really proud of it. This is one of my favorites episodes.

Ellyn takes center stage in this episode where every scene involves water of some sort. From a swimming pool, to the rain, to a fish tank in the background. Ellen Pressman made her directing debut in this episode. Courtesy ABC Photography Archives.

Ellen Pressman: For the opening scene I think I used an Enya song and then I used a Ricki Lee song, "It Must Be Love," for their date. Those were songs I chose and they were approved.

Ann Lewis Hamilton: I like the scene where they are playing Outburst and naming famous couples and Gary called out, "Ellyn and Jeffrey." None of them could keep a secret. I read it again and was surprised how bittersweet it was. I loved Ellyn. I wanted her to have happiness because she was such a mess. The Jeffrey relationship seemed so fated from the beginning, where was it really going to go?

Ellen Pressman: There was something that people didn't really like about Ellyn and I wanted people to fall in love with her deeply. The water was the unconscious mind. I tried to show that love supersedes everything else. Now as a married woman, I may not agree with that. I was a young woman and there was a lot of sexuality in the way in which Ellyn was portrayed at that time. There was that little moment where he discovered her tattoo. That was something I added. There are things that are underneath that people don't see on the surface.

Ann Lewis Hamilton: I think it was a coincidence that we introduced Billy Seidel (*Played by Erich Anderson*) in this episode. I can't remember if Ed and Marshall knew that she would end up marrying him. He was an actor that I knew before. They seemed to fit together really well. I liked their blind date. I think the script said, "He is a nice guy, but that's just it, he's just a nice guy."

Episode

53

"Fathers and Lovers"

Directed by Peter O'Fallon

Written by Ramsey Fadiman and Winnie Holzman, Story by Ramsey Fadiman

February 13, 1990

Melissa feels like a child when she interacts with her father in Winnie Holzman's first writing credit "Fathers and Lovers". Winnie also penned the following hour about Ellyn and Jeffrey moving in together. Courtesy of Kenneth Zunder.

"Her Cup Runneth Over"

Directed by Timothy Busfield

Written by Winnie Holzman

February 20, 1990

Winnie Holzman: I came into the situation smack in the middle as a real Johnny-Come-Lately. I was a wife and mother in my thirties watching the show at home with my little one. I was the abject fan. When I was hired on the show there were things that I wanted to see happen. It was almost like a wet dream for a fan. The other writers didn't have that privilege because they were making the show. When you are making it, you are deep inside of it. When you are watching, it is a different feeling. It's pouring over you.

Winnie Holzman and her husband, Paul Dooley, both worked on several shows with Ed and Marshall. Photo Courtesy of Winnie Holzman.

Tim Busfield *(Director, His directorial debut)*: I directed Winnie Holzman's first script and I wish I had done a better job. I was not up to par with Kenny and Peter in directing. I am not really proud of the work I did. I was very green. In moments I would get some good stuff. When you first start directing there is just so much math. They gave me one and I did a good enough job that next season they gave me two episodes.

Winnie Holzman: I had just gone through a big soul searching time when I first met Richard Kramer. I felt completely open. I wasn't jealous anymore. I was able to say to him, "I think what you are doing on television is brilliant. I have never seen anything like it." It never crossed my mind that he would let me write him a spec script. I was just thrilled to meet him. I was in a very innocent place in my life. I just wanted to talk to somebody who I thought was doing amazing work with no agenda.

Polly Draper: Ellyn was not equating herself very gracefully in that situation. I got Jeffrey, but now I have to deal with the daughter. In Ellyn's eyes, a horrible daughter, but she was a regular teenage girl.

"Good Sex, Bad Sex, What Sex, No Sex"

Directed by Scott Winant

Written by Jill Gordon

February 27, 1990

Scott Winant: Jill wrote the episode and we worked on it together. It all stemmed from a conversation in Hope's kitchen where Melissa talked about having sex and how none of the other characters were having sex. Then we went and looked at each one of their stories and the reasons for that.

Melissa always felt guilty about dating Lee. This comic episode about the status of the character's sex life ends in sadness for Melissa. Courtesy of Carol Gepper's TV Guide Collection.

Corey Parker decided to leave the show for a new ABC series called Eddie Dodd with Treat Williams. The series didn't last. Courtesy of Carol Gepper's TV Guide Collection.

Melanie Mayron: My car broke down and a mechanic in Santa Monica told me a story about how he had dated an older woman. She broke up with him at one point because she knew their age difference was too great. She thought he would break up with her. The story was so moving to me that I pitched it to Ed and Marshall. They wrote that Melissa breaks up with Lee. It was from that story.

Corey Parker (*Lee*): ABC offered me another show for more money. I had a family to feed so I started shooting the new series. So, they broke up Lee and Melissa. I really felt guilty because I loved *thirtysomething* and working with Melanie. The decision to leave wasn't fun on any level. In hindsight, I wish I would have just stayed on the show. The series I left for was not picked up.

Scott Winant: The toy turtle that blocked Gary and Susannah from having sex was a huge deal. God, did I get in trouble for that too. It was my Rube Goldberg experiment. I actually owned that turtle for awhile.

The turtle was Gary's adversary. He couldn't escape it. There was this one moment where the turtle got loose and started to roll across the floor. I wanted to use, and I am going to admit this even though I wouldn't admit it then, I wanted to do a *Jaws* (1977) music cue. That is of course John Williams and I couldn't use it. I said to Stewart Levin, "Can't we do something that sounds like it, but has a different set of chords?" So, he wrote something similar. Sure enough we got a letter from the lawyers. I can't remember how it was resolved. We definitely got caught. I thought we had changed it enough that it wouldn't trigger anything. I'm surprised about how vigilant they were.

Jill Gordon: Once again, I went out and interviewed everyone I knew, as well as strangers on the street. I polled their opinions on what constituted good sex and bad sex. My favorite line came from a man who said, "Bad sex is sex in jail."

Scott Winant: I did everything on the show before I did it in real life. Ed and Marshall were both married. I was younger and I hadn't, but by the time the show ended I was married and I was having my kid. So, I did my *thirtysomething* on camera first, then I did it in real life. Whereas Ed and Marshall did it in real time.

Episode 56

"The Other Shoe"

Directed by Ken Olin

Written by Joseph Dougherty

March 20, 1990

Joe Dougherty: "The Other Shoe" comes out of the *thirtysomething* tradition that you can be angry at someone you love. I was particularly happy with Tim Busfield. I loved when he just yelled at his cancer stricken wife and told her the truth.

Ken Olin (*Director*): Joe brought a lot of that to the episode. He was so different and a unique individual. He has a challenging personality and had different assumptions compared with other writers. That was a cool aspect of the series. This sensibility wasn't the same as the "mailbox scene" written by Susan. And yet, somehow it was all possible on the same show.

Scott Winant: I remember I had to get Susanna Hoffs from The Bangles to sing the song "Cry Like A Rainstorm." We couldn't afford the original recording by Linda Ronstadt, so we recorded our own.

Joe Dougherty: I didn't pick the song or have anything to do with Susanna Hoff. Songs became a disease in the nineties with obtaining rights. Scott was Mr. Music, so he must have picked it.

Patty Wettig: I was on top of the car with Katherine Cortez (*Cancer patient Beatrice Holt*) screaming at the airplanes going overhead. Ken directed it and as an actor it was one of my top three favorite scenes to do.

Ken Olin: We shot that airplane flying over Nancy and Katherine on the back lot and then mapped an airplane over them. It was a composite

Nancy bonds with a fellow cancer patient as she leaves Elliot and children behind in this dark script penned by Joe Dougherty. Courtesy of ABC Photography Archives. The Lisa Mercado Fernandez Collection.

shot. They were both so great in that scene. That was when the show started to get more muscular and darker. I think Joe Dougherty had some influence on this. Joe used to call it, "Plot-like substance." It was going on with DAA and it was going on with Nancy's cancer. There was just more. That episode was really good. It was dark, ambitious, and intellectual. It had some serious thematic exploration of a terminal illness. Patty was so out there brilliant. She was amazing.

"Three Year Itch"

Directed by Victor DuBois

Written by Ann Lewis Hamilton

April 3, 1990

Ann Lewis Hamilton: It was so hard to remove my marriage from the show. I think a spouse resents the other one when someone is too busy. We are still married but I am not kidding when I say my husband thought, "Thank God" when the show ended. My feeling that his work intruded was certainly a real aspect of our marriage. I am sure he would say the same thing about me. I wrote a scene where Michael shaved pregnant Hope's legs because my husband had to do stuff like that. He would shave my legs or wash my hair. I was always big on stuff like that. I think there is something so intimate about it without it being sex. I like that episode. It feels like real marriage.

Michael focuses on asking for a raise and Hope focuses on her new crush, John Dunaway, as the struggles in the Steadman marriage start to become apparent. Courtesy of Carol Gepper's TV Guide Collection.

Mel Harris: I think what we saw on *thirtysomething,* certainly with Michael and Hope, was a steady progression of the ebb and flow of a loving marriage.

Liberty Godshall: I think Hope lusted in her thoughts with John Dunaway (*Played by songwriter JD Souther*) and that was the point. She wanted someone else and that was big enough.

Susan Shilliday: At that moment, JD Souther was interested in a career in acting. There may have been a Peter Horton connection. He was laid back in an Eagles sort of way.

Ann Lewis Hamilton: I remember coming up with the infidelity train and just how hilarious I thought that was. Just a bunch of people having affairs. It is dated now. There is a Donna Rice reference.

Mel Harris: When I was pregnant on screen, that was really all me. Hope was a walking walrus and having another baby. It is a very hormonal, emotional time. It is hard to deal with when the person you love isn't paying attention to you. It is very easy to think about whether there is something better. Maybe it is just a flirtation. In the scope of how we are rating that in the *thirtysomething* hierarchy, I would say Hope doesn't cheat on Michael.

Susan Shilliday: Hope was not cheating on Michael anymore than Michael was cheating on Hope with DAA by the depth of his involvement in his work or friendship with Elliot. If her attention strayed from Michael, it was not cheating on him.

Ann Lewis Hamilton: I think we tried to connect the subplots. It was such a collaboration with Ed and Marshall. There was Michael and his journey at work. There was Hope who felt very distant from Michael and tried to find her own way. When she could get a job in DC, Michael was like, "You would leave?" It was their disconnection. There was always an A story and a B story.

Ken Olin: I loved Mel. She was so gorgeous and great to work with. I got to kiss Mel all day. She was the troop leader. She would organize things. Wives in general have a lot to deal with. Michael was a very idealistic version of the Jewish husband. For a lot of women, he was the perfect husband. He had a strong feminine side and was loving.

Mel Harris: I see the relationship as good and bad. Both parties were culpable. I think for Hope she thought, in the end, that the person she started with maybe wasn't the person she liked as much. She still loved him, but I don't know if she liked him as much. She didn't like the drive that came out of facing the financial challenges in their ad agency. You can look at it and make it logical, but when you are looking at emotion and love it is often a different thing.

Ken Olin: People do not give Mel enough credit. She would walk into a scene in a rehearsal and organize within three minutes where she would have to feed a baby, make a cake and get dressed while delivering lines. When women have to do these things in their real lives it puts them in a bad mood.

"I'm Nobody, Who Are You?"

Directed by Richard Kramer

Written by Winnie Holzman

April 10, 1990

Winnie Holzman (*Writer*): There was a time in my life when I felt like everyone was passing me by. I realize now, looking back, that everything was perfect and I was just living my life but it is very tempting to compare yourself to your peer group at certain times in your life.

Richard Kramer (*Director*): That episode was about Gary feeling less than. There was a big change between Gary and Michael because Michael had become this big man. Gary had a slight contempt for Michael, so it was complicated. Peter Horton was really wonderful at playing those two levels. It is reductive to say he was a Peter Pan character because he wasn't. He was a barometer for the truth that some of them were losing contact with, particularly Michael.

Peter Horton: Gary felt that Michael sold out. He was jealous of him. Michael had a family. Why can't I grow up? The way to not face that shortcoming was to be critical of what Michael had done. Gary didn't want to face his own panic that he wasn't capable of doing it. He meant it when he criticized Michael, but deep down it was his own panic. These relationships and the writing were so wonderfully convoluted.

Richard Kramer: I did a double focus of the waiter behind Gary totaling up the bill. Gary didn't have enough money to afford dinner at an expensive restaurant and Michael was full of money. When Marshall saw the scene he said, "Very visual." It was a visual moment that told the story. That episode was about not having money in real life. We were all doing very well on the show and were becoming conscious of peers who were not doing as well.

Ken Zunder (*Director Of Photography*): I was interviewed for a magazine and talked about the lighting. I said, "I am not trying to make the women look glamorous. I am trying to make them look natural." The next day we were filming in a restaurant and Mel Harris grabbed all the candles from all the tables and put them on her table. I said, "What are you doing?" Mel said, "I want to look glamorous." (*Laughs*) There is a difference between looking good and looking glamorous. She was not supposed to be a Hollywood star, she was supposed to be Hope Steadman and Hope Steadman looked good.

Winnie Holzman: I had a decade where my colleagues were becoming more successful than me. I have had some success, but I have also seen what is underneath that longing for success. It really is about giving yourself permission to risk and fail. What are we without the risk of failing? We are just trying to be popular. That would be a very empty life. One of the reasons I was writing this episode was because I had written a musical called *Birds of Paradise* that Arthur Laurents (*West Side Story, The Way We Were*) directed. It was treated roughly by the critics and it closed after two months. I was asking myself those hard questions. What is my purpose? Should I even ever write again? They were real questions to me. It would be very natural that I would write something for *thirtysomething* that would ask questions about success. It's not success if you let other people tell you that you are a success. That is so empty. I was able to see that I wanted to define success for myself. I didn't want a bunch of strangers who write for the papers to define it for me. That took months and years for me to come to, but it became a very important lynch pin in my life.

Richard Kramer: I have to tip my hat to Winnie. It was a gorgeous, hilarious script. We had great editors and as directors, we were in the editing room at every moment. I remember just laughing at the jump cut from Hope and Susannah fighting to Susannah being in the bath tub. Thank you, Winnie Holzman for that.

Winnie Holzman: My experience with my women friends is that when you meet somebody who you start to feel close with, you get intimate right away. It can happen in a second in a ladies room. That is one of the reasons that women's friendships are so combustible because they do happen very quickly. It's zero to sixty. They were fighting, then she was taking a bath at Hope's house. I had set it up that Susannah didn't have

Gary and Susannah struggle with being new parents with a small bank account while Michael and Hope are flush with cash. This episode has an argument between Susannah and Hope that ends up in the bathtub. Courtesy of ABC Photography Archives.

hot water. They were deprived. They were feeling less than. She was also a new mother and if there is one thing a new mother wants, it is to just take a bath by herself.

Patricia Kalember: Taking a bath on a set is never as comfortable as you think it is gonna be. The water was cold. They had female writers that had a female perspective. They had male writers to have a male perspective. The scenes with Elliot and Michael and their business had such a male spin on it. They let the women do their thing too. Sometimes women don't say it enough. We don't communicate, it can be very "Mean Girls" if you are not communicating.

Winnie Holzman: I got a little bit of push back from the actresses. They didn't say it to me directly because I never spoke to the actors directly back then ever. I had heard maybe through Richard that they were uncomfortable with the idea that Hope was talking to Susannah while she was in the bathtub. I thought it was really weird because it was such a feature of my experience with women friends that we would do things like that and it wouldn't mean anything.

Mel Harris: Things would be in the script and I would say, "I don't think a woman would do this" and they might have a very real example where it happened.

Winnie Holzman: Obviously, when you are writing a show like *thirtysomething* people are going to come at it from their own experience of life. People are going to have polarized reactions to it. We were encouraged to be authentic about our lives and that just came right out of my life.

Patricia Kalember: I think people aren't one thing or another. Life is messy and people are crazy and surprising. So whenever I hear an actor say, "My character wouldn't do that," I want to smack them because you don't know what people are capable of. I love the messiness of life. You've got to find the fun and that is where the life is.

Winnie Holzman: I had a whole thing in my mind about Hope and Susannah for that episode because I didn't want it to be like "Oh, they've just accepted each other as friends and it's all been so effortless." I wanted there to be a fight between them and discomfort between them. It wasn't realistic that Gary would bring this new prickly woman into this very tight inner circle and she would just be accepted by the women. I wanted to show a progress. What would get them to the next stage of development of their connection? To me that had to be some kind of discordant fight. That would tumble them into a new understanding of each other.

Mel Harris: Susannah was a challenging relationship for the characters. I don't know that I would say Hope felt inferior to her, but that she thought Susanna thought that she was inferior to her. Even with Hope staying home and not going off to work, Hope wasn't insecure in her intellectual capabilities. Susannah ends up with Gary, God bless her. It was interesting to see a devoted bachelor with a family. It broke lots of women's hearts.

"Arizona"

Directed by Edward Zwick

Written by Susan Shilliday

April 17, 1990

Ed Zwick (*Director*): Susan and I formed a close collaboration in those years. She even wrote a few movies for me later. "Arizona" meant a lot to me. It was challenging in the creation of an entire other ambient reality where we put Michael and Hope at her parent's condo in Arizona. It was challenging in that it evoked a very personal experience for me visiting Liberty's parents.

Susan Shilliday (*Writer*): "Arizona" in some ways is most directly based on my own life. I can say it now because my parents are no longer with us. The experience of when your parents are living a life that is so different than yours that it is hard to find the connections anymore. The alienation you are feeling because you can't go home again. It is the place where they don't have to take you in again.

Ed Zwick: It has always been our supposition that you never know what anyone's marriage is about because no one really knows what your marriage is about.

Susan Shilliday: They were watching the marriage of Hope's parents which wasn't really what they thought it was. You never know what is going on in someone else's marriage and it is never easy no matter how easy someone might make it seem.

Mel Harris: I look like a beached whale in "Arizona." I gave birth six days after I finished that episode. There was an ambulance right outside the stage. I was huge. It was a really interesting script to me because some-

Ken Zunder checks the light as the cast gets ready to play a scene in Melissa's loft. Like many scenes on the show they are laying around and moving back and forth to keep the shot interesting. Courtesy of Kenneth Zunder.

times late in the season you don't always get what you might think of as a great episode. I liked the dynamic of the parents.

Ann Lewis Hamilton: "Arizona" is unbelievable. It was a really amazing bunch of writers. Susan was from another universe or something. My respect for her is huge. "Arizona" just blew my head off.

Ed Zwick: My favorite moment was when they were sitting on the patio. Michael picked up the binoculars and he was being such a dick. He was looking at the different people, then he came upon Hope and she was just staring at him. We screened this episode at the Museum of Television and that got huge laughs. The episodes really did play comedically like we wanted them to in front of an audience. I am not sure if people at home laughed as much at the series.

Charlotte Stewart (*Played Peggy York*): I don't know why, but I acted a little outrageous for my character. I don't know if they kept it in or not. At one point when I was talking, I just burst out laughing and Ed gave me the weirdest look. I remember filming at the golf course location.

Brandy Alexander (*Production Designer*): Ed directed an episode where I had to make a California golf course look like it was in Arizona. He used a super long lense because he was playing around with an unusual way to shoot a conversation that was set around a table. He wanted to have interesting angles. I had two eight foot tall cactuses from the greens department. I had to move them around on golf carts. Because his lens was like a 200 lens, you couldn't just place the cactus in a normal landscape. I would have to look through the camera before Ed shot to see where the out of focus cactus should be placed. Then I would call out to the guy driving the golf cart, "Move fifty feet to left!" Ed would laugh at me because it was so odd. I only had two cactuses to play with and I had to sell Arizona with them.

Ken Zunder (*Director Of Photography*): It wasn't as simple as how could we shoot this differently? It was how could we tell this story in a non traditional way. The actors suggested things, I could suggest things. It could come from every side of the camera.

Mel Harris: We were in year three as actors. We all knew what a gift we have been given with each other. It was great. The physical part of being nine months pregnant at that point was tough. I sat down a lot in between scenes which was not my normal MO. I remember I had a big caftan on.

Ken Olin: How do you play insecure when you look like Mel Harris? You are stunningly beautiful, have a great body, and get to be married to Michael Steadman. Now you are gonna bitch? What is her problem? She had to face a lot of that which wasn't fair.

Patty Wettig: That was where Hope and Michael visits her mom? I don't really remember that episode. I'll have to watch it again. I think we were all possessive of our own episodes.

Ken Olin: It was Ed and Marshall's show so whatever issues they were having with their wives was put on the show. These were very formidable women. If you were married to Liberty, Susan or Patty, these are ambitious, smart women who happened to be raising all of our kids. They were going to have some problems with the way their husbands were working fifteen hours a day. I don't know how much of that slipped into the show.

Ed Zwick: It came very close to the bone talking about something that we didn't talk about as much on the show which was so latent. Just how much the commitment to the work cost us in our marriages. It is one thing to write a television show, but it is doubly hard when you are working with your spouses and it is triply hard when you are also trying to have the life you are describing. In some sense, you are sacrificing it to have a show about it.

Susan Shilliday: There was usually a two page outline that contained the beats that had to happen in the episode. They pretty much let me write what I wanted to. The idea that they were struggling and would have fights that were interrupted was certainly there.

Ed Zwick: That particular episode was very much about the gulf that was growing between Hope and Michael and the cost of his connection to his work and her complaint about that. His complaint about her lack of support for him. It was, in some sense, an echo of what all of us had to deal with and that would include Scott and Jill, Ken and Patty and all the marriages on the show that were strained by the experience itself. That episode feels like marriage because we were all looking closely at our own.

Mel Harris: I don't know if Hope vilified Michael. I think she wondered if he couldn't work at DAA, be successful, support the family and continue to be engaged as the Michael she knew. Maybe a little more carefree, the Michael that laughs and throws Janey in the air.

Marshall Herskovitz: I think their marriage was in danger but I don't think it was doomed. There is a difference. I think there are a lot of people who would tell you that the vast majority of marriages that succeed have gone through periods of great danger.

Joe Dougherty: I wanted to do *thirtysomething* because it was a show that said you could be angry at someone you love. "You are in this house for twelve hours a day, anger is gonna happen. You are going to figure this out and the fact that you didn't right away is okay. Stay in the room." We just kept people in the room.

Ken Olin: It was never for me to question whether Hope was or wasn't a bitch. I played what was written. At the end of the day, it is an unfair

Michael and Hope started the series as the perfect couple. Three seasons later the issues that have built up come to a head in "Arizona". The last episode of the series that Susan Shilliday wrote and Ed Zwick directed. Courtesy of ABC Photography Archives. The Lisa Mercado Fernandez Collection.

thing because the wife is put in the position of having to get her husband to tow the line or take more than her fair share of responsibilities. There was never a time in four years that I wasn't crazy about Mel. I know that is how Patty felt about Tim. I know Mel felt the same way. We were just trying to play a couple in their early thirties trying to navigate careers, babies and life.

Ken Zunder: There was a little rivalry between *L.A. Law* (1986) and *thirtysomething*. I am not sure who did it first, but both shows would throw in a line to say, "*L.A. Law* is on." Then on their show they would say, "We have to be home to watch *thirtysomething*." It was just an acknowledgement that those were the two popular dramas on the air at the time.

Ed Zwick: There was also something in it that I always wanted to do. There was a very long silence at the end of their fight. You don't want to have silence on television because people get upset by that and change the channel. I wanted to allow the silences to land and grow between them.

Susan Shilliday: The moment at the end where they are dancing is all about marriage. That was my last episode because I started writing a feature. It wasn't that I wanted to leave *thirtysomething*. I had other things to write. At the same time, I felt I had probably said what I wanted to say on the show.

"Going Limp"

Directed by Melanie Mayron

Written by Hugh O'Neill

May 1, 1990

Melanie Mayron (*Director, her directorial debut*): "Going Limp" was one of the few episodes that was a stand alone episode. You could follow along fine because it was about Elliot getting to direct for the very first time. There were so many scenes in it that according to the producers, it was going to take two days longer than what we usually shot. So, I had to move a lot quicker and really have those two days fall under eight days. I was sort of doing an homage to François Truffaut (*French Film Director*). He did the film *Day For Night* (1973) which was a story of a film crew shooting a movie.

Tim Busfield: This is the episode that people talk to me about the most. That is a fan favorite. I loved it, too. It was all Melanie. She was so great. She is such a dear friend. She had not directed yet on *thirtysomething*. It was her first day of directing and we were on location. We were at the food truck. Kenny was there. I said to Kenny, "I am not sure how to play this." The way they had written Elliot wasn't how I direct. I am not that guy. Kenny says, "Maybe read it again and find a way." Melanie rolls in repeating our names and talking really fast. Kenny backs behind Melanie and indicates to her with his eyes mouthing, "Play that." I put my arm around Melanie and said, "Tell me more." I walked her to the set with my breakfast and I basically just played Melanie in that episode.

Susan Shilliday: We brought in some new writers because the guild had a bizarre rule where you had to have a certain amount of outside writers which does not exist anymore. Ed and Marshall wanted to give other people shots, but it didn't always work out as well as it did with Winnie

Elliot gets his directorial debut as a character, while Melanie Mayron gets her actual directorial debut with "Going Limp." Meta much? Courtesy ABC Photography Archives.

Holzman. I did an extensive rewrite on "Going Limp." It was originally written by Hugh O'Neil. My guess is that Joe did some work on it as well.

Joe Dougherty: I don't think I worked on "Going Limp." I was very possessive about Miles, but I don't remember working on that one. If Susan did a rewrite, it is unlikely. There would be no reason for anyone to rewrite her.

Susan Shilliday: I probably wrote a lot of Elliot's' real panic and Nancy's response to it. I don't remember if I did the stuff on the set.

Tim Busfield: The reaction of how Elliot came home wasn't sort of how Susan saw it. Elliot being drunk and saying it was a disaster. That was me just being Melanie. I am much more laid back.

Episode 61

"The Go Between"

"The Towers of Zenith, Part 1"

Directed by Scott Winant

Written by Joseph Dougherty

May 15, 1990

"Samurai Ad Man"

"The Towers of Zenith, Part 2"

Directed by Joseph Dougherty

Written by Joseph Dougherty

May 22, 1990

End of Season 3

Scott Winant: "The Go Between" was a very stylized episode, but it worked from a character point of view. Joe Dougherty had this idea that computers were running in secret. I am very cinematic. I studied montage in school. I wanted to do these match dissolves. They were playing pool and I faded from a cue ball to a computer. It was so funny because the computer was one of those two inch tape machines spinning and flip cards were going through. I thought it was the height of sophistication and if I showed that to my daughter she would say, "What the hell was that?"

Mel Harris: I thought Miles Drentell and Michael Steadman were really sort of oil and water. Yet it drove Michael to aspirations that I don't know if he had in the beginning. He always wanted to be successful, but not to the level of drive that being in Miles's circle created.

The two part season finale focuses on Michael and Elliot trying to take over DAA from Miles Drentell. Courtesy of Carol Gepper's TV Guide Collection.

Joe Dougherty: I thought of Miles as Dickensian. He was very Ralph Nickleby. His voice was, "I need the best I can get from everybody and I am gonna get it. I will pit them against each other. It is nothing personal; just because you couldn't do the job it doesn't make you a bad person, just insufficient for my needs." That was how he got to where he was at DAA and that was how he got vulnerable. He didn't create alliances and had to create them quickly.

Ken Olin: With Miles we made a version of how harsh the world could be. I dug it. It was a cool world to play in. What was Michael like in that world? What was Elliot like in that world? It was different. Since Michael was who he was, he was going to succeed in it. But let's make it harder for him. As an adversary, let's give him someone who doesn't play by the rules. You can't trust Miles's rules. He was a bad guy. I don't remember him ever being a genuine mentor. He was ruthless and a little evil.

Joe Dougherty: Michael was going to be okay because of something else that happened on an airplane. He had that terrible experience on an airplane in "Legacy." In "Samurai Ad Man" he told Hope a story about watching a baby fall off the seat when he was flying back from California. He had an entirely different experience with it. He said, "I am a Dad. I can do this." I think that is the place where he started to get better.

Ann Lewis Hamilton: Joe wrote all these fantastic DAA episodes and I got to write the ones that he wasn't available to write. Writing Miles was so delicious. Everybody wanted to write him.

Joe Dougherty: When Elliot said, "Miles can't hurt me. He can't hurt my kids, he can't hurt my wife." Michael was envious of that attitude. Michael still wanted to fix that. People who don't know the show well used to say it was a soap opera. I would get really bent out of shape by that. Soap was a pejorative term to me. Maybe I have grown soapier or I am more confident in what we actually did. People who don't have any sense of *thirtysomething* only know it is a pre-Seinfeld drama. A soap about nothing.

The end of part 1 has Michael and Miles sitting in front of these screens moments after Michael fires Elliot. Part 1 won Scott Winant an Emmy for directing. Courtesy of Brandy Alexander.

Scott Winant: I identified with the writer I was collaborating with. We all recognized that Joe had an affinity for telling the Miles Drentell story. He intended to have Michael make a run for DAA. There was a scene where he was standing in the doorway of the bedroom and he did something with his suit. Hope confronted him and he lied to her. It was actually a big moment in the show. It was Joe saying that Michael was putting on his armor and getting ready to go to battle.

Joe Dougherty: It was very much like me to make that armor reference and for Scott to pick it up in the script. I think the deeper Michael got into the corporate espionage the less comfortable he felt about it. The takeover doesn't happen and that was basically an Ed and Marshall thing. It was drama 101. Failure is much more interesting than success. Throw a big rock into the pond and write the ripples. The USA Today didn't review this episode in the entertainment section, they reviewed it in the Money section. I was pleased with that.

Winnie Holzman: I thought Paul Dooley was incredible as Bob Spano. He is my husband, of course. It was possible that Joe thought of him because of seeing me all the time. It was possible that they got Paul on his own merits, but I don't remember why they cast him.

Joe Dougherty: I just remember everyone saying wouldn't it be wonderful to have Paul Dooley on the show. He was great. I wish I could have done more Paul Dooley but that wasn't who Bob Spano was. It was calm Paul Dooley.

Paul Dooley (*Played Bob Spano*): That was fun. It was a two parter. I am lucky my wife worked for that show. I also got to do *Once and Again* and *My So-Called Life*.

Joe Dougherty: People quote me the Miles line, "The decimalization of time is arbitrary." They ask me what it means. I tell them they will have to ask Miles. When you see Michael in the back of the limo with Bob Spano, you realize, he is doing it again. He is looking for another dad. He hasn't figure it out. He's still doing the pattern. He just picked another dad.

Ken Olin: I don't think Michael was even looking for that.

Miles Drentell's office is a set piece that is used to play out high drama between Michael and Miles. Joe Dougherty enjoyed filming in this set. Courtesy Brandy Alexander.

Joe Dougherty: When Michael goes to Miles's office at the end of "Samurai Ad Man," that was an eleven hour day. It was before LEDs so we used a scissor arc to create the lightning. They made a lot of noise, so you actually couldn't speak during lightning. I'm not afraid to write a six page scene. You can do it if you have the people who can play it. That was what I liked about Miles and Michael. There were about three different scenes laying on top of each other. Then the teacup rattled. Miles was rattled. There was the coffee cup that turns in "Michael's Campaign" and Stanley Tucci lost his job. There was the teacup that rattled and you heard that Miles was nervous.

David Clennon (*Miles Drentell*): People like Joe Dougherty and Ann Hamilton really got into that office political scene and created a boss that was really formidable. Your leading men couldn't walk out because he was too powerful for them to get away with that. The writers and producers really created a unique character. The plotting was always so smart and full of surprises. It was a real gift to sort of fall into that.

Scott Winant: As a producer, one of things I did was allowed the filmmaker to be unique to the script and each story. Television tends to be about format. Even though I won the Directing Emmy for this episode, my style was completely different from Ed, Marshall, or Peter Horton's style. I encouraged that. I didn't want it to be formatted. I wanted every episode to be unique to itself but true to cinema, true to storytelling.

Brandy Alexander (*Production Designer*): Scott Winant loved to do transitions. He would have a suitcase being packed and then it would fade to the suitcase being carried by the actor or it would be set down in a new location. I always enjoyed helping him with those.

Ellen Pressman: Scott Winant was a master with lens and moves and invisible transitions. The things he does are amazing and he started all that on *thirtysomething*. It takes a certain kind of eye and an ability to work with actors.

Joe Dougherty: I used my wife in that episode. I had met Beverly in New York and she was out here in California and we were an item. I offered her the part of the plumber. I was terrified I would get in trouble because I was seeing her at the time. She got to say, "Are you the guy getting the toilet?"

Marshall Herskovitz: Miles Drentell and the takeover plot turned out in many ways to be a very defining moment for the show. It wasn't just Ed and I. It was a group of people who had very strong feelings about the show.

Season 4

(1990–91)

"Prelude to a Bris"

Directed by Richard Kramer

Written by Richard Kramer

September 25, 1990

thirtysomething *returned for its fourth and final season with an episode where Michael and Hope have their second child, Leo Steadman. Courtesy of Carol Gepper's TV Guide Collection.*

Episode 64

"Life Class"

Directed by Scott Winant

Written by Winnie Holzman

October 2, 1990

Winnie Holzman: "Life Class" came from a very specific place. A friend of a friend just had a hysterectomy. She was going through hell. It occurred to me that Nancy had a hysterectomy and we hadn't even covered that on the show. I knew the challenge she faced.

Patty Wettig: Filming that episode felt like I was in some kind of dream. I truly don't remember the episode that well. Wish I had the episode to watch again.

Winnie Holzman: I knew talking about the psychological and spiritual consequence of losing your uterus was a taboo. People are able to watch subjects together that they would never discuss. Wilson Cruz's character (*Rickie Vasquez*) on *My So-Called Life* helped a lot of people come out to their parents. That is a gift.

Scott Winant: I based this episode on a piece of minimalist music. I asked Stewart Levin if he could hire a few viola and marimba players to do the score. It had nothing to do with the sound of the show, but it was a memorable episode. I used Beethoven in that same episode.

Winnie Holzman: Scott and I connected on *thirtysomething*. I remember writing "Life Class" and hoping he would direct it. I wanted a dream like quality and fluidity to the episode. I wanted to show what it was like for Nancy to be watching that beautiful woman's body. I wanted there to be a sensuality to it. He really connected to it. That was the beginning of our relationship. It got very connected with the pilot of *My So-Called*

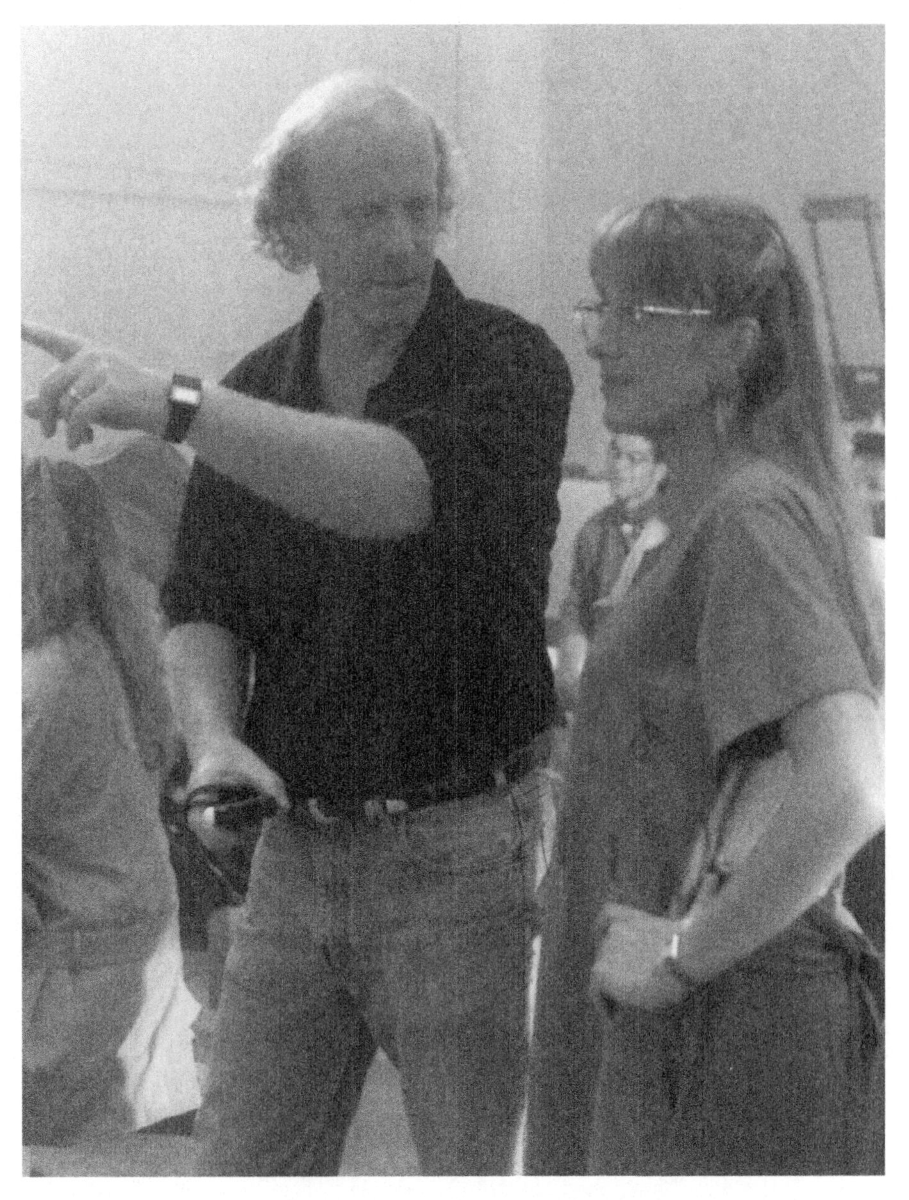

Scott Winant directed this artful hour written by Winnie Holzman. "Lifeclass" has Nancy struggling with her hysterectomy and lack of a sexual drive. Courtesy of Kenneth Zunder.

Life. It just seemed like a natural fit. He added so many touches, visually. He was very creative visually. In "Life Class" there was a romantic quality that I loved.

Winnie and Scott would collaborate with Ed and Marshall again on My So-Called Life *starring Claire Danes as Angela Chase. The series would last only seventeen episodes but would become a cult favorite. Courtesy ABC Photography Archives. Todd Huppert's Collection.*

Scott Winant: Winnie and I ended up partnering after that. We did a movie, we did *My So-Called Life* together. Those were all wonderful things that occurred as a result of *thirtysomething.*

Winnie Holzman: I loved the scene toward the end when Hope said she admired the way Nancy was with her kids. That is a very intimate thing that women don't alway say to each other. Sometimes you can really admire the way a woman is as a mother and almost want that for yourself. The legal department at ABC wouldn't let Nancy say, "I don't care if it was the red M&M I ate when I was five." They changed it to jellybean. Don't even get me started. It was so lame-ass. I guess M&M's felt strongly that they don't cause cancer. At the time there was a rumor about red dye #2 causing cancer. Now we just feed our kids that for breakfast.

"Control"

Directed by Ellen S. Pressman

Written by Ann Lewis Hamilton

October 9, 1990

Ann Lewis Hamilton: Melissa and Miles was not my idea. "Control" wasn't my idea. That is one I have never watched again. I don't know whose idea it was. I wrote it and I remember David Clennon (*Miles*) and Melanie were very good in the episode, but it was really strange. In retrospect, it seemed like kind of a good idea but maybe not really.

Ellen Pressman: I was talking to Ann recently and she was telling me about that episode. I had to remind her that I had directed it. That is how bad our memories are.

Melanie Mayron: That episode got a little rough. There was almost a date rape scene. It was an unexpected turn. I think they wanted to use the characters they had and try to mix them up. I think that if something worked on the show then Ed and Marshall moved forward with it. I don't think it was something that they wanted to continue.

Joe Dougherty: My memory is that one of the problems was that we shot and held it because of the writer's strike. There might have been too much time to think about it. I remember that being Ann and Ellen's frustrations. We finished it, everyone looked at it and there was too much time to think about it. My memory is that it may not have gelled as it was supposed to. That is a value call of mine. It's not my script. It might be selective amnesia on my part. I remember the angst about the episode, but I can't quote what happened there.

Ann Lewis Hamilton: I liked the idea of exploring more of Miles' personal life, but that probably wasn't the best way to do it.

Ellen Pressman: I don't think I believed that storyline was true. It wasn't authentic. It was really difficult for Melanie, David and I. We were all conflicted and we were the people who had to make this believable. Maybe it was my own personal views that were getting in the way. Part of my idea about directing is that it is an archeological dig to really understand what is going on in the script. I don't know how onboard we all were, honestly. I don't think it was my favorite episode.

"Distance"

Directed by Melanie Mayron

Written by Joseph Dougherty

October 16, 1990

Melanie Mayron: I know the opening shots of the clock ticking and the short cuts were my idea. This was my second time directing and I went with Ingmar Bergman. He had static shots and moments like still photography. You are sort of making moving poetry.

Patricia Kalember: Melanie was a real actor's director. So great to work for and is still directing to this day.

Melanie Mayron directed an episode that focuses on Ellyn and Gary. Ellyn breaks-up with Jeffrey over the phone. The call was staged as one long shot. Gary finally ties the knot with Susannah. Courtesy ABC Photography Archives.

Melanie Mayron: The good thing about directing Gary and Susannah's wedding was that I knew Peter Horton so well. It was wonderful to be able to work with him in that way. Patricia Kalember is such a wonderful actress. Melissa is Melissa and Melanie is Melanie. Melanie the actor was directing her second piece. It is work. What I love about it is that it is all creating and all storytelling whether you are in front of the camera or behind the camera.

Joe Dougherty: I have seen this episode miss titled in print as "The Distance" and it is just called "Distance." The distance was the mileage between New York and Philadelphia. Distance was the space between two people. There is a world of difference in those two titles.

Patricia Kalember: I think I shot the pilot for *Sisters* (1991) and it wasn't picked up right away so *thirtysomething* had some time to figure out how they were going to write me out before I left.

Joe Dougherty: We could have sent Susannah to New York because of *Sisters*. I don't remember it being that kind of decision. I thought it was more part of the story. Greater minds than me might know if it was a contractual thing.

Patricia Kalember: I was very conflicted. *Sisters* was a good project and I really liked the other women but I loved doing *thirtysomething*. The difference of being a regular on *Sisters* compared with doing a few episodes on *thirtysomething* was financially more lucrative. With two kids at the time I had to weigh that decision. It wasn't easy.

Polly Draper: Gary loosened Ellyn up and then he married an Ellyn type person. Susannah was very hard-assed.

Joe Dougherty: I had the commonwealth of Pennsylvania fax us the civil ceremony because those were the only lines I wanted in the marriage scene. I said, "I will not write the scene. I will put these four people in the room with a Justice and all I am going to do is have them say the civil marriage ceremony." I put a fish tank in the room because there was one in there when I married my first wife. I wanted to honor her with a fish tank. What you are looking at when you see them is a desire to just find the basics. Then Gary puts his wife and baby on a train and doesn't know what it means because maybe they shouldn't have been married.

Melanie Mayron: What I loved was them on the train with the train tracks and they say good bye. Susannah goes to New York and Gary stays home right after getting married. There are some really wonderful moments in that episode.

Peter Horton: Gary ended up marrying a girl he wanted to fix and make whole. As opposed to Melissa who was right there and loved him. She would have been his best friend as well as his wife. He just couldn't let himself have that.

Patricia Kalember: I think it was instilled in Susannah that she needed a purpose in life and had to make a difference in the world. Her move to New York wasn't selfish. There was something that told her that women are not supposed to be dependent on others.

Joe Dougherty: That episode also has the telephone conversation where Jeffrey breaks up with Ellyn. I wanted her to be as naked as we could do it. It was a terrible phone call, so I wanted to take away everything that we could take away from her. Let's take her makeup off, wet her hair, and let her sit there in a towel.

Melanie Mayron: I remember Polly and I came in on the weekend. We got the keys to her bedroom set. It was a big monologue and I didn't want to interrupt it with a cut. She is a top notch stage actor. If she just goes and we do the whole monologue in one shot it could be so powerful. So, we worked together on how she would sit on the bed and when we would push in.

Joe Dougherty: Melanie shot it in a way that got the most you could get out of it. It was meant to be one single piece. I wrote it fragmented for Polly and she was magnificent. I used to joke with Polly that the way you wrote for Ellyn was that you couldn't do compound sentences. You wrote clauses that were stitched together.

Ken Zunder (*Director Of Photography*): We used to build a very large dance floor which let us move the camera all around. It was very common to spend quite a bit of time rehearsing the scene to figure out how to tell the story without cutting the camera.

The romance between Jeffrey and Ellyn ends off camera in a three minute, one-sided phone call that was shot in one long take. Courtesy of Carol Gepper's TV Guide Collection.

Melanie Mayron: Two days later when we were on the stage with the crew in her bedroom I said, "This whole scene is gonna be in one shot and there are a lot of moves." Everyone looked at me. They put down what is called a Vin Dance Floor which is a smooth floor that the camera can move on easily and stay in position. We had twenty-one camera positions in that one monologue. I have never done that again, but with Polly I could. We just did it a few times because she knew it so well.

Ken Zunder: The pressure was on the actors and crew to do a oner. They all loved the challenge. You don't want to be the actor who blows a line three minutes into a take and they have to do the entire scene again.

Joe Dougherty: I think we rolled it like three times and then Melanie was happy. One of the memories that I take away from the series isn't the episodes. It is finishing that scene of her sitting on the end of the bed. To this day, I remember hugging Polly, I remember the smell of her eye makeup and the glycerin that was put on her shoulders that made her look wet because water would dry too quickly under the lights.

Melanie Mayron: The series was about bringing the minutia of life in front of the lens. There wasn't a crime of the week, it was about life. In life, when you are talking to someone, they are not always in front of you. They turn, they walk, we are following them. I thought there was something powerful about not always filming people from the front.

Polly Draper: I loved my part. It was when Ed and Marshall got some single people to write for Melanie, Peter and I that our parts really got a lot more resonance. Winnie Holzman, Joe Dougherty and Richard Kramer were so brilliant writing for the single characters. We were initially foils for the married couples, but as the seasons went on, we became rounded characters in our own right.

Joe Dougherty: There was a lot of plot in that episode. One of the things that is wrong with television, and I was aware of it when we sat down to the commentaries for the DVDs, was that when we started *thirtysomething* the episodes were forty-nine minutes in four acts. Now they are forty-one minutes broken into six acts. An hour of drama on MTV is thirty-nine minutes.

Episode 67

"The Haunting of DAA"

Directed by Joseph Dougherty

Written by Ann Lewis Hamilton

October 30, 1990

Ann Lewis Hamilton: Ed and Marshall had a master plan for the first season. The second season they had sort of plotted out what they wanted it to be. Before the third season, I know we gathered and they asked us what we wanted to write. Joe and I talked about doing a haunted house episode that became the "Haunting of DAA." They had done holiday shows like the wonderful Christmas episode. Let's do Halloween. Something bizarre like Miles telling a kind of ghost story that was strange and interesting.

Joe Dougherty: I used a Laurie Anderson song, "The Day the Devil" in "Haunting of DAA." I am not sure if is still on the DVDs. The nice looking gentlemen with the beard that is getting fired is Nick Meglin one of the editors from *Mad Magazine*. He gave Ann and I artwork from *thirtysuffering*: a *MAD Magazine* parody. When Mad Magazine spoofed the show. That was it, we were famous now.

Nick Meglin: (*"Nick," Editor of MAD Magazine*): The art Joe mentioned was my personal paste-up from a panel that appeared in the story to which I added my friend Drucker's caricature of me so that it looked like I was one of the stars of the show for my fifteen second appearance. It was Ann who wrote my cameo into the script. I played "Nick the Art Director" who gets fired in a segment directed by Joe. Ann subsequently referred to me in another script where Michael and Elliot mention me as a possible rehire.

This Halloween episode has ghosts and costumes but it really focuses on Michael having to become the boss and fire employees. Courtesy ABC Photography Archives.

Ann Lewis Hamilton: I had sort of forgotten that I had written some of the episodes where Michael and Elliot fall apart a little. I was looking at "The Haunting of DAA" and how Michael is sort of forced to fire people. Michael as what it means to be a boss. That is kind of small but wow, that is really interesting.

MY MAD-VENTURE

BY NICK "NICK" MEGLIN

(Left and right) For Nick's holiday greeting that year, Mort Drucker added his caricature to a copy of his opening panel art. Drawn by Mort Drucker for MAD Magazine. Courtesy of Mort Drucker and Nick Meglin.

As a *MAD Magazine* editor, we have to see movies, TV shows, etc. that capture a wide audience when creating our satires. When we saw the ratings jump on *thirtysomething*, we were confident we had a viable target. When Frank Jacobs, a freelance writer more known for his clever poem and song parodies, finally submitted a brief synopsis that focused on the heavy dosages of baby boomer angst being distributed among the seven major roles (each portrayed by an especially talented actor), *thirtysuffering* was born.

When the satire, brilliantly drawn by *MAD*'s premier caricaturist Mort Drucker, appeared on the stands we received many fan letters and phone messages, but none like the call I received from Ann Hamilton and Joseph Dougherty, two of the top *thirtysomething* writers. It appeared that everyone

connected to the show enjoyed our spoof to the extent that Ann and Joe (both MAD fans since their teen years) wanted to secure the original art as a surprise holiday gift for Edward Zwick and Marshall Herskovitz. As mutual admirers, the three of us had instant rapport, but there was no way to satisfy their wish inasmuch as all original *MAD* art was maintained by the magazine. However, I was able to send them a large print of the opening double page spread to frame for the show's creators.

Once they had received the print, the duo called again to thank me, and they invited me to visit them on the *thirtysomething* set. When I arrived on the set, Timothy Busfield shouted, "The *MAD* guy's here!" and the rehearsal literally stopped dead. Many of the cast members gathered around and I answered as many questions as I could before they had to resume work. I was invited to stay for lunch and attended the first reading of the subsequent week's script later that afternoon. It was a day I'd never forget.

But the saga didn't end there. Several months later, Ann called to tell me that Joe would be directing her next script in which an agency's art director gets fired. Since my gray beard looked "art director-ish," would I like to play the part? I'd even have a line or two of dialogue. I pushed up the date for my next visit and booked plane tickets that night.

I showed up on the set at the required time and was ushered to the section of trailers that had each of the character's names taped to the door: Michael, Hope, Gary, etc. and then saw one that read "Nick" -- how they came up with that name for me is anybody's guess. My own trailer! I was costumed by one person, another sat me down for make-up. As I was ushered onto the set, the extras in their special waiting area stared at me with obvious "Who is this guy?" expressions. I spotted Joe behind a camera and repeated Gloria Swanson's "I'm ready for my close-up, Mr. DeMille" line from *Sunset Boulevard* which he, being a great movie

Nick Meglin got to act with Ken Olin and Tim Busfield in a Halloween episode. Courtesy ABC Photography Archives.

buff, appreciated. I was given a classic director's chair with my real/stage name taped to the back and cracked up when I saw they had placed it between Ken Olin and Timothy Busfield. Being a nervous rookie, Joe wisely prepared me for my first time at bat by telling me that they weren't taping the first run through of my "getting fired" scene and since this was a montage with only music and no voices being recorded, I was to improvise dialogue apropos to my anger at Michael for canning me. I did just that, throwing in a few profanities like any self respecting method actor would do. Joe said, "Thanks, we'll need you back in half an hour for the "Elliot makes nice" scene." The sneaky bastard had the camera going the whole time and felt he had secured what he wanted. Alone, I wondered if I should insist that the publicity department refer to me as "First Take" Meglin and should I sleep with sunglasses on that night? No doubt that the damage had been done -- I had gone Hollywood!

Ann assured me she'd write a "Nick gets rehired" scene in one of the next season's shows, but alas, this was to be the final season. The gang at *MAD* teased me relentlessly afterwards, blaming my performance for the show's demise. They may have been right! As for Ann and Joe, we remain close friends to this day.

■ ■ ■

"The Guilty Party"

Directed by Norman Seeff

Written by Winnie Holzman

November 13, 1990

Winnie Holzman: Marshall and Ed created that Hope went to Princeton. I went to Princeton. She had a daughter. I had a daughter. Her daughter never spoke, but nevermind that. I could identify with Hope. Maybe I was just giving her my traits and Hope wasn't exactly that guilt ridden. I think there is a way that you can feel guilty towards everyone you love because you can feel you are coming up short. I think it started with the party and then it snowballed inside her. It is really hard not to wrestle with guilt as a parent. We had very different relationships with our children than our parents had with us. Everything I wrote with *thirtysomething* was stuff that I was thinking, obsessing and worrying about. That is where "The Guilty Party" came from. That was my spec script. Like any spec script I was writing something that I had no idea what their plans for the show were. I didn't know their inner circle. Once they decided to buy it, which was life changing for me, then I went back in earnest and spoke with Marshall and Ed. I got notes and direction of where to go with it. I came into the job and there is Richard, Joe, Susan, Liberty, Ann, Ed and Marshall. I had to write from my fucking soul. Writers are competitive. I've got to come here to play. I have to show up. I've got to exceed what I even think I can do. It is that whole cliché that if you play tennis with someone that is better than you then you are gonna become a better tennis player. That was my story. Richard is such an incredible writer. He brought me in. I wanted to somehow measure up, so I was working overtime.

"Photo Opportunity"

Directed by Ellen S. Pressman

Written by Racelle Rosett Schaefer

November 27, 1990

Photo Opportunity focuses on Melissa's career and her sister. The casting couldn't have been better than Gale Mayron, Melanie's actual sister. This photo shows them on the set of "Going Limp." Her sister had a cameo in that episode. Courtesy of Melanie Mayron.

Episode

70

"Never Better"

Directed by Ann Lewis Hamilton

Written by Joseph Dougherty

December 4, 1990

Ann Lewis Hamilton *(Director, her directorial debut)*: Ed and Marshall encouraged people to direct. I wanted to do it, but it was very scary because they were really good directors. The fear of failure was big. I knew I didn't want to direct my own script. So, Joe and I switched.

Polly Draper: Joe is such a good writer. That writing is so beautiful. I loved the moment of Billy teaching Ellyn to draw. Then Gary and Ellyn pulled the prank on Michael and Hope to make them think we are sleeping together. There was a kind of a sexual tension, like a teasing thing. Our friendship evolved like it does in life.

Joe Dougherty: Probably, if Ed and Marshall had known the prank was going to be as goofy as it was, there might have been more push back. It had a very retro feel to it. It was a little goofier but I think it is a nice piece of parsley on the plate. That was the year Ann and I traded up. She wrote "Haunting of DAA" and I directed it and I wrote "Never Better" and she directed that. We thought what would happen if we did this?

Polly Draper: I had no idea Erich Anderson (*Billy Side*l) would come back. I think they liked our chemistry together. He was just a one shot deal initially.

Joe Dougherty: Ann and I would sit around and talk about how the series was arguably becoming too articulate and that we both started to think about ways to find a simpler reality between characters. We

"Never Better" has Ellyn falling in love with Billy Sidel. Gary and Ellyn also make Michael and Hope think that they are having an affair in a story that pokes fun at how shows always have male and female friends date. Courtesy of Carol Gepper's TV Guide Collection.

thought about friendship between men and women, how do you play that? How do you be there for someone? How can we depict a friendship between a man and a woman, especially two good looking ones like these were?

Episode **71**

"Guns and Roses"

Directed by Ken Olin

Written by Liberty Godshall

December 11, 1990

Liberty Godshall: I loved this episode. It just keeps on resonating with me on so many levels. I didn't know if Nancy would live or not when I wrote it. I hadn't known anyone who had cancer at that age. I was thirty-one and I hadn't had a friend die. I am not sure the technical aspects are correct but it feels like a journey to touch on the fragility of life and to touch on what makes life matter even more. If I were to write that episode today, I would have more fear and panic for everyone. We know the trail better now.

Patty Wettig: I remember while I was filming Liberty's episode I had come home and went to bed. I woke up after sleeping for a little bit and I thought, "Do I have cancer? Is that real?" It probably only lasted twenty seconds. It wasn't very long. I couldn't remember if it was actually me who had cancer or not. It freaked me out. It was the only time that has ever happened to me as an actor. I went into the office and said, "I don't think I can do this much more." Some place in me kind of crossed over.

Ken Olin: It wasn't until the very end that Patty had a moment of confusing herself and her character. At that point it became enough already. It just became too integrated in her life. But as a director, I loved the visual stuff of a coffin shutting on her. There was no part of me that confused my actual wife dead in a coffin from ovarian cancer with my wife the actress and timing the piece of string to pull the top of the coffin shut in sync with the camera. I just didn't confuse those. If it worked, it was the giddiness of how cool the shot was. It was funny to me to be able to pull off an effective illusion. It was the enjoyment of film making.

The Westins have to face the idea that Nancy may not survive her battle with cancer in an episode that was so real it made Patty start to confuse her character and herself. Courtesy ABC Photography Archives.

Liberty Godshall: I liked using her illness as a way to get back to that little girl who was painting and hiding away under the dining room table. I love the theme that was in "Love and Sex" when Hope witnesses a slice of passionate life. Here, Nancy witnessed a part of Ethan that a mother never sees, a first kiss. I love what you can learn when you eavesdrop on other people's lives. She realized she didn't want to miss anything. She didn't want to give up.

Ken Olin: I became emotional by how moving I found Patty's performance, but there was no part of me that wanted to pull back from it. I wanted to push more to realize all she could do. Some of the scenes she did were so truthful and the size of what she would speak about was amazing. I loved directing those episodes. What a privilege. Part of it was because they were Patty so they would let me direct those episodes. There were a couple of scenes I really helped with, but most of the time I didn't have much to do with her performance. She won a couple of Emmys for it. She did incredible work and was recognized for it. All of the writers got to write about it. Everyone got their shot at it.

Elliot breaks down in the break room at DAA with Michael in "Guns and Roses." Michael wins an award for a commercial while Elliot faces the fear of losing his wife. Liberty chose to have a B story that shows life is rarely fair. Courtesy of Brandy Alexander.

Patty Wettig: I wasn't very self-conscious at the time. I wanted to trust a director that they had an outside eye. When Ken, Scott or Peter directed they were very involved. They were not sitting on the outside and just observing. If Ken directed he watched the scenes while he mouthed the lines along with you.

Liberty Godshall: The B story in that episode was Michael winning an award because life is so unfair. That is how it happens sometimes. It would be great if success was traded off between those who deserve it. A lot of times success begets success by the mere fact of it. It is not fair but really true.

Joe Dougherty: I miss "The Water Is Wide" by Karla Bonoff on the DVDs. I think that song, in so many ways, was the true feeling of what we were doing. I have a hard time listening to that song without crying. The first couple of years they were only buying music rights for ten years. Maybe that is a statement of how long they thought we would last.

Liberty Godshall: I was so disappointed that was my favorite song on earth. I always picked my songs. I was emotionally waiting for it when I recently watched it and then it wasn't there. I am sure that Karla would want it on the episode.

Episode 72

"Happy New Year"

Directed by Victor Du Bois

Written by Richard Kramer

December 18, 1990

Richard Kramer: One of my favorite shows that we did was "Happy New Year." An act of it was based on *The Dead* (1914) by James Joyce. I remember that Polly Draper and I went to see the movie and we were blown away by it. What that episode is about is the ultimate unknowability of other people. Michael has to accept that there is a part of Hope's life that he has no access to. That episode is about privacy. It is about allowing someone to keep a part of themselves to themselves and that is a loving act.

David Marshall Grant (*Russell*): All the actors were firing on full cylinders at that point. It was a great feeling to be integrated in that world. Everyone was so astonishing on that show. It just holds up as an honest portrayal of human beings. I knew it was my last episode and it was bittersweet for me.

Richard Kramer: Constraints are very freeing if you use them right. We had gone over budget on the two previous episodes. We were always conscious about being responsible because it wasn't our money. They told me just write it all in one house because we didn't have any money. That freed me in a way. I can't get out of this house, but how do I make it interesting to not be able to get out of this house. That is much more interesting than do anything you want.

Tim Busfield: One of my favorite episodes was the New Year's episode where Nancy didn't come to the party at Michael's. Elliot showed up with a bottle of tequila and by the end of the episode Michael had to take

The show became available on DVD in 2009. Many of the episodes have commentaries as well as interviews with the cast. Some of the original music has been changed on the DVDs due to legal rights. Courtesy of Shout Factory/Scott Ryan's Collection.

him home. I loved the opportunity to play a character who was a blackout drunk. I sat on a staircase talking to Mary Kay Place (*Played Patsy Klein*) where I took a shot of apple juice. I made it sort of bounce like tequila can do back up to your Adam's apple. I made the camera operator go outside and throw up.

Richard Kramer: A good actor is a good custodian of their role. We used to warn outside directors not to come in with any preconceived ideas because the actors are not going to go for it. They know their characters better than your shot plans. The idea that Elliot was a child of an alcoholic is certainly something we might have set up in the first season and then forgot it. But Timmy would remember it because they were so alert to who they were.

Tim Busfield: Elliot certainly was the child of an alcoholic in the sense that he was trying to please everyone. So much of the fun of Elliot was pushing the envelope on boy behavior. Elliot was a step back in humanity for me. He faced some sort of drinking confrontation and he had to stop at some point. Playing a drunk on *thirtysomething* had to be totally different than a drunk on any other show because it had to be really, really real.

Richard Kramer: I remember how amazing it was to go down to see that winter landscape where they don't have snow. I could just put it down on paper and it would be done so beautifully. It just freed your imagination.

Brandy Alexander (*Production Designer*): The snow was a combination of snow blankets, plastic, and snow shavings. Since I grew up in New York, I was always appalled when effects people would shoot the snow foam and it would stick under the branches. I said, "No, snow comes from the sky and falls down, it doesn't shoot up from the ground." I did a lot of hands on work whether it was snow or leaves because I wanted it to look like my childhood did. We had a great efficient crew.

Richard Kramer: I remember vividly Mary Kay Place standing on the ledge listening to the cast sing "In My Life." That brings back her entire memory. She plays that without a word.

Episode 73

"Melissa and Men"

Directed by Randall Miller

Written by Winnie Holzman

January 8, 1991

Winnie Holzman: "Melissa and Men" is my favorite episode, for sure. The way Marshall, Ed and Richard placed a Jewish woman on the screen at that time in a way that was so complex. She was not reductive or a stereo-type. I don't know if that has ever been done again.

Melanie Mayron: It was so groundbreaking in a way. There still aren't many stories that have a Jewish girl as the main character. It is great that it got to happen.

Winnie Holzman: It meant so much to me as a Jewish woman watching it, seeing the way they let her be a real person. They let her be sexual, be attractive but also have doubts about that. It was so beautiful and inspiring to me.

Melanie Mayron: Winnie's writing was magnificent. I remember the line when Melissa looks in the mirror and says, "I'm old." Someone in their thirties looks at herself and thinks she isn't twenty anymore so she is old. I can't believe I said that line then. What would I say now? I've earned it now, but not then? That is Winnie's writing. Who writes that honestly? She wrote Melissa so well. That episode is really the history of all Melissa's lovers. It was something that just doesn't get done on television.

Winnie Holzman: I like the fight that Gary and Melissa had. If you lose a friend suddenly it's often how it is. The last interaction was not that good. That could be a gift for Melissa. I picture that for the rest of her

Melissa's love life and her art is the focus of what Winnie Holzman calls her favorite script, "Melissa and Men." Melanie Mayron had to play many sides of Melissa from comic relief, to fantasies, to heart breaking fights like the one she has with Gary in this episode. Courtesy of Kenneth Zunder.

life when she cares about someone she will let them know. She won't walk away from someone and not say, "I love you." I like that entire script.

Melanie Mayron: I didn't know that those fights would be my last scenes with Gary.

Ellen Pressman (*Producer*): The photography that we presented as Melissa's work was a photographer that I found named Deborah Roundtree. That was one of my jobs to find the artist. Her work was really interesting because it wasn't just straight photography.

Melanie Mayron: Winnie Holzman is such a great writer and you know, she wrote the book for *Wicked*. I've seen it five times.

Episode 74

"Advanced Beginners"

Directed by Deborah Reinisch

Written by Liberty Godshall and Winnie Holzman

January 22, 1991

Liberty Godshall (*Played Madison, co-wrote script*): I just had fun writing this off-beat free spirited girl. Marshall and Ed kept saying they couldn't find anyone to do the part. The date of the shoot was approaching and it was getting scary. They said, "You don't have the luxury of refusing. You are playing the part." So, that took the onus off it. I was scared to death because I had stopped acting. Polly was so amazing and generous to work with. She was really responsible for anything I did right. She is such a pro.

Polly Draper: Liberty is wonderful. She is a beautiful person and a beautiful writer. Liberty played Billy's old girl friend. We all knew each other very well and it was perfect to have her play that part. I was happy to have her.

Winnie Holzman: I loved Liberty playing Madison. She was wonderful in that part. We didn't sit in a room and write together. She must have started the script and asked me to finish it. I can't imagine why else that would have happened. I think I did write a lot of that script. I loved writing Madison.

"Sifting the Ashes"

Directed by Martin Nicholson

Written by W.H. Macy, Steven Schachter and Joseph Dougherty

February 5, 1991

Tim Busfield: The actor has to be open to whatever direction the writers want to take a character in. I have this conversation as an executive producer with young actors who say, "My character wouldn't do this." I say, "Hey, I didn't know on *thirtysomething* that I was Catholic until year four. I didn't know that my wife and I would get back together. I didn't know we'd have to play a cancer story. I didn't know any of that when we started." I think it's really important that the actor stay open to the writer's muse.

Joe Dougherty: I remember getting flack for Elliot saying to Michael, "I have forgiven you for killing my lord." in an earlier episode so his religion was there. William H. Macy and Steven Schachter wrote the first draft. I never even met them. Ed and Marshall asked me to rewrite it. I think I added the Catholic part because "Father Tierney" was the name of the priest in my parish in Long Island. I may have been driving that bus a little bit. Part of that episode was me working through my Catholic stuff. His faith came out of trying to figure out what was going on with Nancy. I think Elliot's mother was drinking in their draft and I put her in the program.

Tim Busfield: I told them my mom was an alcoholic and Eileen Brennan (*Played Elliot's Mother*) showed up and she was an alcoholic. You had to be really careful what you told them. She was a great actor. She listened to you. Actors that are really good listeners end up being great film actors. I really did luck out with her as my mom and Eddie Albert as my dad.

Joe Dougherty: What good is Catholic guilt? Can you show Elliot pray? Can you show him talk about this? You just didn't ask those questions on television at that time. Father Tierney (*Richard Brestoff*) talked about faith not being a salad bar and you were either in or you are out. He paraphrased C.S. Lewis with you really do not know how strong your faith is until it is a matter of life and death. Then Elliot says, "I can't come back." Father says, "How long can you stay outside?" There is a lot in that episode I like. I know Ann and I talked about the way to pull off talking about faith was to start with someone who you would never suspect. Who would initially be embarrassed to admit it.

Tim Busfield: I was not raised Catholic. I was raised as a sort of soft Christian like so many Americans and my views by that point had already leaned more to the Eastern philosophy. To play a character who was searching for an answer was fantastic. I understood it. It was deep and fun to play.

Joe Dougherty: I think there was an awareness of where we were going with Elliot. I know Ann's decision to do the scene with Elliot in the stall in the following episode was her decision. She wanted to do that right. I must have finished writing "Sifting the Ashes" and then immediately started on "Fighting The Cold." I don't know how I physically could have done that. I guess I was younger then.

Episode 76

"Second Look"

Directed by Ken Olin

Written by Ann Lewis Hamilton

February 12, 1991

Peter Horton: A friend of mine sent me the article from the February 12, 2016, *Washington Post*. I opened it up and saw this picture of myself from *thirtysomething*. I thought I had been in a time warp, then I read the article. It was twenty-five years ago to the day. "Second Look" is kind of a beacon on that show. The idea really came out of the fact that I wanted to be a director more than an actor.

Scott Winant: Ed and Marshall wanted to be honest about the cancer situation. They were intending for Nancy to die. That was the approach that we all agreed on. We started to see that people were invested in Nancy's health.

Joe Dougherty: I think early on in the process Nancy was going to die. The reaction from the audience and from people whose lives had been touched with cancer wanted her to survive. It was very important to a lot of people for a lot of reasons that she survived. I do remember a mid-course correction.

Patty Wettig: You had so many women who were fighting this disease who were writing in saying, "let Nancy live." The writers adjusted the storyline. No one wanted to put out something that would make people going through cancer feel worse.

Scott Winant: Our obligation to the audience was to keep true to what we believed as artists. If they want a happy ending, I don't feel any

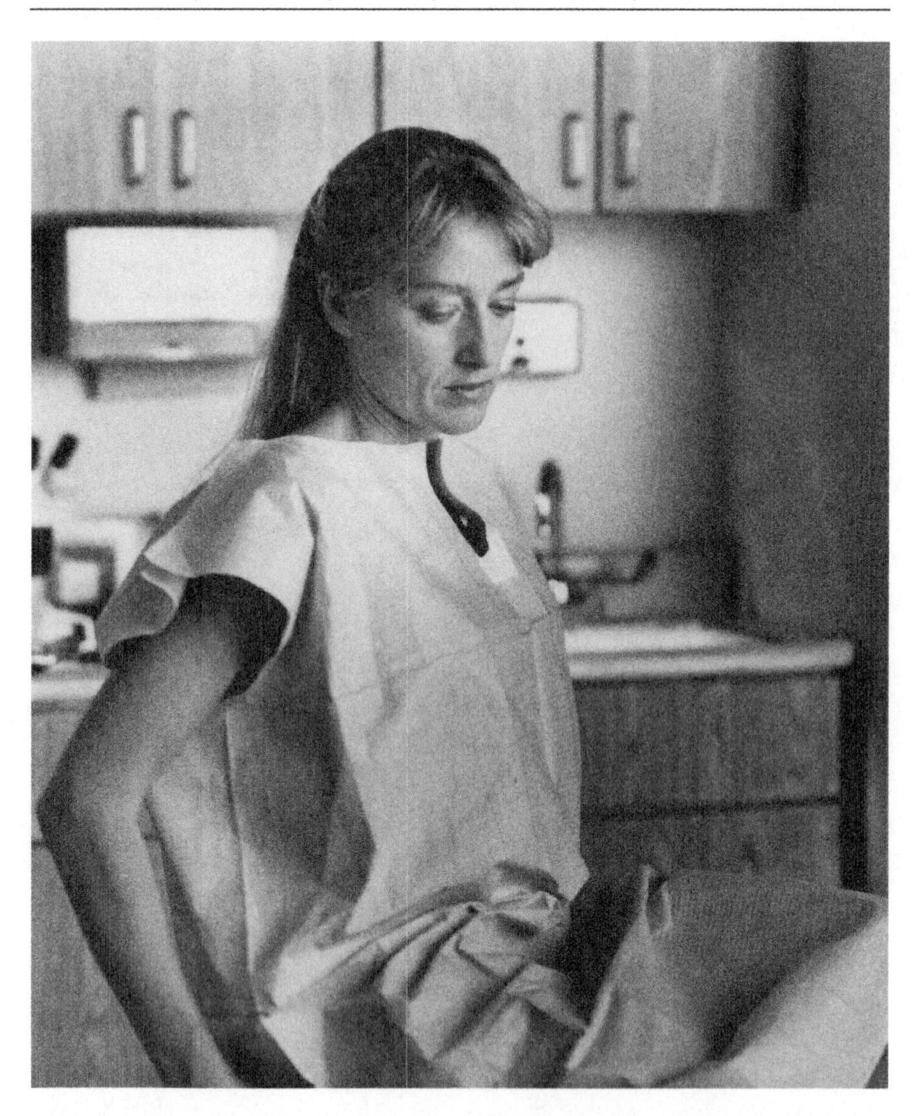

"Second Look" brings the cancer story to a close in a shocking way that is still talked about all these years later. The Washington Post did a 25th anniversary article about this episode in 2016. Courtesy ABC Photography Archives.

obligation to give it to them. We wanted to talk about illness in an honest way. The odds of someone surviving with the kind of cancer that Nancy had was unlikely. It was getting tough because we were getting correspondence from people who were ill who were finding strength in Nancy's ability to fight.

Tim Busfield: I hoped Nancy would die. That's what you wish for as an actor. That's all you really want is stuff to play that's interesting. What isn't interesting is to play the checkout person at the grocery store saying, "Do you have any coupons?"

Joe Dougherty: Her survival became more important for us to deal with than the tragedy of her loss. If that had happened, then it would be a story about Elliot and the kids and that would have been the soap opera. We were enlightened that Nancy should struggle and then survive.

Scott Winant: I remember that it was something that Ed, Marshall, Joe, Ann and Richard really argued about. I think there was one side that felt they shouldn't kill Nancy because it would have devastated the people who had invested in her and another side that said we couldn't be dishonest. We have an obligation to be truthful.

Marshall Herskovitz: We went through a year of agonizing of what to do with Nancy's cancer. Whether we had a responsibility to people who had cancer or whether we should even care about that as artists. We had so many talks about whether she should live or die. The solution was to have Gary die. We always knew that someone would die. We realized this was a solomonic solution. We would save Nancy, but that someone else would have to die.

Patty Wettig: At the beginning of the third year they told me I would die halfway through the fourth year. I wouldn't be back for the fifth year. We did the whole third year thinking I would die. I certainly had nothing to do with them deciding to take out Gary.

Marshall Herskovitz: We figured out of all the people that Horton would be the most okay with dying because he wanted to be a director. Early in the fourth season we called Peter. "We have something to say, we are not forcing this on you. We want to get your feelings on this. We are thinking of having your character die." He was worried that it was something about him. He wanted to think about it and then said, "Yes, I am game." Then it became a big thing about keeping it a secret.

Scott Winant: Now here is the truth of what happened. This was us being loose cannons. The network and the studio were told that Nancy was going to die. Although conversations had been had with Patty Wettig about exiting the show early, a new set of conversations had to start with Peter Horton privately. We wrote an episode where Nancy died. We gave that script to the network and to the studio. We held an act of the script that nobody saw, even people on the crew didn't see it.

Ed Zwick: We decided we would spare one person while the other was cruelly taken. That was another expression of that very painful reckoning that we had during the emotional year that Marshall and I had back in the early eighties.

Brandy Alexander (*Production Designer*): We actually shot in a real morgue in a closed down hospital in a really bad neighborhood. When we were scouting, we weren't sure who was actually going to die. The ac-

Ann Lewis Hamilton (Writer) and Ken Olin (Director) were both nominated for Emmys for their work on "Second Look". Tim Busfield won for Best Supporting Actor in a Drama. Courtesy of Carol Gepper's TV Guide Collection.

tor's didn't know. Ken said, "I want to get up on the table, let my character die." They knew whoever died was going to get more attention. The actors wanted to have the juicier part.

Joe Dougherty: We had some security problems. Ed wrote some phony scenes that killed another character just in case it got out. He enjoyed that part tremendously.

Ed Zwick: I think I wrote it in a night. It was like automatic writing. I just blasted something out. I am sure it was as horrible as anything could possibly be. I just decided releasing misinformation would be a great thing to do to people who wanted to steal our thunder.

Peter Horton: We were trying desperately to keep it out of the press. It was in the wind that someone was going to die and everyone thought it was Nancy. They wrote a dummy script that leaked that Polly got hit by a bus or something.

Polly Draper: We were sworn to secrecy. They put out a fake script that said Nancy died. So everyone was mourning her already and then she is fine, but oops, your friend dies.

Scott Winant: The boys, being that they were really courageous, didn't tell anybody. They just went ahead and wrote an alternate ending. We didn't really release the new pages until we were in production on the episode and that is what we shot. It all came to a head. I think at that point ABC and MGM were just happy that it worked. I really got spoiled because network notes are really the bane of my existence and why I don't do broadcast network pilots anymore. At least I try not to because it is hard to tolerate their notes. On *thirtysomething* the notes were minimal. There was so much respect for what the boys did.

Patty Wettig: When I sat down to read "Second Look," I knew Gary was going to die. We were a little ahead of it. Seldom did we get a script that we weren't a little privy to by then.

Melanie Mayron: We all found out at the table reading. We sat down and started to read the script and, oh my God, during that hour we all found out that Gary died. It was unbelievably shocking.

Ann Lewis Hamilton (*Writer*): I think "Second Look" was my favorite script that I wrote because it was written after I had been on the show for a long time and I knew the characters. We would do outlines with Ed and Marshall and by then it was such shorthand. We knew what was gonna happen. Nancy was going to have surgery, it was going to be good news, Gary was gonna die and we would have to deal with that. It was really simple. The outline was like a page. I have a vague memory that when the first cut came in it was like fifteen minutes too long. A lot of scenes had to be edited out.

Ken Olin (*Director*): We were all supported when we directed. So, it wasn't the pressure that a guest director would have felt. Whatever pressure there was came from within. We had all done so much together it was like a band. Mel didn't come in and try to compete with a riff that Tim and I did in a scene any more than I would have tried to tell her how to feed the baby or move around the kitchen set. It was a band that had been together for four years.

Ann Lewis Hamilton: There were more scenes with Nancy and her children before she had the surgery. There was a scene with Gary on the phone talking to Susannah and reading *Goodnight Moon* to his daughter.

Peter Horton: I remember distinctly when we shot the last scene on the porch. I knew it was the last scene I would be alive on the show. I had conflicting feelings about it by then. I really did have to bury that in my system. I knew that moment would be significant and remembered. I didn't want to tip it. I wanted the surprise to land. It was hard to do. It was sad and a lot of emotions were going on that couldn't be there. It had to just state the facts.

Ken Olin: No one was going to play the first half hour with any extra weight. We all would have known not to tip that Gary was going to die in that episode because we were all in sync. The thing for me as a director was how do I illuminate those aspects?

Melanie Mayron: In the script they didn't write a reaction for Melissa. The piano bench was the only opportunity. It was silent and she sat at the piano. I knew that the last time she was with Gary they threw plates at each other. They were so angry. I just felt she would be so guilt ridden.

I thought it had to be all of that at once coming like a flood.

Ann Lewis Hamilton: Melanie had such a great face. She killed me in "Second Look." It was all Melanie because she didn't have any lines when she sat at the piano, she just cried. I think that was in the original script. That scene really hurt because she and Gary were kind of in a bad spot and she didn't get to say goodbye.

close up

THIRTYSOMETHING (CC)
10 PM 7

SECOND LOOK

First came the shock of discovery. Then came the trials of the operation and chemotherapy. Now Nancy (Patricia Wettig) awaits the verdict of her biopsy results as she faces her second-look cancer surgery.

Ken Olin (who plays Michael) directed the episode. Gary: Peter Horton. Elliot: Timothy Busfield. Dr. Karen Silverman: Patricia Heaton. Hope: Mel Harris. Ethan: Luke Rossi. Nurse: Cheryl Carter. Nurse: Kathleen McMartin. Eleanor: Elizabeth Hoffman. Melissa: Melanie Mayron. Ellyn: Polly Draper. Britanny: Lindsay Riddell. (60 min.)

Patricia Wettig

This review in the TV Guide really says nothing because no one knew what was going to happen in this episode. Even the Network and Studio were kept in the dark until the last moment. They wanted no one to know what the twist ending would be. Courtesy of Carol Gepper's TV Guide Collection.

Melanie Mayron: It's an actor's moment and Ken let me have it. That was what was terrific about having Ken direct. He knew to just stay there for what was happening and give it the time.

Ann Lewis Hamilton: Ed and Marshall were very democratic in how they would hand out big scripts. It was kind of the luck of the draw that I got to kill Gary. My dad had died ten years earlier and I never liked on television when death is too Bergman. I wanted to write about the simplicity of it. I wanted people to say, "Gary's dead. Gary's been killed." When my father died very suddenly of a heart attack, there was not a lot to say except, "My father died." It was the simplicity of the lines that I really like.

Tim Busfield: I absolutely loved that scene that Kenny shot in the bathroom when Elliot broke down in the stall. I haven't seen it in twenty years, but I remember a lot of it.

Ken Olin: The morning after it aired, I went to drop off my kids at school and Steven Spielberg was there dropping off his son. He said, "Hey, Ken, that was a really good shot in the bathroom last night." That was cool. He wasn't like, "Gary died, what the hell?" He just mentioned a shot of Tim in the bathroom stall.

Peter Horton: There was a scene where Michael came to identify the body where I was dressed up in death make up. I was inside of a body bag, inside of an actual morgue drawer. It was awful to shoot it. I got in the bag, they zipped it up, someone slammed the morgue drawer. I layed in the dark and thought, "Ken better open that door and get me out. I am getting a preview of what death is." It was a very creepy feeling to be in there. Ken did a good job of directing that episode. It was demanding for him as an actor as well as a director. He ended up fulfilling both roles pretty well.

Ken Olin: Originally, Scott was going to direct, but he wanted to direct Jill Gordon's next script and I wanted to direct "Second Look," so we switched. The night that I decided to do the phone call in one shot was one of those times I could feel my whole body vibrate. I tried to figure out how to do it in a way where the experience of that phone call would translate emotionally. If I did it in one, then the emotional evolution of the shot would be the emotional evolution that Michael went through.

Patty Wettig: When Ken got the phone call about Gary dying, he asked if I would watch to make sure his acting was okay. He did the scene, looked at me and I said, "Nuh-uh. Come here, Ken. I know you are directing and you've got another scene to get to and you are filled up with everything. This is a pivotal moment. You need to find this within yourself, completely. You can't act this. This moment matters."

Ken Olin: Did Patty tell you about my acting in this shot? I figured she did, she usually does. I said to Patty, "Can you be there?" Normally, I wouldn't need that because we had playback. She was watching and I remember doing it and it was technically right. Everything that needed to be done was done. I walked over to the monitor and she said that. It was a moment of going, "Yes, it is a very cool shot, but now you need to stop being a director and be an actor because you are not there." It had

Patty Wettig was there to assist Director, Ken Olin, with his acting in "Second Look." She felt Ken was focusing on the shot more than the emotion. Ken tried again and nailed it in an emotionally charged scene at the hospital. Courtesy of the Dan Steadman Collection. US Magazine.

to be done so elegantly and simply. I had pulled off the camera work, but not the acting.

Patty Wettig: I just remember willing that moment for him. He took a few minutes. He walked away and then came back. He did the scene again and it was beautiful.

Ann Lewis Hamilton: I think that episode was directed so well. Ken's performance is so good. I still don't know how he directed it and gave that performance. Patty is fantastic. I like that Mel Harris sort of chooses denial and anger. Tim Busfield just kills me.

Tim Busfield: I did submit it for my Emmy award that I won. They put it on the Emmy certificate that you get for a nomination.

Ann Lewis Hamilton: When they find out Nancy was gonna be okay and Michael and Elliot were in the hospital room, I wrote dialogue for them to basically say they were so happy. Ed and Marshall said, "No, that is not the way men behave." Men say, "God dammit, she's not gonna die, now I can't run off with a cheerleader. That sucks." It is another great example of how, on some shows, no one would say that. They would just rewrite you or it would go on the air wrong. But they were like, "No, this is male behavior."

Patty Wettig: When I turned away from the window and say it is just an empty parking lot. I can barely even say that line now. (*Starts to tear up*). You don't think those moments remain in you but it is still in there. I couldn't speak those words not even once before we filmed it. It felt like all four years came down to the moment when she turns from the window and tells Elliot that she is cancer free. That was a moment that I don't think anyone else could play the same way. It isn't like a film where you only have six weeks. We had lived with those characters for four years. It felt like the complexity of four years and all the layers of this marriage.

Ann Lewis Hamilton: Ed was especially brilliant. Ed said, "It would be fabulous if we see Gary and Nancy linked at the beginning of the episode." We added the scene where Gary goes over to pick up the children's books. Ed said, "It would be great to find a children's book that has an applicable quote in it." I went to Ed and said. "I was thinking about the quote at the end of *Through The Looking Glass*. I mean, I like it but, you know, it is kind of obvious. Maybe it is dumb. In a wonderland they lie dreaming as the days go by." I read that to Ed and I thought he was going to yell at me and say it was horrible. Ed said nicely, "You're an idiot. It's perfect."

Peter Horton: I remember I got on my bike and rode away. It was very cold. One of the last times it was ever cold in Los Angeles. I have so many people thinking I died in a bicycle accident because the last scene was me riding away on a bike. I've had to correct that for twenty-five years.

The last image we see of Gary is him riding his bike, but his death is actually a car crash. Courtesy of Carol Gepper's TV Guide Collection.

Ken Olin: Gary riding the bike at the end was not scripted. I wanted there to be an image of Gary at the end that was life affirming. When you said Gary was killed in a car, I even thought he was killed on a bike. Which is so fucked up. So even I mixed it up. Now, I am wondering if maybe I shouldn't have put the last shot of him riding a bike.

Ann Lewis Hamilton: I really like how everybody thinks he died on the bike. I still have people telling me, "He was riding his bike." I say, "No, he was in a car accident." People forget that. But I do like the idea that viewers and Michael, at first, think he was on the bike.

Ken Olin: When a viewer is watching the episode that last image resonates in the way it was intended. I don't think the last shot is confusing. They see that last image and don't think about the words, they think about Gary on a bicycle. It is the memory. Michael says very clearly to Hope that Gary was killed by driving a car. The intention of that was something that I added. I wanted that image while she is reciting *Alice In Wonderland*. I wanted the image that we would remember Gary by to be a beautiful image.

Ann Lewis Hamilton: The last scene in the original script was Nancy and Elliot walking away and it didn't end with Gary. I think that it is absolutely perfect to end with Gary on the bike. That is a great example of the collaboration I had with Ken.

Ken Olin: That shot to me is who that character was. It is a beautiful shot. I felt like it was emotionally ironic. We also haven't seen Gary. We weren't going to show him dead in the car. As a coda, doing that is more emotional. Seeing him that way, you would feel how much he would be missed. Even though Steven Spielberg didn't mention that to me. He

"Second Look" may be the ultimate tearjerker of an episode. Patty Wettig couldn't rehearse her lines before filming in fear she would break down. She got choked-up just discussing this episode twenty-five years later. Courtesy of ABC Photography Archives. The Lisa Mercado Fernandez Collection.

didn't say, "What was that shot at the end? I thought he died in a car crash?" (*Laughs*)

Ann Lewis Hamilton: Peter was ready to be dead and then I think he started to realize what it meant. It was very sad. I have some hate mail saying, "How could you kill Gary Shepherd, shame on you!"

Peter Horton: When Gary died, there was a six month period of time when I got a sense of what it must have been like to be Michael Jordan. There was this onslaught of emotional attention. People had really been quite shocked and moved by it. It is an odd blessing to be the guy who died on *thirtysomething*.

Melanie Mayron: The night that "Second Look" aired was the only time we all got together to watch. Everyone came over to my bungalow in East Hollywood. We had a pasta dinner, some wine and watched it together. It was the first time we got to see it and there we were all together. It was a really special night.

Peter Horton: I had this weird sensation when it aired. We had shot the show. I couldn't tell them all. I was sworn to secrecy by Ed and Marshall, but I couldn't quite help it. We decided to gather at Melanie's house. Tim Busfield turned to me while watching and said, "I have this weird feeling like we are all in an airplane that it is going down and one of us just jumped out with a parachute." It was an odd moment. I wanted it but when it happened, it was a moment of real sadness and second guessing. Did I do the right thing?

Polly Draper: Peter was devastated. He kind of suggested that he die. He thought it would be kind of fun and then he was crushed. I remember he said to me, "You are not mourning me enough. Everyone is talking about me and all you say is 'come to my wedding.' You really should be mourning me more."

Peter Horton: Ellyn definitely wasn't sad enough. She hadn't really fulfilled the sadness of the moment.

Patty Wettig: I think the cancer storyline took off much more than they had expected. That it would affect people as much as it did. I don't think cancer had been explored in such an intimate way before. The writing of those episodes were all incredible. Every writer who wrote about it went into a deep place and I was grateful. As an actor, these episodes are among my favorites that I ever acted in. I was the lucky recipient of such beautifully written scripts.

Winnie Holzman: The day after it aired. There was a tiny coffee shop near Radford where I would get a sandwich. There was a lovely and adorable Korean woman behind the counter who had seen me all year and never said a word to me. She said, "Why did you kill Gary?" I didn't even know she knew what I did for a living.

Polly Draper: When Gary died, my father was in New York and my sister was in San Francisco. My sister called my father and said, "Hey, did anything interesting happen on *thirtysomething* tonight?" My father said, "Nah, some guy died, but Polly was barely in it. It was hardly even worth it." Then my sister watched it and found out that Gary died and was like, "Dad, what do you mean nothing happened!" He only cared about my character.

Goodbye, Gary Shepherd

By Peter Horton

It was 11:00 on the night of February 12, 1991. I flopped into the driver's seat of my tin can of a green Land Rover, slammed the door and sat silently. That was it. Gary was officially dead. I knew that because, like millions of other Americans that night, I had witnessed it. Had just seen it on TV at Melanie Mayron's house, along with the rest of the *thirtysomething* cast. In fact, we had all gathered there to witness it together: clutching and savoring the last few moments of normalcy in the world of Westons, Steadmans, Warrens and, yes, Shepherds. Because tonight Gary was officially gone. Killed in a car crash on the Schuylkill on his way to celebrate the good news of Nancy's recovery.

From the moment I had heard the plans to kill off Gary, through the desperate attempts to keep the news from the press, even through the actual shooting of the episode, I had held it like a dream, a concept, a cool TV shocker, even a career choice to finally get back to directing full time. But now, as I sat in my car, it crash-landed in my gut. Like, well, a death. This goofy, earnest, lovable guy I had the privilege and sheer joy of playing these last four years, was gone. And to my great surprise, I, too, was heartbroken.

These days my 14-year-old daughter needs a vintage jacket to go with her retro Halloween costume of a girl from the '90s. She asks if I have something she could borrow from that "old" show I used to be on? So I open my guest room closet door, reach in, and as I pull out Gary's green and tan baseball jacket, musty and slightly moth eaten, I still feel that tinge in my gut. That wisp of an ache. I guess I'll always miss Gary Shepherd, and for that, I couldn't be more grateful.

"Fighting the Cold"

Directed by Joseph Dougherty

Written by Joseph Dougherty

February 19, 1991

Joe Dougherty: I have a strange sense of knowing what Ann wanted to do in "Second Look" with Elliot. I know that Ann and I talked about his faith which would have influenced "Sifting the Ashes." There was an awareness of where we were going. If you look at Elliot from "Legacy" on, it was all about taking stuff away from him and seeing what was left. There was a logical progression from "Sifting The Ashes" to what he said to Michael about faith in the basement in "Fighting the Cold." After these two episodes, our stock line was Ann killed Gary and I buried him.

Ann Lewis Hamilton and Joe Dougherty worked closely on the three episodes that take Elliot from a passive catholic to an active one. Today they edit an online writing magazine called Hot Valley Writers. Courtesy of Ann Lewis Hamilton.

Patricia Kalember (*Susannah*): I think it was one of my favorite episodes to do. It was written so well and came naturally to be able to play it. She didn't confront the world the way most people did. Joe did such a brilliant job of writing someone who had so much going on that they can't show anything.

Melanie Mayron: It is interesting when women share a man. They both have intimate knowledge of someone and of each other as well. Every actor has a different process, I was just zeroing in on where I thought Melissa would be.

Joe Dougherty: That was the only scene in the series between Melissa and Susannah. Melissa was so furious that there wasn't even a scene where she talks to the woman. I just love Patricia in that scene. She did things in there that are just, oh boy. The thing about not being able to finish a sentence and her pushing the door in Michael and Hope's room. I remember how happy Patricia was when I told her Susannah started smoking again.

Patricia Kalember: I have three kids so imagining loss isn't that difficult, but what is really difficult is imagining the loss and then not being able to show it. You just know if someone touches you, you will be on the floor. They would cut and I would have to go cry and then pull it back together.

Joe Dougherty: The axiom is don't have the actors cry because you want the audience to cry. In that episode there is no weeping. It just happens. They can't contain it, so it leaks out their eyes. I couldn't see Polly's tears on the monitor, so I didn't know she'd started to cry during her speech until I said cut and walked onto the set.

Patricia Kalember: If you don't let yourself cry it will drive you crazy. Susannah is not exhibiting normal behavior. It is very difficult to take care of her.

Joe Dougherty: I remember the slate and I printed the first two takes of everything when they moved over to the window seat. They just knew what it was. Melissa and Susannah sat on that window seat, they didn't need anything. They barely needed a camera. I wanted to save the tear for the end when you saw Susannah through the window. It was the best directing that I did on the show. I played Snuffy (*Music Composer*) the Charles Ives song "The Unanswered Question." I wanted the score to feel like that. It was nothing like "The Unanswered Question." I just wanted that kind of longing. None of the original themes were in this episode. It was all new music. There was one cue too many in there. I didn't want music under Susannah saying, "He changes you and then he goes." I remember Ellen Pressmen saying, "You need a cue under there." Part of me thinks it was a little too on the nose. It bothers me less now than it did then.

Patricia Kalember: They let the writers write their own voice, who they felt the characters were. Richard's writing is gonna have a different voice than Joe or Ann's. They let them express themselves as writers which is why everyone liked working on the show.

Joe Dougherty: There's a theatricality which is sometimes missing from television drama. I didn't want to just cut into flashbacks. I wanted the light to lead it. Which is why when you are on Nancy's face, you hear it first. Nancy watches them come in the back door. I changed the light on her face first because I wanted to put her in the light that came with the scene. I remember walking into Ed and Marshall's office and I said, "I don't think we can do the main title." I told them, "I would like to do a new set of credits with a different theme." They said, "Go do it." If they had to explain that to the network I never heard anything about it. They understood why I wanted to do it.

Episode

78

"The Difference Between Men and Women"

Directed by Timothy Busfield

Written by Winnie Holzman

February 26, 1991

Tim Busfield: Ed and Marshall told me, "William Wyler said mood spelled backwards is doom and we just 'mooded' the show in a hole. Between 'Second Look' and 'Fighting the Cold' we have to pull the audience back out. So stupid, light, comedy, pedestrian transitions is what we need." I felt like, "Guys, I want to do our show." I don't think this episode will go in anyone's top eight-four list. Ed might have done a really good job with it. I didn't feel like I had crushed it. I do like having Chris Mulkey (*Billy's friend, George*). I think he did a great job of making that dark world of a bachelor party. I remember Ed liked how I blocked Ellyn pulling Billy's boots off while they are having an argument. Erich and Polly were great in that scene.

Winnie Holzman: I think there is a psychological trip to it. When something happens in your inner circle you do go into shock and it is quite a while before you are dealing with it. We have Michael think he sees Gary. It never occurred to me when writing it that I should be concerned that it is after the funeral. I was just trying to write it as real as I could. I don't remember that episode as clearly as some of the others, maybe that is the reason.

Episode 79

"The Wedding"

Directed by Scott Winant

Written by Jill Gordon

April 9, 1991

Scott Winant: I composed that entire opening sequence and montage to "Going To The Chapel of Love" by The Dixie Cups. That song is controlled by Phil Spector. They don't license that song. I was getting freaked out because I really didn't want to go with another song. So, I personally was calling on it all the time. They said, "Look, unless you talk directly to Phil Spector, you are never going to get the rights to it." We were already

Jill Gordon wrote the wedding script that is told as a flashback. Her husband, Scott Winant, directed the hour. It ends with a musical montage to the Ray Charles classic, "Come Rain or Come Shine." Courtesy of Kenneth Zunder.

Ellyn's wedding takes place at Michael and Hope's house. Cast members can be spotted in attendance in this never before seen photo from Ken Zunder. Courtesy of Kenneth Zunder.

up to the sound mix of that episode and I still didn't have the rights. I mixed it in anyway. Generally we had an eight day turn around before it was actually on the air and I had nothing in the show other than "Going to the Chapel." Through sweet talking his secretary, I got Phil on the phone and got the rights. We negotiated a no perpetuity deal on that song and that is why it ended up getting pulled out of the DVD.

Jill Gordon: (*Writer*): It was challenging to work with Scott. I was so thrilled when he finally got his first break to direct on *thirtysomething* and I was always his biggest fan, until he directed one of my episodes. While I still remained his biggest fan, I quickly came to the conclusion that it would probably be better for us to live as husband and wife, rather than work together as director and writer. I'm delighted to say, we are still married all these years later.

Polly Draper: I had no idea Erich Anderson (*Billy Seidel*) would come back. I didn't know that I would get married at the end of the show. They didn't really tell us much.

Scott Winant: I can't remember if it was a plan in bringing him back. People were so invested in our characters. When Ellyn got married, there were people who had invested in her being single and felt it was a betrayal.

Patricia Kalember: I came back for that shot of me attending the wedding. At that point, I was doing *Sisters* so they had to squeeze me in. I remember going for the day.

Ellyn and Billy get married making her one of the few characters that actually gets a storybook happy ending as the series starts to wrap up. Courtesy ABC Photography Archives.

Richard Kramer: We had to recast Ellyn's mother. My guess would be that Betsy Blair lived in England and we might not have had the money to bring her back.

Corey Parker (*Lee*): The show I left for didn't get picked up. They offered to bring me back to *thirtysomething*. Richard told me that Melissa and Lee would get married and have a kid. I was so excited. Then two days later, it was announced *thirtysomething* would not be picked up.

Scott Winant: I love the Ray Charles song "Come Rain Or Come Shine" and I love Polly. She was so beautifully emotive in that scene. Unfortunately montages take forever. You have to set up all these different angles and you never have enough time to do it. We were working in the days of film so every time you attempted a speed change to slow motion down you had to make sure you have the proper camera body so that you can over crank the film. Very complicated stuff you can do now without much effort at all.

Polly Draper: I had so many people calling up asking me where I got that wedding dress and those earrings. The phone was ringing off the hook. There was a lot of sweetness on that day. I loved when Scott Winant directed episodes because he had such love for the characters. Those two were a nice match. Billy was a kind of down to Earth guy and wouldn't put up with a lot shit from Ellyn.

Episode 80

"Closing the Circle"

Directed by Richard Kramer

Written by Paul Monette and Richard Kramer

April 16, 1991

Richard Kramer (*Writer, Director*): Paul Monette (*Co-writer*) was HIV positive and he needed to write an episode to keep his insurance active. So, we let him write the first draft of the episode. Then I rewrote it for the episode we shot. The idea was to discuss the aftermath of a death. I wanted to write about mourning and how hard it is to let someone go. I really felt the friendship between Gary and Michael reflected my friendship with Ed. It wasn't something I was conscious of back then.

Ed Zwick: Of course I am that person and Richard is that person, but so is Marshall. Hope is also all of the different women who worked on that show. We found the personal in every possible moment to let it form the fiction. If that helped Richard to write and capture that emotion then for that moment it was true.

Peter Horton: I was off the show by then, but here I was back and playing this part where I was only in Michael's head which pained me to no end because I had to be Ken Olin's imagining. It was this sad slow goodbye to the show.

Richard Kramer: How is Michael dealing and how is he gonna let Gary go? I remember Ken and I crying when we shot the goodbye scene with Gary. For whatever private reasons, it just got us. Peter and Ken had such a warmth between them personally. They were not just actors coming in and saying lines. There was a removal of a barrier between character and actor.

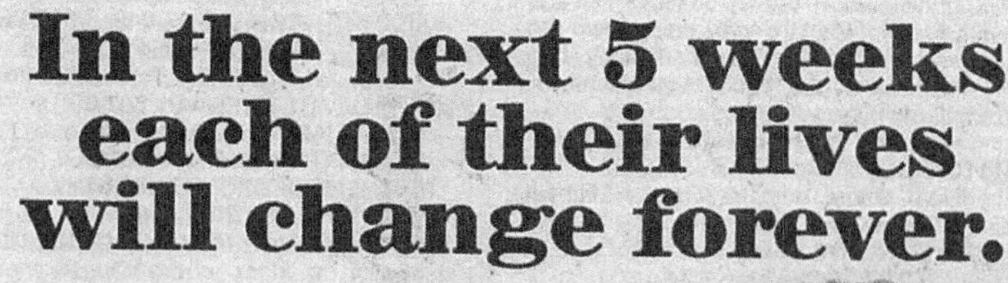

With five episodes to go, ABC started to promote the end of the season. At that point, no one knew it would turn out to be the final five episodes of the series. Courtesy of Carol Gepper's TV Guide Collection.

Ken Olin: That last year was tough except for the directing which I was really into. I really liked acting with Peter Frechette in "Closing the Circle." I loved him. That was the one episode I really got it together as an actor. As much as everybody brought a lot to that show for the first couple years, doing it for that long, we were tired. The toughest thing about *thirtysomething* was we could never cut to a car chase. On *Hill Street Blues* we could cut to the car chase. We could only cut to scenes about people and relationships and life. That gets tough.

Richard Kramer: I told Ken when we were filming this episode that I finally figured out what his character was about. Michael was trying to

Gary comes back as a ghost for Michael to say goodbye to. This was Richard Kramer's final full script for the series. He also directed the episode. Courtesy ABC Photography Archives.

figure out how to live his life in an impossible world. When Michael went to Gary's house to help Susannah, that was the first time I figured out what film directing was. The last cut in that scene was to a very wide angle of him outside and she closed the door on him. She had resisted his help in the scene. We pulled way back off the set to get the shot. I wanted to show his incredible isolation. The moment was not about the two people together. It was him realizing he was alone and dwarfed.

Patricia Kalember: I don't remember my last episode very much. How do you end something? How is any ending satisfying? Everybody thinks the end will be a big thing and sometimes it just ends.

Richard Kramer: I realized that at the end of writing *thirtysomething* for four years, that in one way or another I had always written the same story. I think basically every writer has one story within them that they keep trying to excavate without even really knowing that they are doing it. By the time we did the commentaries on the DVDs, it was so many years after and I was able to see a pattern. It shows up in my other work, as well, almost always, hiding like a mouse behind a wall, tiptoeing out when I'm not looking. My subject is acknowledgement, the need for it, how it feels not to receive it, how it can appear in the most unexpected places, and the most surprising ways. I can't get away from it; it knows where I live and it always says "we've met before."

"Out the Door"

Directed by Mel Harris

Written by Ann Lewis Hamilton

April 30, 1991

Ann Lewis Hamilton: The relationship of Elliot and Michael was so interesting. Miles was the devil and he represented everything that you think that you want. Michael had such success. He had everything, and yet he didn't. He was losing Elliot. He was losing one of his best friends.

Elliot finally leaves DAA in Mel Harris' directorial debut, "Out The Door." This leaves Michael behind with Miles . . .for now. Courtesy of Kenneth Zunder.

Michael knew that deep down. He was clinging to "this is what I thought I wanted." Elliot was still kind of immature, but he was trying to follow his heart. Elliot just almost lost his wife. He had reevaluated things and what he thought was important, wasn't.

Mel Harris (*Director, her directorial debut*):: The woman who was supposed to direct "Out The Door" got sick. They called me four days before we started shooting and asked if I could do it. I said, "Of course I can, I am a Harris woman." I did it and had a ball. I loved directing. It challenges other parts of my mind. To have Kenny and Timothy as my stars and going at each other, what more could one ask for? I can't believe I got that one.

Episode 82

"Hopeless"

Directed by Mark Harris

Written by Liberty Godshall

May 7, 1991

Liberty Godshall: When my son was about three, we were going out for dinner and there was a homeless man who came up to us. My son asked, "Where is this man's mom and dad?" I think we have numbed over that reaction now. There are so many homeless people everywhere. There is this tacit agreement to not go into it. That theme was very big in my life but to be frank, I don't think it played well. This episode was such a downer. I did win a Humanitas Prize for writing it.

Episode 83

"A Stop at Willoughby"

Directed by Timothy Busfield

Written by Joseph Dougherty

May 14, 1991

David Clennon (*Miles Drentell*): After the Gulf War, they had the guts to do something that challenged the whole mindset. It was an episode about a guy who was yanked from a beer commercial because he appeared at a protest against the war. The episode explored the relationship between advertising and propaganda.

Miles gives a speech about how advertising links the war to making consumers feel good about buying products. This speech shakes Michael to his core and makes him quit DAA. Courtesy of the Dan Steadman Collection.

Joe Dougherty: Miles's speech about advertising was written during the first Gulf War. That was Miles just basically taking Michael apart. I am very pleased with the speech. During the second Gulf War somebody put it up on Youtube. Clennon and I have spoken about that often over the years. I really wish I had been wrong. I am not that smart. It is not so much that I wrote it, it was that the pen was there to catch it. I am astonished that they let us say it. I have no idea if there was any push back or not. Ed read it and said, "This isn't biting the hand that feeds you, this is ripping it out of the socket." He was so excited to say it like that. He just loved it.

Ed Zwick: We all looked at the show as this sort of bully pulpit. There we were on television able to write what we wanted and no one was giving us notes. We were our own editorial board as to what we should write about. Joe had some very strong points of view. The idea that you could be rhetorical through a character was really fun. The idea that a character could hold forth in that way was good for the character and it was what Joe wanted it to be. It was who Joe was.

Joe Dougherty: I am amazed that the speech is in there. I don't know if you would be allowed to say it today. No one could believe they let us say it. Maybe it worked because it was Miles and he said it in this heightened language. He twists the knife so well by saying, "I thought you knew what you were doing because you were doing it so well." It was a reaction to the Gulf War and today everything is worse. It is just as relevant. It's like being in 1976 and saying *Network* was good but it was a little over the top. To me, Miles was stating the obvious. I just hoped that someone would notice what was happening, but none of it has changed.

Marshall Herskovitz: ABC never communicated with us about the content of our shows. We didn't get notes from them. They never would comment on a speech we had a character give. The only people that ever contacted us were Standards and Practices.

Joe Dougherty: I was so tired when I wrote that episode. Before Miles came to the house, Melissa came out of the kitchen and she had a plate of watermelon. She said, "Where is the gouda?" I was so exhausted at that point that I had no idea what I was writing. I thought, "No one is going to let that line go through." But no, props got a big plate of watermelon.

Tim Busfield: You can see that I was figuring out directing a little bit more. I was starting to shoot what fit the story. Ed was much nicer to me on this one than he was on the first two. David Clennon and Kenny were so good in the scene in the bedroom where Michael quit. Joe Dougherty had written such a beautiful scene.

Joe Dougherty: Miles never took his coat off. That was Miles saying, "I am here but I am not here. I am still outside. I am not in your house. I am not gonna take my coat off. I have been in the lower porting of your

This is the prop beer that was made for this episode. The campaign was for Durstin Gold. Joe Dougherty kept this prop from a script that took on the Gulf War which had just ended. Courtesy of the Joe Dougherty Collection.

house but I am now upstairs. I am in your flipping bedroom, pal. I am in the space where you have had sex with your wife and I am standing here asking you to come back to me. Don't be a fool."

Tim Busfield: I just remember that I broke the scene in the bedroom down mathematically wrong. I had them in too many angles. All I remember is the sweat and panic that it was taking too long to shoot. I had boxed myself into a corner and I had to make sure the actors were really comfortable with that scene. It is not one of those scenes where you can tell them exactly where they stood. It was important to be sure that the actors owned how they played it. Today, I would have handled it better.

Joe Dougherty: When Michael puts his pants on, he was really putting on his pants. The spell is broken. He figured out what he can and cannot get from Miles. He understood what Miles did to him.

Ken Olin: I put my pants on in front of Miles? I don't remember that at all. That is fantastic.

Joe Dougherty: Then Michael paraphrases Raymond Chandler to him. My future work doesn't have to be particularly good, it just has to be mine. That was the scene. You are in my bedroom, I don't care, I am putting my pants on. I am done. Miles knows it is not going to happen. So his exit line actually isn't as strong as he would like it to be. I think he says, "You're a fool and you don't know what you have done." It is very Milesian. Miles walks down the hallway, and then your wife comes and holds you and you say what have I done? Then Joe went home.

Episode
84

"Melissa in Wonderland"

Directed by Ellen S. Pressman

Written by Winnie Holzman

May 21, 1991

Melanie Mayron: Melissa wanted to reinvent herself. She had a place with that group. She wanted to be her own person, not Michael's cousin or Gary's old girlfriend. She wanted to stand on her own.

Liberty Godshall: After rewatching this, Melanie Mayron should have had a spin-off immediately.

Ellen Pressman (*Director*): There was a lot of pressure about that show because the idea was that it was a potential spin-off for Melanie's character. Winnie was writing it. It was an episode that wasn't really in our vernacular. It wasn't a lot of fun. Ed and Marshall were just done. It was hard on everybody. I was aware that they were trying to end the series and it was a really tumultuous time.

Melanie Mayron: It was an adventure. She was going to go out to California and seemed to be the one that was following her dreams.

Ellen Pressman: Scott was directing the next episode, so that contributed to the craziness. I am on the set for "Melissa" and he is prepping "California." Scott was everything to everyone and very supportive, but if he was prepping, he was not there.

Some in the main cast wanted the show to continue and some wanted it to wrap up. All that mattered was what MGM wanted and they did not want the show to end. Courtesy ABC Photography Archives.

Episode 85

"California"

Directed by Scott Winant

Written by Marshall Herskovitz, Edward Zwick, Liberty Godshall, Susan Shilliday, Joseph Dougherty, Winnie Holzman, Richard Kramer, Ann Lewis Hamilton

May 28, 1991

The Series Finale

Scott Winant: Ed and Marshall basically decided that they had told all the stories. They wanted the show to end. They contrived for that to be the last season. They never shared this with the studio or the network. They were oblivious that Ed and Marshall were going to end the show. I was one of the only people who was totally in the loop.

Tim Busfield: Marshall and Ed kept the winding down really quiet. I don't know how much we all knew. They wanted the show to end without letting ABC or MGM know. The truth is that Ed and Marshall didn't want the show to continue because their contract was up. My contract was up with theirs.

Brandy Alexander: I remember Ed saying, "I went to college for four years. I did *thirtysomething* for four years. I am done."

Ed Zwick: This speaks to our own ridiculous sense of ambition, but we wanted to move on. We felt that we had said all we wanted to say about these people. We were in serious risk of repeating ourselves. We had come to it with the dream of being filmmakers and that was what we were able to become.

Marshall Herskovitz: It was our intention to end the show because after four years we felt that we didn't have anything new to say about these characters. We were desperately afraid that we would start repeating ourselves. However, MGM, who actually owned the show, wanted us to go another year. We wrote the episode sort of unilaterally which clearly would be the end of the series.

Scott Winant: Ed and Marshall wanted all the writers to participate. They wanted to split up the episode and give each act of the finale to a pair of writers. I was going to direct. I knew exactly what the end shot would be. I was going to shoot it in a way that would kill the show. We didn't tell anybody.

Ann Lewis Hamilton: I think I wrote an act with Joe. I don't even have a copy of the script and I have not seen the episode since it aired because it was such a sad time. If there was a DAA component, I suspect Joe and I wrote it.

Joe Dougherty: I remember Ann and I jumped at the second act because we didn't want to set anything up and we didn't want to pay anything off. My memory is that Scott asked me to come in and rewrite the Miles material in the other acts.

Scott Winant: In the end, there weren't a lot of people there. Ed and Marshall weren't there. I don't think Joe and Ann were there. Winnie was a staffer at that time. She was doing a lot of the heavy lifting. Winnie and I became very close in that last season.

Winnie Holzman: I think I wrote Act 2. I wrote my part with Richard. The only thing I remember is a line where I have Hope talking about being in bed and pulling the covers over her head. I don't remember a lot about "California" because it was jammed out. It was a hard time for me personally because the show was ending and my dad was dying. There was a lot of emotion in my life at that time.

Richard Kramer: I remember I wrote the line for Hope, "How long have we been talking to each other like this, like lawyers?" That was a line that we all liked.

Tim Busfield: There were basically eight writers on the show. The thought was that Ed and Liberty would write an act, Marshall and Susan,

Joe and Ann, Winnie and Richard but that was too many writers on one script. You can only have two paid writers.

Scott Winant: What you are supposed to do is turn in a memo to the Writer's Guild Of America (WGA) with whomever is writing the episode. This was where Ed and Marshall made a misstep. In order to get eight writers to do a single episode, you have to get a waiver from the WGA. They really wanted to do this, so they wrote a letter to the WGA saying, "We would like to have eight writers on this script because it is the final script of the series." The problem with that is, the memo goes to the WGA and the studio at the same time. I told Ed and Marshall, "If I send this letter you are telling the studio that you are ending the show. Have you told them that?" They said, "No." In basic Ed and Marshall fashion they said, "Just don't send the note." So, every day the script coordinator, Mary Helfrich, would come in and say, "They are asking for the memo of who is writing the season finale. I can't keep putting them off." I was prepping to direct in a few days, so we sent it.

Tim Busfield: They didn't know that a copy of the memo was going to go to MGM. When David Gerber, who was running MGM television, got that memo, he called Marshall and Ed and said "I'm suing you guys. We need the show to go on longer."

Scott Winant: It only took a couple of hours until the president of MGM called me up. They were going to file a lawsuit against Ed and Marshall. David Gerber was pissed. He said, "You don't work for Ed and Marshall, you work for MGM and if you ever hope to have a career after this, you'll listen very carefully to what I am telling you. They are in breach of contract. You are not to continue on this episode. You are to prep only the first act and you have to rewrite the script so that it is open ended." I said, "I can't do that unless Ed and Marshall tell me I can do that."

Ed Zwick: The studio owned the show. The show was produced for ABC. It was the studio that stood to gain the most by another year of the show because they would have more episodes for syndication. The network was willing to have us end it the way we wanted to, but the studio threatened us with a lawsuit for violation of our contract. We went on to do three more series for ABC. It wasn't the network who were villains in that regard, it was the studio. They were the copyright holder.

The Logo for Marshall and Ed's company, Bedford Falls. They went on to produce Once and Again, Relativity *and* My So-Called Life *for ABC. Courtesy of Bedford Falls.*

Marshall Herskovitz: The studio did not want the show to end. ABC was sort of undecided. I think they would have probably preferred for it to go another year. The studio was angry with us because we had discussed this with the network without bringing them into it.

Scott Winant: What they wrote that upset the studio was that Michael was going to take a job in California. Hope was going to move to Washington, DC. Hope and Michael were going to split up. The last shot was going to be a moving van in front of their house pulling away as they went their separate ways. I had already ordered a crane so that I could pull back and show the whole neighborhood which at this point was built on the back lot. I was going to crane up and then I was going to pan around and show Studio City. Pretty much saying that it has all been a fake and the show is over. Ed and Marshall went forward with this.

Marshall Herskovitz: The original ending showed that Michael and Hope couldn't resolve the idea of moving to California. She decided she wasn't gonna move. It was not stated explicitly but it was implied that they were probably going to get a divorce. You would really have a sense that this whole story and group of people were all over. That is what the studio wanted us to change.

Brandy Alexander: All the characters were moving away. They created no place for the series to continue. Hope and Michael put their house up for sale and did a yard sale. It gives me goose bumps just thinking about it.

Liberty Godshall: There was a shot of the empty rooms in the house. I have chills thinking about it. It would have been so much better than what actually aired.

Ann Lewis Hamilton: There was a different ending. I think that Ed and Liberty wrote the last act. There was something about a garage sale. The ending was just sublime. It was the end of the series. It was elegant, and I think the network said, "No. It is too final. We want to leave it more open ended in case the show continues." It was like a film. Ed and Marshall had seen four years of something and they had ended it. I could be making that up completely, but I don't think I am.

Ed Zwick: I know that we had imagined that Hope and Michael would at least, for the moment, separate. That sounds familiar. That could be true. I know I wrote it, but I can't remember what it was. It would never have been our nature to end it with absolute finality. The idea that Michael might say, "I am gonna go to California." and Hope says, "I don't want to do this." That sounds right. It might be what Liberty and I might have written.

Joe Dougherty: I know the end I wanted. I remember pitching it to Ed and Marshall. Michael and Hope go to California together. The last image of the show would be the empty house and just hear audio tracks from scenes that had played in the different rooms.

Tim Busfield: They had to change the ending because the studio said, "We see what you did. You broke up Michael and Hope. Elliot and Nancy moved to California, so they're not in the same town anymore." There would have to be brand new sets built which would cost millions of dollars.

Polly Draper: They wouldn't let us do a real ending because ABC wanted the show to continue and Ed and Marshall wanted it to end. We never got to shoot the one they wrote. I don't even think I read it. ABC wanted it to be open ended. It wasn't really the way the show should have ended. I have a vague memory of them doing something where the camera pulls back and you see it was a set and the audience realizes that we were just characters. I think the aired ending wasn't a really well thought out ending because they had another one in mind.

Marshall Herskovitz: It's not a question of regret. We had no choice. It was a contractual responsibility. We would have been sued. There was nothing we could do. Our lawyer said we had to comply, so we had to re-write and move things around. In our minds, we didn't know if the show was going to be over or not. We had to take out any reference that would make it seem like the show was ending.

Scott Winant directs the final episode of thirtysomething while a fight waged with the studio. Courtesy of Kenneth Zunder.

Scott Winant: The boys held out for three or four days with lawyers involved and all this stuff going back and forth. Luckily, Winnie and Richard were there and we rewrote the script so it was open ended. Michael comes back and choses to stay with Hope. I was location scouting in Santa Monica and I would point to stuff and say, "I may use this and may use that." I would come back and tell Richard and he would try to write it in.

Ken Zunder: Twelve different versions of that script came out between April 3 and April 22. The last was a double green version and probably came out the day before we finished shooting the entire episode.

Ken Olin: It would have been nice if we could have spent as much time on the final episode as we did on the first episode. It is an hour of television from people who didn't have anything else to say. They were contractually obligated to put another hour on television. So, they wrote something that could be the end.

Ken Zunder (*Director Of Photography*): They go to California for Elliot to shoot a commercial and they named the cameraman in a scene Kenny Zunder. They asked me if I wanted to be cast as the camera man. I said, "Hell no, I'd rather have an actor play me." Elliot says, "I got Kenny Zunder to shoot it." They cast someone younger who had a full head of

MICHAEL
Yeah, pretty weird, huh? How's the thing going?

ELLIOT
It's going okay, it's good, we start tomorrow. Kenny Zunder's shooting it, did you know that?

MICHAEL
Hey, that's great, good for you, it must be--- going great.

Ken Zunder, the actual DP, is mentioned in the final version of the script. Courtesy of Kenneth Zunder.

hair. Some of my wife's friends who hadn't met me said to her, "We saw your husband on TV last night." We shot that scene at the actual advertising agency Chiat\Day.

Susan Shilliday: We had to wrap it up somehow. It wasn't the best episode. It was open ended. Are Hope and Michael gonna make it? Who knows. I think they make it for awhile, maybe get divorced much later.

Ken Olin: I don't even remember the last episode. Did it seem like they were gonna get divorced? It got kind of weird. I don't feel connected to the end of the series. Ed and Marshall were done. In exchange for their next show, ABC let it go. Today, ABC would make us do it for three more years. I was done. Patty was done. Peter was done. That is what that episode felt like; everyone was done. It is hard to believe that the consummate feeling is that Hope and Michael aren't together. The experience of *thirtysomething* has to be Hope and Michael are together and Elliot and Michael are together.

Liberty Godshall: I think the show is the love story of Michael and Elliot. That is why they wrote the original ending that Michael goes to California with Elliot.

Ken Olin: I think in the end, the Elliot and Michael love story is the one that is sustained because Ed and Marshall are still working together. I think the Michael and Elliot relationship went through a lot more color than Michael and Hope ever did. The partnership between Michael and Elliot was profound.

Marshall Herskovitz: It's like when comedians say, "I went out and killed." We had some desire to kill the audience and I think that this desire to end the show in such an emotionally violent way came out of that overarching sensibility that we were working under at that time. Looking back on it, I am not sure I would agree with it now.

Joe Dougherty: I have never watched "California". The only reason I am saying that publicly is that I understand there is at least one other writer that hasn't watch it either. I think part of it is that we were all a little wired by the end of the fourth year. I embrace my arrogance as a younger writer. I was personally finished when I completed writing "Stop at

"California" focused on the status of Michael and Hope's relationship. Some writers remember they were split up and some remember they stayed together. What did happen in the script that MGM banned from being filmed? Read on. Courtesy of ABC Photography Archives. The Lisa Mercado Fernandez Collection.

Willoughby". The ending of "California" went through a lot of machinations because of studio pressure.

Marshall Herskovitz: Ed and I were much darker in our view of the world and life at that time. I think it pleased us at that moment to say that this whole thing was gonna be blown up. Looking back on it, I am not sure that we would necessarily have to do such violence to the fabric of the show in order to end it. I am not sure I regret the way it ended now because it is more in keeping with what the show was. The show was full of love. People disagreed, there was ambivalence, there was anger, but it was full of love.

Ann Lewis Hamilton: I can't believe Marshall said that, of course he did. It was all about love.

ABC's Tuesday lineup from 1987-1989 was Moonlighting *followed by* thirtysomething. *Courtesy of Carol Gepper's TV Guide Collection.*

A Fifth Season?

Patty Wettig: We thought we were coming back for a fifth season. We had heard rumblings that Ed and Marshall were going to leave and maybe Richard or Scott were going to take over. I don't think Ed and Marshall wanted to turn their baby over to someone else.

Scott Winant: That was a real rough week. I always used to say that for about five years I don't remember sitting down. I was constantly in motion, in crisis mode. When it all ended I was exhausted. ABC still wanted to pick it up. I was put in an awkward position because Ed and Marshall were gonna step away and between Joe and Richard there were people who wouldn't have minded to take on the show, but only if I came back.

Ann Lewis Hamilton: There was so much going on behind the scenes. Was there going to be another season? Ed and Marshall had their film career. Certainly there were writers that could have continued it, but it wouldn't have been the same. Ed and Marshall were that show.

Scott Winant: To Ed and Marshall's credit, they came to me in person and said if I wanted to take it over, they would not begrudge me. They wanted me to know that. David Gerber and I used to battle every week on the budget or other issues. All of a sudden, he wanted to be my best friend. It was like a scene out of *thirtysomething,* he took me to the Bel Air Hotel for lunch. He offered me all this money and talked about how important it was that the show continue for a fifth season.

Tim Busfield: Bob Iger, who was running ABC, called me on my giant suitcase car phone in 1991 and we talked about the fate of the show. I said, "I didn't know if I wanted to go back if it was going to be like *Moonlighting* (1985) and it was going to change so drastically in the last year without Ed and Marshall." *Moonlighting* was one of the best shows ever for the first three seasons and then fell apart. I didn't want that and Ed and Marshall didn't want that. We all wanted to go out on top.

Peter Horton: Had Gary lived for a fifth season, I am sure he would have grown up, cut his hair and got a job. He would have had to have changed.

Polly Draper: Ellyn would have divorced Billy in the fifth season. They would have had marriage troubles. She seemed like one of those perennial single women. It would be cute to see someone like Ellyn as a mother because she would be so inept and try so hard.

Patricia Kalember: Susannah might have married a wealthy Bloomberg and got him to fund all of her progressive yearnings. Maybe Melissa and I have a lesbian relationship? (*Laughs*) The possibilities are endless. We find Gary again through each other.

Melanie Mayron: I would hope that Melissa and Lee got together. Corey Parker and I are still in touch on Facebook so that is a plus. I wanna believe what Gary's ghost said, that they end up together and have a kid.

Ann Lewis Hamilton: I would wonder more about Elliot and Nancy. Would they really last?

Tim Busfield: Yeah I think that Elliot and Nancy probably made it. Although, I don't know if Elliot would be mature enough to handle Los Angeles. I think that would have been his downfall. I don't know if being in the land of opportunity of drugs, alcohol and sex if Elliot could have withstood that.

Patty Wettig: Of course he said that. Why does that not surprise me? (*Laughs*) I know that Mr. Busfield really well. He cracks me up. He is so funny. Ken loves him, too. He is the person that we have shared a love for. We were both madly in love with Tim.

After 85 episodes the show went off the air, but the cast remained very close. Most of them have worked together behind the camera or guest starring on one of their shows. Courtesy ABC Photography Archives.

Liberty Godshall: The series ends with Michael looking at some things about himself for the first time. It took him almost destroying his marriage before he looked at them. I think Hope and Michael probably don't make it. They probably divorce. I feel like they had their relationship.

Ann Lewis Hamilton: My vote is that Hope and Michael stay together because my husband and I have been together for thirty years. There are ups and downs and we are still together and happy, even though he is glad the show isn't on anymore.

Mel Harris: I think Hope was in a take a break mode. I don't know that she was willing to throw in the towel, but some space was really something they both needed. It doesn't mean they still can't be a couple, just that they needed a break.

Scott Winant: In the end, I turned the network down and they cancelled the show. I felt like I had too much respect for Ed and Marshall. I always tell my wife that had they come to me maybe two or three weeks later after I had rested, I wonder if I would have said the same thing but I was so exhausted. I was still a zealot and so it didn't even occur to me. That would have been a huge payday for me.

Patty Wettig: Ken and I had taken the kids to school and went out to breakfast. We were eating and our waiter came over and said, "I heard your show was cancelled." We didn't know. No one had called us. No one had told us. We were shocked. That was how we found out. At the time, I can't say we were devastated by it. I felt we had done four great years. You just don't realize that it is going to be really hard to find something else to do as gratifying as those four years. I was ready to move on. What were we thinking?

Joe Dougherty: It was rough and we were exhausted. I have survived twenty-six years without watching "California" and if I watch it, then I can't have not watched it. My sole memory of that episode is watching dailies with Scott, watching the sun go down behind Tim and Ken. Scott got to be there for sunset and there is this one seagull that flies in through the background between Michael and Elliot. Let that be the last image I see of these two guys. Then Scott yells, "Cut."

California, Here We Come?

by Scott Ryan

From 1985 to 1989, ABC aired ground breaking shows like *Moonlighting, China Beach, Twin Peaks,* and *thirtysomething*. Each show, in its own way, took a swing at tearing down traditional television storytelling norms. *Moonlighting* talked to the screen and spoofed the mainstream detective series that, at the time, littered the television highway. *China Beach* put a flawed female character front and center, made her an alcoholic and jumped time periods in the final season. *Twin Peaks* had dreams, demons and dancing dwarfs that were shown with no explanation provided. Viewers were asked to either make sense of it or change the channel. In many instances that is exactly what happened with all of the series, viewers just changed the channel. The viewers that did stick around were a different kind of television viewer that didn't want simple answers to simple questions.

ABC was programming as if it were a cable channel from the future. They were allowing producers to take risks instead of playing it safe. Without knowing it, they were creating the model that HBO, FX and even Netflix would eventually follow. How long could an American broadcast network keep that kind of brave programming on the air? Not long. On May 21, 1991, ABC cancelled *China Beach, Twin Peaks* and *thirtysomething* at the same moment. This marked the end of the brief period where a major network tried to do more than sell bars of soap. One year later, HBO would premiere *The Larry Sanders Show*. It would become the first cable show to win a primetime Emmy in one of the major series categories. (*Rip Torn, Best Supporting Actor in a Comedy, 1994*) Cable would become the leader of quality programming until streaming services stepped into the ring to become the next contender.

Throughout the first eight-four episodes, the studio and network left Marshall and Ed to do as they pleased. Yes, they made them stay within the boundaries set by the censors, but on plot points, they left them alone. It can't be a coincidence that the one time the studio got involved with plot, was the one time the series felt false to the viewers, writers, and actors. Had everyone just let Marshall and Ed end the show as they desired, *thirtysomething* might have been able to have a perfect series finale. What if MGM had not interfered with the original script? Couldn't the staff had written themselves out of the ending and done a fifth season if the network decided to bring the show back? With writing, anything is possible. There could have been countless possibilities that reunited this group of friends. On the flip side, why force an artist to continue with a story that had reached a natural ending? The only answer is for money.

None of it mattered anyway as ABC canceled the show. To make matters worse, they made the decision to cancel a week before "California" even aired. So, had they been able to film the original ending, it would have played as a series finale with an actual ending instead of playing like an unresolved finale. It is mind boggling to think that they forced them to write an open ended episode which watered down their final idea only to cancel the series before the ratings were even in. A clear indication of what happens when art is shaped by corporations, lawyers and businessmen. While most of the cast and crew were ready to move on, it would have been nice to allow fans to see the intended ending.

During my interviews, everyone had differing opinions about what actually occurred in that original script that upset MGM. No one could remember because no one kept the script. That was until I talked with Ken Zunder. For over twenty-five years the script sat on his shelf just waiting for me to call. Ken was nice enough to scan it and send it to me. Marshall was even nicer to give permission to publish the intended ending here. In an email, Marshall not only said I could print it, but that he would never sue me. I am pretty sure there is no greater endorsement in the entertainment industry than that. After all these years, fans can finally read what is the ending of the story for the Steadmans. It doesn't disappoint.

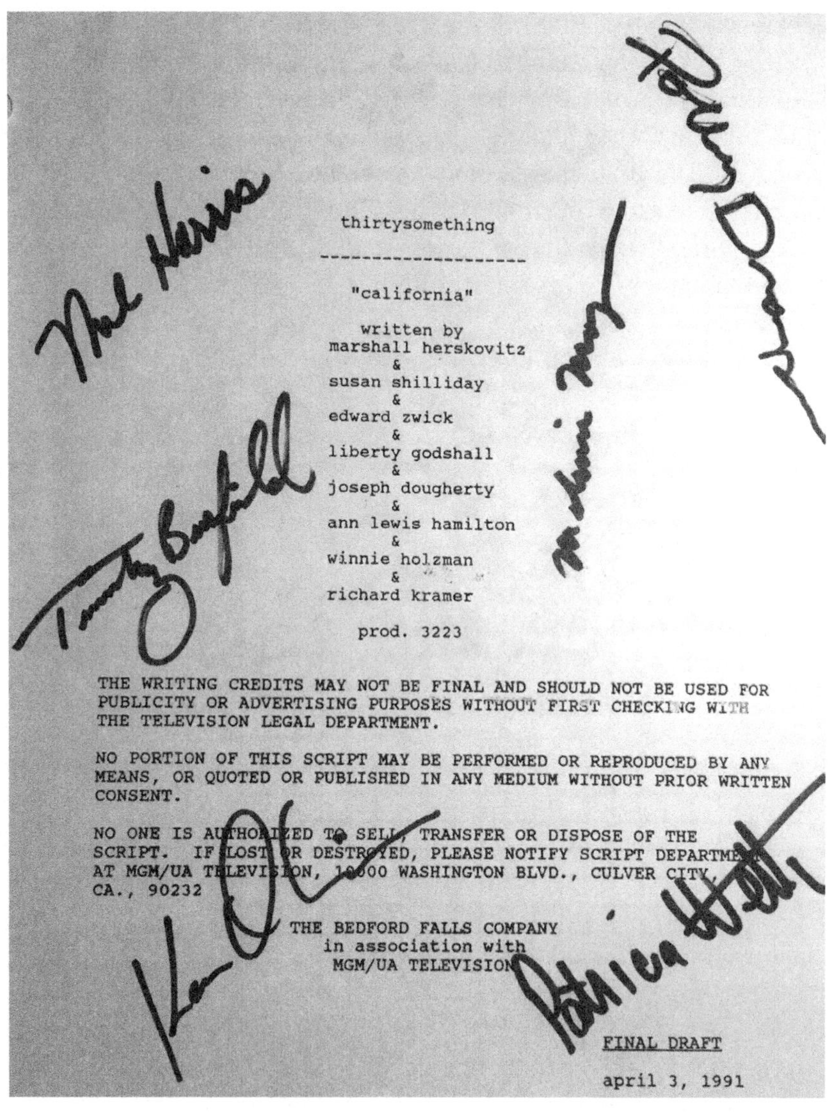

thirtysomething

"california"

written by
marshall herskovitz
&
susan shilliday
&
edward zwick
&
liberty godshall
&
joseph dougherty
&
ann lewis hamilton
&
winnie holzman
&
richard kramer

prod. 3223

THE WRITING CREDITS MAY NOT BE FINAL AND SHOULD NOT BE USED FOR PUBLICITY OR ADVERTISING PURPOSES WITHOUT FIRST CHECKING WITH THE TELEVISION LEGAL DEPARTMENT.

NO PORTION OF THIS SCRIPT MAY BE PERFORMED OR REPRODUCED BY ANY MEANS, OR QUOTED OR PUBLISHED IN ANY MEDIUM WITHOUT PRIOR WRITTEN CONSENT.

NO ONE IS AUTHORIZED TO SELL, TRANSFER OR DISPOSE OF THE SCRIPT. IF LOST OR DESTROYED, PLEASE NOTIFY SCRIPT DEPARTMENT AT MGM/UA TELEVISION, 10000 WASHINGTON BLVD., CULVER CITY, CA., 90232

THE BEDFORD FALLS COMPANY
in association with
MGM/UA TELEVISION

FINAL DRAFT

april 3, 1991

The main cast signed Ken Zunder's script of the original version of "California." The script was written by all eight main writers. Read the ending for the first time ever. Courtesy of Kenneth Zunder.

The first three acts of the script are very similar to what aired. The episode begins with Michael saying he is not going back to advertising. Chiat/Day calls and invites him to California where Elliot and him decide to start a new business. Hope does not want to go to California, says she won't move and decides to go to Washington, DC to take a job. Here is where it gets interesting. All the writers talked about how Michael and Hope split. In fact, they did not split. They stayed together. Just like in the version that aired, Michael came back to Hope and they had a similar scene where he said he will support her and follow her to Washington, DC. The aired episode ends there, however the original script went on. Thanks to Marshall, Ed and the other six writers, everyone can finally read the true ending of *thirtysomething*...

Excerpt from the first draft of "California"

Written by
Marshall Herskovitz, Susan Shilliday, Edward Zwick, Liberty Godshall, Joseph Dougherty, Ann Lewis Hamilton, Winnie Holzman and Richard Kramer

Outside Mile's office, Elliot finds Michael wearing jeans, a t-shirt and tennis shoes.

MICHAEL

Hey.

ELLIOT

Nice suit. Is this some kind of reverse psychology for Miles or do you have a death wish? (*re his sneakers*) I thought I was the one living in California.

MICHAEL

You are.

It doesn't take a genius to sense that something's wrong.

ELLIOT

You aren't?

Michael shakes his head. This is hard.

MICHAEL

I can't do it.

ELLIOT

Sure you can.

MICHAEL

I mean… I won't do it.

Elliot sits there a moment and lets it sink in.

MICHAEL

But you can. You don't need me out there

ELLIOT

This is on the level?

Michael nods. Elliot sits back and closes his eyes.

ELLIOT

On the way in from the airport I stopped by and took a deposit on my house. The guy's a lawyer. It's a good price actually.

MICHAEL

It's the right move. For you.

ELLIOT

You remember that moment in *2001*? When the guy's out there in space and somebody cuts the cord that's holding him to the ship?

MICHAEL

I'm sorry. You hate me again.

ELLIOT

Because you decided your marriage is more important than hanging out with me on the beach? (*looks at him*) I hate you.

MICHAEL

Can I still invent some kind of flimsy pretext now and then to get out of the house and come visit you in California?

ELLIOT

No.

MICHAEL

Will you write?

ELLIOT

Me?

MICHAEL

Call?

ELLIOT

You know how expensive that is?

MICHAEL

I really want to thank you for making this so easy for me.

Elliot turns and looks up at him. This really is goodbye.

ELLIOT

I love you, man.

MICHAEL

If everybody loves me so much, why do I feel so terrible?

Elliot puts his hand on Michael's knee and they sit there together and this is how we leave them We dissolve to the Steadman kitchen - day, where a real estate agent is taking the listing for the house as Michael tries to hide the peeling wallpaper.

AGENT

And what exactly did you say is wrong with the plumbing?

Dissolve to the Steadman bedroom - another day where Hope, clad only in a bra and panties is putting on makeup at the bureau when the agent breezes in with an older couple in tow.

HOPE

Oh. Hello…

Dissolve to the sun room- another day where Michael sits at the desk, staring at a piece of paper. Hope perches beside him.

MICHAEL

We could counter.

HOPE

We could also maybe never get another offer.

They look at each other. Michael signs and hands her the pen. Dissolve to Janey's bedroom - another day where Hope and Michael kneel on the floor, packing up stuffed animals. Finding a dusty old bear under a chair, they stop and spontaneously embrace. Dissolve to the Steadman house - another day. Hope is overseeing the dregs of a garage sale on the lawn. Melissa haggles over a lava lamp with a tall man in plaid shorts while Ellyn browses through a pile of old sweaters.

ELLYN

Hey, this is mine.

HOPE

It is not.

ELLYN

It is, too. Yours was the blue one with the Peter Pan collar.

HOPE

Here, take it.

Ellyn holds the sweater up to her face and smells it.

ELLYN

Don't go.

HOPE

Ellyn...

ELLYN

I know, I know. It's just - finally, I do the one thing you've always wanted me to do. I'm this married person now, okay? And...who am I going to have to talk to about it?

HOPE

We'll talk.

ELLYN

I know.

HOPE

Melissa'll be here.

ELLYN

What can she possibly know about life? She's single.

Hope swats her. Melissa joins them, holding a lava lamp.

MELISSA

The guy in the plaid shorts is gonna bite for this baby, I can feel it. How much?

HOPE

Michael's the merchandiser. If I had my way we would have given it all away years ago.

Melissa calls out to the man in plaid shorts.

MELISSA

I gotta go talk to management.

She heads into the living room where boxes are stacked against the walls and most of the furniture is gone. Movers enter and leave, lifting sofas and scraping a dolly across the hardwood floors. Michael is wrapping a glass bowl in newspaper.

MELISSA

(*re the lava lamp*) How much?

MICHAEL

That was an expensive piece.

MELISSA

Two bucks?

MICHAEL

Try three. But settle.

MELISSA

(*yelling outside*) I'm working on him.

She sits on top of a box and watches him.

MELISSA

Almost done?

MICHAEL

Any minute.

MELISSA

When does the truck get there with your stuff?

MICHAEL

They say they'll have us all moved in by tonight.

MELISSA

Hope says it's a nice house.

He nods. Stops. Considers.

MELISSA

But not like this one.

They sit there for a minute.

MELISSA

There's absolutely no reason to get emotional. It's only two hours away for God's sake. The metroliner goes right to Union Station. (*he just smiles at her*) It's good for me you're leaving, you know. High time I got the hell out of here, myself. I'm thinking New York to start. Then L.A. maybe. Paris. (*shrugs*) I'll probably stay right where I am and still show up for bagels on Sunday.

MICHAEL

(*gently*) No, you won't.

MELISSA

No, I won't.

She leans her head against his chest. He kisses the top of her head.

MELISSA

I absolutely refuse to say goodbye.

MICHAEL

Just when I tell you to go, you leave me.

Fighting back tears, she breaks the moment.

MELISSA

Hey. I'm losing a customer.

She gets up and grabs the lava lamp, calling out as she goes.

MELISSA

I went to the mat for you, pal. Wait'll you hear this deal.

Michael stands there suddenly very conscious of the silent space around him. As he walks across the gleaming floor we flashback to the moment from "Housewarming" when they are all huddled together in a circle. Back to the sun room. He pauses, as if he can hear his father talking to him about the model car. In the kitchen Gary and Ellyn cook dinner. On the stairs, Hope carries Janey up to bed. And so on and so on from room to room, the memories brim and overflow. Until, once again, he find himself back at the front door. The real estate agent is standing with an attractive young couple - open faces, holding an infant- reminiscent, in spirit at least, of Michael and Hope, years ago.

AGENT

I'm sorry. We thought.

MICHAEL

It's all right. We're out of here any minute.

YOUNG HUSBAND

If you'd rather…

MICHAEL

No, no. Go ahead.

YOUNG WIFE

Thanks. Really. We're just...so excited.

MICHAEL

Go on.

Michael steps outside as they head in. Hope joins him on the porch and puts her arm around his waist. Together, they listen as the young couple's laughter spills out of the house.

HOPE

Ready?

He nods. Together, arm in arm, they walk away and we hold on that lovely house one last time. Fade out.

THE END.

And In The End...

Tim Busfield: I miss the writing every day of my career, absolutely. I miss that character every day. It was a high point for me. It was difficult for all of us for it to end.

Melanie Mayron: The writing is universal. It is timeless. Fashion and technology changes but people are people and love is love.

David Clennon: I can't think of anything on television that matched the consistency and quality of the writing of *thirtysomething*. If you know

The cast reunited in 2009 on Good Morning America. Courtesy ABC/Photofest

something about acting, then you know that you are not going to shine with mediocre material. You've got to be supported by quality writing.

Jill Gordon: The time I spent with Ed and Marshall has helped me every day on my own series. It is the lessons they taught me about being honest over slick, that challenges me to work harder and dig deeper. It was the respect they showed me as a writer, that reminds me every day to thank my colleagues. No one was like them.

Liberty Godshall: During the making of it, the blur factor was huge. I don't know how they did it. I had a lot of dinners with Ed and our son. He was an amazing father through all of it. It was a huge work load. They hired amazing writers and actors, but the sheer physical will of getting a show out every week. I don't know how they did it.

Ron Lagomarsino: I just remember at the time I felt so lucky to be a part of it. I can't think of any other series that touched on the day to day in that particular way. I am blessed that was the beginning of my television career. It helped me get to direct pilots like *Picket Fences* (1992) with David E. Kelley.

Ken Zunder: I learned to make it good on the set and not in the editing room. Give the audience credit for being smart. Let them figure it out. Sometimes television takes the obvious and hits you over the head with it.

Susan Shilliday: I am really proud of the work I did on the show. I feel that I am very lucky to have worked in television at that moment. We helped take one step further than what had been done on television before and I am proud of that.

Mel Harris: I consider *thirtysomething* my Master's degree. I did a body of work that I am really proud of, I was paid well and made life long friends. Any one of us can call any of us and say I really need a favor and everyone would be there. We know that and it is a really lovely thing. For me, it really changed my life.

Winnie Holzman: It is a privilege to have people receive your work in a way that goes deep and is heart felt. I try to write from my own heart. I was taught that by Richard, Marshall, Ed and Arthur Laurents.

The series may have ended with an open ending, but Ken Zunder (Pictured here with Patty and Melanie) kept the original scripted ending on his book shelf for all these years. Fans finally get to read it with Marshall's permission for the first time. Courtesy of Kenneth Zunder.

Patricia Kalember: I discovered that you could do television to great satisfaction and I never thought that was possible. This was before cable shows. Back then doing television the way Ed and Marshall did it wasn't normal. They took time, they did it intelligently, they didn't get network notes. They really did little movies and were the first ones to do it, along with *Twin Peaks* (1990).

David Marshall Grant: I think what *thirtysomething* did so brilliantly was examine the ordinary and expose it to being extraordinary. Every moment is filled with contradiction and drama. Russell and Melissa's friendship was, for its time, very shocking to see. I think you have to give credit to Ed, Marshall, Richard and the network for changing a lot of people, including me.

Richard Kramer: We sort of felt like we invented an opportunity within commercial interrupted, language restricted network television that was unique. Everybody was working together, sometimes without words. We just understood each other. That was so unique and we all knew at the time that it was not likely to be repeated in our lifetime.

Peter Horton: It was a series in a particular moment in time. What none of us could see coming was the dissolution of a centralized television system. Where it went from having four networks to now where we have 420 scripted shows on the air that are competing with all the social media and technology that has emerged since then. Never again will there be something quite like that where there was a centralized focus of the country on something that had such a unique voice for the time.

Melanie Mayron: You go on sets now and the entire cast and crew are on their iPhones. We were all hanging out and sharing stuff on the set.

Liberty Godshall: People's sensibilities have changed. Our attention spans have changed. Most shows are so plot oriented just trying to titillate people.

Richard Kramer: Television has changed from something you watch to something you have to catch up on.

Liberty Godshall: It has been an incredible earthquake in my life to rewatch the series. It was emotional and I didn't expect to take the journey I took. The series is about putting a lens on a group of friends in a certain decade of their lives. You can't help but be slammed with what is going on culturally and economically.

Ed Zwick: When Liberty said she had been watching them, what so struck me was how I miss those people. How we should all get together and have dinner.

Liberty Godshall: This makes me want to write sixtysomething. Life is so much richer than we ever dreamed it would be and it is all part of the puzzle. Divorce and getting through life with scars is really the hard part. The stuff you think was the hard part at the beginning isn't the hard part. There is so much to be mined from it and where they all are. It would be very rich to write about it now. I need to talk to Marshall and Ed about that.

Patty Wettig: There is no "still." I don't think like that. It is fiction. I don't engage on that. When it was over, it was over. So, when people talk about a reunion, I don't know how that would be. I don't think I could have been more present in those years but I have spent no time in my life afterwards imagining what would have been had my character gone on. I miss it and I am very proud of it.

Marshall Herskovitz: Right now the answer to a reunion show is no. To me, it is a prescription for disaster. Fans would be happy to think about it, but not sure they would be happy when they saw it. I do feel that some of these things may exist better in memory than in real life. I don't know. We did have a serious discussion about it six months ago where we thought maybe there was a way to do it. So, I wouldn't rule it out, but I don't think we are ready to do it yet. It would inevitably be as much about the next generation.

Peter Horton: Tim, Ken and I became such great friends. The star of the show were the scripts so we had no drama among the cast. It was with the writers where all the drama was.

Melanie Mayron: All of us loved each other and respected each other as actors. We just generally were thrilled to be on the show. There would be a few times a year where there would be a party episode and we would all be together. We would all be talking and the poor directors couldn't get our attention. Those were like the best of times.

Polly Draper: I have this really sweet memory of all of us sitting in the Michael and Hope living room playing "In My Life" by The Beatles. We were just all there and having so much fun, laughing together and singing that song. Anytime that song comes on the radio, it brings back so many memories.

Tim Busfield: What I take with me from it is that I got to be a band mate with Ken, Mel, Patty, Melanie, Peter and Polly. I feel like I was part of a band that put out records everyone liked while we played. I will cherish it forever.

Ken Olin: I was lucky to be working with that cast. I was basically married to Mel and Tim and then would go home to Patty. That was amazing.

Ed Zwick: When you do a television show you are in such a bubble. It is kind of cool that after time goes by that you have this notion that there is some lasting resonance from that. Much more than I remember the specifics of the stories, I remember the feelings we all had of the enterprise and our connections to each other; the struggles, the fights, the problems, the friendships. I was overcome by a very wistful recollection of just how in it we were. How utterly abandoned we were to it and how unaware we were to it, the fact that it would go beyond ourselves.

Patty Wettig: I loved the experience but it is like getting to an end of a novel. I may want to go back and read it again, but I don't want the novel to continue.

"And Dance By The Light Of The Moon"

Afterword
by Joseph Dougherty

thirtysomething was my first experience on the writing staff of a television series. We made eighty-five episodes over four seasons then all headed off in different directions. As educational experiences go, it was epic. Its lessons are part of everything I've done since.

The thing about television is that it's ephemeral. One of the reasons it's ephemeral is that there's so damn much of it. Sixty-plus years' worth and they're making more every day. It is fleeting. You can own more of it now, and have access to more of it, but it all has the permanence of a traveling tent show. And that's probably the way it should be. That perspective of the temporary is liberating, if you can deal with it. It keeps you balanced as a writer. You realize, eventually, that your best shot at immortality isn't that your work will somehow survive, but that someone will remember something about your work and find it useful and/or entertaining long after you're gone. At least, that's what I'm counting on.

This book gives you some insight into how the thing happened. How it was possible to tell interesting stories while attending the Mad Hatter's tea party.

In many ways, *thirtysomething* came out better than anyone could have expected. The show as it exists, with its successes and failures, its noble experiments and occasional pratfalls, happened because of a profound and goofy alchemy resulting from a bunch of mismatched creative people touring with the same carnival for four years. We all had the sense that what we were doing was at least a little different from what surrounded it and what came before. And, God help us, we took it seriously. We wanted to do it the best way we could. We were all just trying to make our parents proud of us.

We were a mixed bag with very different tastes and sensibilities that occasional collided during the process. But I think what we all wanted was to be as honest in our writing as we could be and put a kind of human experience in front of people they weren't getting anywhere else on television at that moment.

We examined and questioned while having a fine time for ourselves, jazzing around with all the toys we'd been given to play with. We were also, at least partially, in the business of giving people permission to feel the way they felt about their jobs and their friends and their families by showing they weren't alone in those feelings and fears. We couldn't fix anything, but at least we could tell them there was nothing wrong with them because they were frustrated at work, confused about how to be a parent, and terrified that they could be so angry with someone they loved so much.

If you read the contemporary criticism of the show (assuming you can find it since, oddly enough, the episodes have survived, but the reviews have faded) you'll discover we were often hammered for the smallness of what we explored. I never understood that argument. It's as if the critics had never examined their own lives and found them to be an aggregate of small events; slights and pleasures, losses and flirtations. Yes, big things happen to us, but they happen in the context of so much other stuff. The story of Nancy's cancer is a certifiably "Big" television story, but the reason you remember Nancy is because of the specificity of the world around her. Life doesn't stop for us, but maybe, one night, someone will set off fireworks that spell out our name. They won't last, but they'll burn bright. And we'll remember them.

If *thirtysomething* has had an afterlife, if people come back to the series or discover it for the first time, it's because families and work and the mistakes we make out of our best intentions haven't changed all that much.

Television has always been an intimate experience. Once a thing of living rooms and bedrooms, now a thing of tablets and telephones, but always a private sort of entertainment, usually shared in the past tense, as something watched last night or last year or late in the preceding century. I have found that television drama works best when it is about individuals, when it acknowledges its dimensions and embraces the words of W. B. Yeats:

"The history of a nation is not in parliaments and battle-fields, but in what the people say to each other on fair-days and high days, and in how they farm, and quarrel, and go on pilgrimage."

That's what I think we were trying to record on *thirtysomething.* We weren't the first or the last to do it, but we did it at a particular time and in a particular way. A way that was not so particular that what we wrote has lost its meaning.

Inteview Data

Phone Interviews by Scott Ryan

Brandy Alexander 4-27-16
Dana Delany: 4-7-16
Joe Dougherty: 3-5-16
Liberty Godshall: 3-11-16
David Marshall Grant: 3-23-16
Ann Lewis Hamilton: 1-20-16
Marshall Herskovitz: 5-4-16
Winnie Holzman: 12-4-15
Richard Kramer: 2-28-16, 3-30-16
Ron Lagomarsino: 3-12-16
Melanie Mayron: 5-17-16
Ken Olin: 4-10-16
Ellen S. Pressman: 2-21-16
Susan Shilliday: 2-6-16
Charlotte Stewart: 4-30-16
Patricia Wettig: 3-20-16
Scott Winant: 1-25-16
Kenneth Zunder: 5-23-16
Edward Zwick: 5-8-16

Email Interviews by Scott Ryan

David Clennon: 1-26-16
Polly Draper: 4-6-16
Michael Feinstein: 3-23-16
Jill Gordon: 4-25-16

Paul Haggis: 5-11-16
Nick Meglin: 3-10-16
Lenny Von Dohlen: 4-7-16
Scott Winant: 4-24-16

Paley Center Museum of Television 1999 Festival. David Bushman hosted a *thirtysomething* panel. Two quotes from David Clennon were taken from this panel. Courtesy of Bushman and the Paley Center. 3-11-99

thirtysomething Podcast Interviews with Scott Ryan and Carolyn Hendler

Timothy Busfield: 1-2-16
Joe Dougherty: 10-24-15
Polly Draper: 11-21-15
Mel Harris: 1-8-16
Marshall Herskovitz: 12-21-15
Peter Horton: 2-26-16
Patricia Kalember: 2-3-16
Richard Kramer: 9-12-15
Melanie Mayron: 11-29-15
Corey Parker: 4-23-16

The podcast interviews are located at iTunes, Facebook and Twitter @30somethingpod.

Special Thanks

There are so many people to thank for making this project a reality. I attempted to write my thanks with a little bit of sweet and a little bit of sour… just like me.

Carolyn Hendler. My co-host on *The thirtysomething Podcast.* We started this amazing journey together from a late night email chain just talking about the characters we love. Carolyn knows the show backwards and forwards. She co-piloted ten of the interviews with me. You can listen to them on iTunes. We are a great team. One might say she is the lime and I am the lemon.

Richard Kramer. This book exists because of him, plain and simple. His kindness is only eclipsed by the brilliance of his words. He was always willing to help pave the way for me to interview someone. I don't know how to ever truly thank him. Wait, yes I do. I'll suggest you buy his wonderful novel, *These Things Happen.*

David Bushman. An author of the *Twin Peaks FAQ* book and a great friend and mentor. Let me be clear. I am saying I am his mentor. He supported me through this process. I appreciate his feedback and advice. He was a good first reader. He also helped with research at the Paley Center in New York. @TwinPeaksFAQ

Becca Ryan. The artist who created a few of the graphics and designed the front/back cover of the book. She loved getting my assignments as much as she loved hearing me talk about a show from the eighties. Oh, and thanks for being my daughter.

Todd "Huppie" Huppert. Thanks for being a great first reader and giving advice during a rainstorm when the sun was out. That isn't a metaphor, it was a strange rain storm. He is a huge *My So-Called Life* fan and really wants Claire Danes to call him.

Aaron Berman. Check out his book about TV's *Soap*. He was kind enough to get me in touch with BearManor Media and that made all the difference.

Ben Ohmart. He simply responded to my email pitching this book with one word: SOLD. Sometimes one word can change your life path.

Josh Minton. My co-host on *Red Room Podcas*t. He set me adrift into the world of podcasting and life has never been the same. He is my TV partner even if he incorrectly likes *Mad Men* more than *thirtysomething*. I forgive him. Check out our podcast @redroompodcast.

Joe Dougherty. Joe reached out to @30somethingpod and said he was waiting over in the corner when we wanted to talk to him. He may have regretted it when I kept going over to that corner to ask him one more question. He sent me the first pictures for the book. He also wrote a wonderful Afterword for the book. I am thinking he is a Steadman overachiever at heart. Mostly, I have to thank him for "Michael Writes A Story." That episode means the world to me.

Ann Lewis Hamilton. My brick and mortar friend. Thanks for the photos and the wonderful Foreword. I may not have been in the room where it happened but I know Ann was never helpless or satisfied and would not throw away her shot at writing like she's running out of time. What I am saying is that it must be nice to have Ann Hamilton on your side. Your obedient servant, S. Ryan.

Susan Shilliday. I hunted her down through her bookstore, The Montague Bookmill. When I emailed her, she already knew I was coming. My name had filtered through the *thirtysomething* world. Even with that, she said yes to my interview. This book better be for sale in her shop.

Peter Horton. Peter was one of the first to agree to come on the podcast. I appreciated that. He also directed "First Day/Last Day," which taught me how to structure a flashback. His interview was all charm. I wish there was a way I could have transcribed out the coolness that is Peter Horton. Thanks for your essay about dying. Not every living person can write about that.

Marshall Herskovitz. You always hope your heroes live up to your dreams. Talking with Marshall is just what you would want. He was thoughtful and intellectual. He also answered every email I sent him. He may be the smartest person I ever talked to. Hmm, maybe that will offend the rest of the participants. Okay, he was the second smartest.

Ron Lagomarsino. Ron was so easy to talk to. I interviewed him while he enjoyed the sun rise in California. I felt like we were both sitting on his back porch drinking a cup of coffee. He was nice enough to talk to me about my other favorite show, *Picket Fences*.

Ellen S. Pressman. Ellen was a little weary of talking to me. She was the only person that asked, "How will I know you will print what I say?" I wasn't sure how to prove it. I went with because I promise and Richard Kramer likes me?

Timothy Busfield. Tim was the most challenging person to transcribe. He talks faster than Elliot pitches ad campaigns. His story about winning the Emmy was cut from the book but is posted at *The thirtysomething Podcast* on iTunes. Check it out, it is a great story. He also indulged me and talked about *Studio 60* and *West Wing*.

David Marshall Grant. David was so open about his path to coming out on national TV as possibly the first gay best friend. I was very honored that he trusted me enough to share his thoughts on life. I think his interview raised the level of the discussion around "Strangers." I am glad he agreed to be in the book.

Polly Draper. The Polly interview was so much fun. She made me laugh the entire time. In our interview she said, "Thank you for talking about scenes I'm in." I thought that was adorable. She also suggested a TV show called *Last Tango In Halifax* which all my family ended up watching. I really want to be friends with Polly. We need to make that happen.

Ken Olin. Ken wins for longest interview session. He sent me a kind, personal and inspiring email after our interview. It will be those moments that I will remember long after this book is on sale in the half off bin. I also loved when he told me I was making him be Michael Steadman again. Plus, he directed the best episodes of *Alias*. Ken, I am up for an *Alias* oral history if you are.

Melanie Mayron. Melanie was so kind to contact a few of the cast for me. Talking to her was like chatting to a school mate you hadn't talked to in years. She was open to any follow up questions and always made time. She also directed a *Larry Sanders* episode. That gives her major street cred with me.

Mel Harris. When we were interviewing Mel for the podcast, we got disconnected by mistake just when I was asking her about making the mean Hope face. I thought she hung up on us. That was the longest minute of the entire process as we realized we got disconnected. She was a great sport about it and answered her phone and more questions when we called her back.

Ed Zwick. Ed was balancing a Tom Cruise movie and interviews with me at the same time. I like to think he enjoyed his time with both of us equally. If you can get the chance to talk directing with Ed, do it. You will learn a ton.

Scott Winant. Scott is a busy man. I had to hunt him down for three months, but he made the time and was totally devoted to the conversation. He told such great stories, you can tell why he is one of the best directors working today. He also inspired me as a young filmmaker. I stole a Winant wipe in a movie I made in 1999.

Patricia Kalember. She is such an actor's actor. I loved her interview. I wish I could have used more of it in the book. We kept getting off topic and having so much fun. I think Gary made a good choice when he married her. I think I would marry her even if it meant I would be killed off later in the season.

Winnie Holzman. She was so kind and fun. She blew me away when she told me she was taught by Stephen Sondheim. She even talked about

Wicked with me for a little bit. You have no idea the kind of restraint it took to not sing "Popular" to her when she off handedly said the word during our talk. She also made my day when she put her husband, Paul Dooley, (Bob Spano) on the phone. Did I ever tell you that I talked to the person who wrote *Wicked*?

Patty Wettig. She was one of the last people I got in contact with and I feared I might have to do the book without her. I would have nightmares that she would think that I would think that I could do a *thirtysomething* book without Nancy. Her stories were so passionate. The book would be so much less without her. She is also the only one I made cry. Does that make me only 1/7th as good as Barbara Walters?

Liberty Godshall. She is my new best friend. She even said I am her new best friend. She emailed it to me and who am I to disagree with her? I couldn't pick a favorite interview, but Liberty and I really had a heart to heart. I foresee a day when we do the town, get our hair done, and do some shopping while Jen and Ed stay home watching sports.

Kenneth Zunder. Ken saved this book with his wonderful behind the scenes photos. Leave it to the camera man to think of taking photos at work. He also scanned the "California" script to share with the world the original ending of the show. Thank you for keeping this piece of history and I send you a "damn fine shaft of light" for all your help.

Brandy Alexander. Brandy took a chance on a Facebook request and it made all the difference to this book. She shared all her photos and set drawings with me. She went above and beyond for this book. Her pictures are so wonderful. Is there anything cooler than the DAA letterhead?

Corey Parker. Corey made me laugh with his fun stories about being a young actor. He also sent me pictures without me even having to ask. He is an acting teacher in Memphis. Check him out.

Jill Gordon. Jill claimed she didn't remember much, but then was able to give me some great quotes. Her script for Ellyn's wedding is a marvel.

Nick Meglin. Nick generously shared a piece of *thirtysuffering* art from *MAD Magazine* and then wrote an essay about his appearance on the show. It is a true honor to have a piece of *MAD* talent in the book.

Charlotte Stewart. Charlotte was nice enough to take time out of a Twin Peaks Festival to talk *thirtysomething* with me. She also guested on the Red Room Podcast to promote her BearManor book, *Little House in the Hollywood Hills*. Check it out. I like to tell her we are co-workers now.

Dana Delany. Dana is a great person to interview. I think she should let me write her life story. Her picture has been my phone's screensaver for years. She called me on that phone. That was a surreal experience. You can listen to my entire interview with her about *China Beach* at the *Red Room Podcast.*

Michael Feinstein, Paul Haggis, David Clennon, Lenny Von Dohlen. How cool is it that they all emailed me back with information for the book? It shows you how much people loved working on the show.

Scott Saccoccio. Scott was a great contact to have at Bedford Falls. He assisted me with all my needs. Great name by the way.

Thanks to **JoAnne Bagwell** and **John Teehan** for editing and designing the book for Bear Manor Media. You were both so patient with all my changes. Thanks for putting up with me.

Brad Dukes. Brad was very helpful in securing a few interviews from *Twin Peaks* actors. It also was fun to be able to share with someone the experience of what it is like to write an Oral History. @TwinPeaksBook

Carol Gepper. Carol sent me boxes of TV Guides that she was trying to get rid of. It is amazing that one person's junk becomes another person's pictures in their book.

Dan Steadman. I asked him for one picture, he sent me seventy-one. His *thirtysomething* photo collection rivals my *Twin Peaks* collection. Thanks for sharing it with me. I used as much as the lawyers would allow.

Lisa Mercado Fernandez. Lisa let me use her collection of *thirtysomething* photos. She also was a great resource for the show. She was ridiculously supportive of this project. Her positivity and generosity was just what I needed. Check out her book *The Eighth Summer*.

Thanks to my friends **Lisa**, **Holly**, **Stephanie**, **Tiffany, Mel, Rachel**.

Thanks to my **family** and children: **Alex**, **Becca**, **Gillian** (thanks for helping with the pictures)**, Reagan.**

What can I say that will adequately express how much I want to thank my wife, **Jennifer Ryan**? I am very lucky to have a partner who understands that I will often times be lost in finishing the hat. She listened to me talk about each email, interview and each and every step through this book. She helped proof and read over each part. I am thankful every day to have someone who supports me in everything I do. I have been an artist since I was born, but I never had success until I had you, that can't be a coincidence. I love you and half this book is yours, but there is no way I am giving you half the money from this book if we get ever get divorced. Also, I am leaving you all the kids.

Scott's eBook on sale at Amazon and iTunes.

About the Author

Scott Ryan's writing has been published in *The Sondheim Review* and the essay book *Fan Phenomena: Twin Peaks* (Intellect Press). He wrote a comic essay book, *Scott Luck Stories* (Amazon, iTunes) in 2014. He wrote and directed the independent film *Meet Abby* (Amazon). He directed *A Voyage to Twin Peaks* in 2016 (available for rent or purchase at Amazon.com). A documentary about the 25th anniversary of the Twin Peaks Festival, which has played at Twin Peaks events across the globe. He has written two musical reviews performed at the University of Miami in Ohio. He is the host of four podcasts: *Red Room Podcast*, *Scott Luck Stories*, *Big Bad Buffy Interviews* and *The thirtysomething Podcast*. He is told he has been happily married for an amount of years.

Please check out my ebook, *Scott Luck Stories*. It is twenty comic essays from life about parenting, work, and love. You will laugh and actually own a book where I write stuff in it. It is in ebook form only. Follow me on Twitter **@Scottluckstory**.

I am currently starting a *Twin Peaks* magazine with John Thorne called, *The Blue Rose Magazine*, Bluerosemag.com. I am also working on a Buffy oral history with David Bushman. Follow us on Facebook and iTunes at *Big Bad Buffy Interviews*, **@buffyhistory**.

If you love television, check out Red Room Podcast **@redroompodcast.** We have over 100 episodes with interviews, commentary, and high level talk about the art of television.

Follow **@30somethingpod** to hear some of the interviews that Carolyn and I recorded. We talk *thirtysomething* like the show is still on the air.

Like all four Podcast Pages on Facebook
Email me with good comments only at superted455@gmail.com

Scott hosts a podcast about television called *The Red Room Podcast*

Last thought: if I have your attention in this moment, can I pitch you my religion? It is called Kindness. Ignore what you see in the media, on Facebook and on highways. Kindness is out there, you just have to look. Be kind to everyone you come in contact with and have no regard to if you receive kindness back. I promise you that your life will be happier and better. I was kind to Richard Kramer and he was so very kind to me. This book was born from kindness. All of these interviews happened because strangers were kind enough to take time out of their lives to talk to me. In turn, I tried to be as kind as I could to them. Some of these interviews blossomed into true friendships. Kindness, it is the antidote to the media.

Please spread the word of this book on social media. Thanks so much for reading.

Printed in Great Britain
by Amazon

78682336R10220